BADGER

BADGER

IN DRAMA AND REAL LIFE

CHRISTOPHER KENWORTHY

FOR MY WIFE, HELEN,
WHO GIVES ME ALL THE IDEAS

This book is published to accompany the television series *Badger*,
first broadcast in 1999 (Series I) and 2000 (Series II).

The series was produced by Feelgood Fiction in association with the BBC

Executive Producers: Laurence Bowen and Philip Clarke
Producers: Series I: Murray Ferguson, Series II: Annie Tricklebank
Directors: Tom Clegg, Paul Harrison, Martyn Friend and Keith Washington

Published by BBC Worldwide Limited, Woodlands, 80 Wood Lane,
London W12 0TT

First published 2000

ISBN: 0 563 53700 0

Commissioning Editor: Emma Shackleton
Project Editor: Cleo Wright
Copy Editor: Barbara Nash
Art Director: Linda Blakemore
Designer: Isobel Gillan
Picture Researcher: Miriam Hyman

Set in Frutiger by BBC Worldwide

Printed and Bound in France by Imprimerie Pollina s.a. - n° L 80010
Colour separations by Imprimerie Pollina s.a.

CONTENTS

INTRODUCTION **6**

INTRODUCTION

n the winter of 1996, I drove to Northumberland to interview my very first Police Wildlife Liaison Officer (PWLO), a police constable named Paul Henery, a young man who started life as a wildlife artist and, only as an afterthought, decided to add a uniform and Land Rover to his sketch book and brush.

He was, it seemed to me, an interesting man doing an interesting but largely unknown job in an interesting place, and he made a good page feature in the *Weekend* supplement of the *Daily Telegraph*.

PC Paul Henery, the man who started it all.

That one-page feature has cost the BBC more than £6 million so far – and may cost the corporation far more. For it was that feature which inspired Laurence Bowen and Philip Clarke to launch the screen series *Badger*, at a cost of £500,000 per episode. The drama was based on the work of the men and women, who, like Paul Henery, are at the pointed end of wildlife law. They stand between the criminals and the creatures that the criminals regard as theirs to abuse, exploit, kill, torment and torture.

At the last count there were more than 650 men and women PWLOs working in police forces up and down the country. Like Paul Henery they are all passionate about their work, but find themselves an unknown army.

Wildlife crime is the fastest growing area of crime in Britain, possibly in the world. In 1999, the international trade in prohibited wildlife, such as tigers, rhinos and parrots, was estimated to be worth £5 billion – that is, worth more than any other criminal activity except drugs.

Here in Britain, in one single year more than 10,000 badgers were killed by diggers and badger-baiters. Threatened bird species, such as buzzards and red kites, are regularly poisoned by farmers to protect game stocks. Golden eagles, hen harriers and peregrine falcons are targeted by egg collectors and traders in birds of prey, who sell them at up to £5000 a time.

But none of this shows up on police crime figures.

Understandably, the police authorities – which are constantly nagged to make their work cost-effective at a time when they are faced with ever reducing budgets and falling manpower – are reluctant to devote valuable officers and time to preventing or prosecuting crimes which are never going to make their clear-up rates look better.

With the police already overwhelmed with fighting crime against burglars, muggers, armed robbers holding up banks and post offices, pickpockets operating on

Alnwick Castle – built by the Normans, now home to the Duke of Northumberland and his family.

Day in the wild life of a natural copper

Television is going to town on rural policemen. **Christopher Kenworthy** *goes on the beat with a hero from the Blue Light Zone…*

Before PC Paul Henery has even got his coat off, the phone is ringing in his cluttered office at Northumbria police headquarters in Ponteland, Near Newcastle.

On the line is an anonymous tipster with the names and activities of a group of badger baiters at work on the constable's patch. It gets Henery's attention at once. The 32 year old full-time wildlife liaison officer for Northumbria hates badger baiters almost as passionately as he loves badgers.

Henery, the star and subject of next Saturday's Wildlife Cop, one of Channel 4's Blue Light Zone films, is one of a new breed of police wildlife officers. A former wildlife warden and accomplished wildlife artist, he is also Northumbria police's first full-time wildlife officer. Under his guidance, 36 part-time wildlife officers cover his vast beat.

He depends on them just as he depends on the occasional back-up of the firearms team, the helicopter and the tactical support group he may need to arrest violent criminals.

Wildlife crime is on the increase or, at any rate, perception of it is on the increase. Certainly, far more is now reported. Figures collated by the Royal Society for the Protection of Birds indicated that only about 20 wildlife offences per year were noted in the Northumbrian area before Henery set out his stall. Last year, he logged 610 incidents.

The offences he deals with fall into several categories. Badger baiting is the target of his special loathing. "Nobody knows why but the type of person liable to go out and bait badgers is often also associated with violent crimes," he says. "They see wild animals as there to be abused at their pleasure."

"And they do get pleasure from it. It takes a lot of hard work to go out on a Sunday morning with terriers and a spade, dig out a badger and set dogs on it until it is dead. Badgers are powerful and dangerous animals, and these men don't want their terriers hurt, so they maim the badger. They break its jaw or blind it, or maim its legs. And all this for pure sadism; there's no commercial profit in it."

Hard on the heels of badger baiting comes poaching for profit. Henery makes a sharp distinction between a country villager who goes out at night for a couple of rabbits for the pot and the organised gangs out for handsome profits. "Three nights' work with a net and gaff for a salmon poacher can bring in between £150 and £300, which is not bad."

Then there are the organised groups of inner-city thugs who take out four wheel-drive vehicles and "long dogs" (lurchers and greyhounds, which hunt by sight rather than scent) on night-time "lamping" expeditions. They drive on to an estate, catch a deer in the light and drive it down until they are close enough to loose the dogs from a moving vehicle. The dogs run along the beam and pull down the deer, which then gets its throat cut. They can catch three or four in an hour."

"At £40 for a deer, that's not bad money. Most of the venison is sold in pubs, though some goes to hotels, game dealers, even the occasional butcher."

Henery gets extra pleasure out of catching the men who prey on the birds of prey. For some unknown reason, the North-East has the largest concentration of illegal falconers in the country. They take live eggs and chicks from the wild and usually sell them on. There are customers all around the world: Germany in particular is a new and expanding market.

"A peregrine is worth up to about £1,000, a goshawk £800-£1,000, and peregrines lay in clutches of four. That's £4,000 for a night's work."

Already the work of Henery and his wildlife officers is having an effect. Since an illegal dealer was sent to prison for 15 months by Newcastle Crown Court last year – the first in England - Henery says thefts from known nests have sharply declined.

Not so, however, the other enemies of the birds of prey: the otherwise respectable game breeders. "There are lots of wild and beautiful birds like buzzards in the Lake District," he says. "But none in parts of Northumbria."

"A lot of this I put down to direct persecution. Game-bird breeders kill them in the belief it protects their own stocks, but if these people are killing and trapping and poisoning them, that is illegal".

His work has put wildlife criminals in his area on the back foot. In a carefully co-ordinated campaign last year, he raided six egg collectors - outlawed since 1954 - and recorded 3,500 wild birds' eggs.

"The red-backed shrike, which used to breed in this country, has been wiped out by egg collectors," he says. "The trouble is that they take not one egg but the whole clutch. In one collection we found six clutches of red-backed shrike eggs – pretty well the whole breeding population for one year, in one drawer."

There are, however, more pleasurable sides to his work. When he has rescued live wild animals from their criminal captors he tries to release them back to the wild. This is more complex than it sounds: you can't just open a cage and let a group of previously captured birds fly off. The locality may not be suitable, or there might be local birds of prey who would attack them.

Henery has a special favourite in a little owl he found last year. It had damaged wings and plumage and had been kept in a tiny cage in Newcastle city centre.

"I put it in a tree in an area which seemed suitable and last weekend I took the children for a picnic there and I saw the same bird in the same tree. He's obviously settled down," he says.

This afternoon, he has to liberate a collection of bull-finches (these are wild ones but they would raise £50 per bird on the legitimate captive-bred market), visit a sanctuary, call on his most recent rescuees, and check over a buzzard.

The buzzard was being kept in the city centre and driven around in a car, a sophisticated form of cruelty. Now, it sits cheerfully in a special aviary, waiting for its freedom. Next door is a tawny owl recovering well from incarceration in a small room, where it was the pet of an elderly woman.

Today's escapees - some bull-finches, a blue tit and a linnet - are waiting for him. He drives them to a local wildlife reserve and lets them out.

To Paul Henery, it is the abusers who should be in the cage, not the abused.

• *'Wildlife Cop'*, Channel 4, next Saturday, 10.35pm

The original article from the Daily Telegraph.

city pavements, how much time and money can we realistically ask the police to spend on catching badger-baiters and hare-coursers, on investigating developers who may be disturbing bats, or farmers who put down poisoned bait to kill predatory birds and foraging foxes?

The result is a force within a force, a task force of police officers who mainly do their second job, their wildlife job, in their own spare time. But police officers have families just like everybody else, and, even in the normal run of things, their normal day jobs send them home at impossible times. Pressure of work is notorious for the high failure rate of police marriages. So the temptation to think: 'I work hard enough as it is: be damned to the bunnies!' must be very strong indeed.

It is a tribute to the devotion and passion of the Police Wildlife Liaison Officers that this so rarely happens, that so many of them are willing to invest their spare time trying to keep back the despoilers who raid our countryside and our wildlife to line their pockets.

The PWLOs themselves have another argument. They point out that wildlife criminals are not a separate breed from other kinds of criminals. The men who raid banks, mug people and run protection rackets, who make life on some sink estates a living hell, are also the men who dig badgers from their setts in order to kill them slowly by setting terriers on them.

Brutal violent criminals like brutal violent pastimes. Catch a crook who loves making cocks tear each other to pieces, and ten-to-one you have caught a man who loves to beat and brutalize his way through life. Under these circumstances, the work of the PWLO is simply another facet of the work of a beat copper.

Once, police officers were semi-isolated within the bounds of their own area, and this did not matter when criminals, too, tended to operate within their own 'turf'. But these days we have motorways and mobile phones. A badger can be dug out in Cornwall one night and be baited in Cambridge, Carlisle, London or Edinburgh the next. Police patrols which could once creep up on unsuspecting crooks about their crimes now have to run a gauntlet of look-outs who can phone ahead by mobile to tell their colleagues the cops are coming.

If all else fails, the violent men who carry out these violent crimes are perfectly prepared to fight or menace their way out of trouble. A farmer who sees men digging on his land is best advised to keep out of the way, because he could easily end up with a broken head or worse.

Against this background, largely unsuspected by the general public, *Badger* hit our screens with a bang.

Many people, even those who should have had access to accurate information, assumed that Tom McCabe, the PWLO hero of *Badger*, was the product of a BBC think-tank: a combination of the 'cops and docs' school of television, and the huge appeal that animal programmes have for the viewer. 'Bunny-hugging bobbies', they jeered, 'can't go wrong.'

The news that every one of the *Badger* adventures is based on real life, that such police officers are out ranging the countryside every day – and, in the case of Northumberland, what countryside! – caught them and a great many viewers by surprise.

But the characters from *Badger* live, both in real life and on screen, and this book is the story of how they got there.

CHAPTER ONE

THE WHY OF IT

Everyone loves a party and Laurence Bowen, head of drama at Feelgood Fiction, the independent television production company, is certainly no different. But the one he attended in Brighton on 24 March 1996 was a particular beauty.

Lightly hung-over and muzzy, he climbed into the train for the journey back to his London home, only to realize as the train pulled out of the station that he had forgotten to buy himself a Sunday newspaper to while away the time. All, however, was not lost. Spread in a tangled mess on the opposite seat were the abandoned portions of the previous day's Saturday *Daily Telegraph*, and prominent in the pile was the *Weekend* supplement.

It was in the supplement that he found an article about PC Paul Henery, the PWLO for Northumbria.

'I read the article about Paul Henery with great interest,' he says. 'I had never heard of PWLOs before. Even through the hangover, it gave me an idea.'

LAURENCE BOWEN – Executive Producer

Born: London, 17 August 1964, son of parents who were both artists.

Career: Directed theatre whilst at school and Oxford University, worked at the Royal Court Theatre, London, and read scripts at the BBC. Ran the charity First Film Foundation for six years. Hired by Philip Clarke to set up the drama wing of the independent producers, Diverse Productions. Combined with Philip Clarke to buy out of Diverse and set up Feelgood Fiction.

The idea was *Badger*, the story of a Police Wildlife Liaison Officer, and Bowen took the idea back to his colleague, Philip Clarke.

The Clarke – Bowen team had already proved its talent for drama which appeals to the viewing public. The drama *Stone, Scissors, Paper* was widely admired, as was the series *The Hello Girls*. They knew how to put a winning formula together and to their minds, this idea had 'winner' stamped all over it.

They started the process by finding themselves a writer.

'I took the article to Philip and suggested it would make a series, and then I wrote a two-and-a-half-page "pitch" document laying out the idea, and took it to Tessa Ross, head of drama at the section of the BBC which deals with independent productions. She liked it very much, and after discussing who might be the best possible writer to deal with this combination of subjects, we approached Kieran Prendiville.'

Prendiville is a writer with a glittering track record, including the tough, hard-hitting *Roughnecks* series set among the oilmen of the North Sea, and the extremely successful *Ballykissangel*.

And, to their astonishment, he thought that they must be mad: 'I took one look at their idea, and thought: "You have got to be joking! Furry animals and cops! The critics will slaughter us!"

'Then I read it again, and changed my mind. I began to be intrigued. I thought: "Stuff the preconceptions! So what if it does look formulaic? Formulaic is just another way of saying structured and everything needs a structure."'

The cast of **Badger,** **looking cheerful despite the weather.**

Prendiville decided to see for himself and set out on a tour of Britain, talking to PWLOs on the ground and collecting their stories together to form a basis for his own dramatic ideas.

'I met eight or ten of them, including several who work in London, one in Belfast, one in Wiltshire, one in Wales and so forth. I quickly decided that setting the show in London would not work. And after meeting Paul Henery in Northumberland, I knew that his particular patch absolutely demanded to be used.'

In fact, the team considered setting the series in a number of locations including Manchester (where there is a full-time PWLO) and Belfast. The combination of Paul Henery's spectacular home countryside, however, and the fact that Newcastle is home to many fine actors who could handle the difficult Geordie accent helped them to pick Newcastle and Northumberland.

'I also wanted to get out in the countryside again,' says Kieran. 'I had spent months researching child abuse in North Wales for one drama, and the mean streets of Dublin for another. I desperately wanted to get some clean air in my lungs, and the countryside of Northumbria has not been exploited, nearly enough. I know there must be others, but, in fact, apart from *Our Friends in the North*, which was strictly a serial, the last popular series I could remember set there was *When the Boat Comes In*!'

Their next step – and a hugely important one – was to find a star.

Stars can make or break a series. Cast the wrong one, and the finest script in the world and the most beautiful locations cannot prevent what could have been a hit from turning into the biggest turkey ever made. Not only must the star be physically correct for the role, he must also have the right personality or be able to reproduce it on screen.

Physical appearance is crucial. Woody Allen would not look right as Marshal Rooster Cogburn of *True Grit* fame, but John Wayne was born to play the role. What the people at Feelgood needed was a well-known face not too identified with other famous roles, mature enough to have authority in the job of PWLO and young enough not to look played out.

Jerome Flynn might have been made for it. After the huge success of his screen partnership with Robson Green in *Soldier, Soldier* and their combined success with three chart-topping hits, he was already nationally famous and recognizable.

He also had two other assets. After enjoying his success for years, he had recently taken two years out to let his career cool off, and decide for himself the way his future career ought to go. This meant that for audiences, his face was familiar without being stale. He also has an abiding interest in wild animals, and maintains that if he had not become an actor, he might easily have opted for life as a PWLO.

Raised in the Home Counties, he was used to his mother nursing orphaned fox cubs and damaged wild birds in straw-filled shoe-boxes behind the kitchen door, and his childhood playgrounds were the fields and woods behind his home. He already knew how to handle wild animals, and had developed, even as a child, a real passion for the very creatures with which he was now required to act.

They left the casting of the other roles to Di Carling, the casting director, who was responsible for casting hits such as *Undercover Heart, This Life, Out of the Blue* and many others.

She selected Phillippa Wilson to play Steph Allen, the single-parent vet who catches McCabe's heart, Rebecca Lacey from *Casualty* to be Claire Armitage, the Royal Society for the Protection of Birds investigations officer married to McCabe's policeman boss, David Armitage, played by Kevin Doyle, and newcomer Alison Mac to be Catherine (known to all as 'Wilf'), McCabe's unsuspected daughter come from his past to complicate his future.

McCabe needed a sidekick, too, so Di Carling recruited Adrian Bower to play Jim Cassidy, a policeman who is basically only interested in wildlife when it comes with chips.

KIERAN PRENDIVILLE – Writer

Born: Rochdale, 25 December 1947, one of eight children of a local GP.

Career: Started his working life as copy boy for the Oldham Press Agency, making tea and running errands while he learned his trade as a journalist. Moved to Fleet Street as a reporter on national newspapers and agencies, and then joined the BBC. Worked as a researcher and later presenter and reporter on *Man Alive, Nationwide, That's Life, Tomorrow's World, Horizon, QED*. Entered the drama writing world with scripts for *Boon, The Bill, Roughnecks* and *Ballykissangel*. Lives in South London.

CHAPTER TWO

THE HOW OF IT

Once they had their writer and their star, the Feelgood team felt they were really on their way. After his expedition round the country, talking to the officers on the ground, seeing their problems first-hand, Kieran Prendiville felt he was in a position to write the first episode of the new series, plus the 'bible', which is the book of basic facts on which other writers coming after should base their plots.

They took the combination along to Peter Salmon, head of the BBC at the time, and he duly commissioned the series. When each episode is going to cost at least £500,000 that is a strong commitment, but the resulting series has justified Salmon's faith in it.

Kieran Prendiville is a man who believes that people and their relationships are more important and fascinating than things, so it was inevitable from the start that the characters would be the driving force behind his screen police force.

He understands his subjects, though. He has talked at length to the real PWLOs and discussed their problems with them. He also understands their bosses.

'The police hierarchy must think: "How do I show that my men are not wasting their time if their work never shows up on the crime statistics?" So I do know that they need a pretty well-meaning boss if they are going to get some backing.'

In real life, the PWLOs crave enthusiastic backing. They have to run their second job on budgets which can be as low as £80 per year, and, if they want to carry their message to the public in schools and village halls, have to do all the work themselves.

They are supported by a healthy and vigorous network of exhibit exchanges, which means that sometimes North Wales's collection of illegal gin traps is lent to South Cambridgeshire, and Edinburgh's birds of prey pictures turn up in a PWLO exhibition in York. But very often individual officers, with their families pressed into service to help, do the work themselves.

There is also a country-wide exchange of information. South Wales's illegal hare-coursers may visit Oxfordshire's wide-open pastures confident that their local PWLO is safely left behind in Wales – but their vehicle numbers and descriptions have gone before them, and eyes which follow their progress down the motorways on a sunny Sunday morning know who they are and where and why they are going.

The fact that these officers were pretty well unknown to the public before *Badger* is, to a certain extent, their own fault.

'I know that they were unknown,' admits Prendiville, 'because I had never heard of them myself. You look at the ingredients you put into a series, which in this case was cops and vets – and you think to yourself: "This seems like it was designed by a committee!"

'The trouble is that these cops have no conception of television marketing and analysts. Say to them that they are a paradigm of a BBC Sunday evening series and

Rebecca Lacey and Jerome Flynn star.

they will laugh in your face. They say: "What are you talking about? I spent last night freezing my buns off trying to stop someone stealing eggs from a cliff face in Northumberland. What's cosy and Sunday night-ish about that?"'

To Prendiville, the best aspect is not the job – although that is real and works – but the people who do it. These people are passionate and dedicated in real life, though they would scoff uncomfortably at the descriptions if presented with them, and it is not difficult, on screen at least, to give them passionate private lives.

Tom McCabe (Jerome Flynn), former marine, divorced and now living by himself in a stone cottage in Northumberland and nursing a damaged badger back to health, is tentatively exploring a relationship with local vet Steph Allen (Phillippa Wilson). Steph – known to all in the series as Steph the Vet – has a broken marriage behind her, and a son called Liam (Scott Karalius), who still hankers after his father. McCabe has to work hard to get the boy to accept him. However, in Series II, he is just succeeding in this when who should turn up from London, sleek with success, driving a state-of-the-art Saab motor car but Ralph (Conor Mullen), the boy's father.

In any case, McCabe's affections are being tugged at by the already married Claire Armitage (Rebecca Lacey). Claire spells trouble in several different ways. She is obsessive about her work as investigations officer for the Royal Society for the Protection of Birds (RSPB), and constantly on the lookout for people who want to abuse birds – and, to be fair to her, there are plenty of them around. She naturally expects McCabe to back her up, which, from her point of view, means him coming running whenever she calls.

In turn she is married to McCabe's boss, Inspector David Armitage (Kevin Doyle). Their marriage is going through a rocky patch, just when McCabe suspects his romance with Steph is running into trouble. And Armitage doesn't like animals anyway, which means he has little time for McCabe and his wildlife duties which he tends to find ridiculous.

And then there is the question of Catherine (Alison Mac), known to the whole world as 'Wilf' after the footballer, because her surname is Mannion. Catherine is McCabe's eighteen-year-old daughter, who, unknown to him, was born to his wife after they separated.

'What happens to a man in middle age when he discovers he has an eighteen-year-old daughter he knew nothing about?' says Prendiville. 'She's old enough to blame him for leaving her mother, so, with the best will in the world, he has terrble trouble coming to terms with her. And then his partner (Cassidy) starts making moves on the daughter, and he can't come to terms with that at all.'

In Prendiville's complex, intense, emotional world, nothing is as it seems.

But then, McCabe also has to deal with the equally complex world of the wildlife officer. Jerome went to see Paul Henery, the real-life PWLO for Northumberland, straight away.

'I never intended McCabe to be a portrait of Paul,' says Jerome, sitting on the wharf at the edge of the Tyne where the unit filmed some of its most gritty footage featuring scenes which involved a badger-baiting session. 'But when I met Paul I realized I was not going to have any trouble finding the character. When he told me about his job in fact I realized I did not have to look for anything. It was there. I saw very easily that if I had not become an actor, I could have ended up doing something exactly like this and been very happy at it.

'I connected with his passion and was inspired by his commitment. Hopefully this series will increase the awareness of wildlife crime and will save animals from suffering.'

Of Paul Henery, he says: 'He exposed the amount of wildlife crime going on in his area, and he takes it as seriously as any other crime.'

JEROME FLYNN – PC Tom McCabe

Jerome was an inspired choice for the character of McCabe. Physically, he looks right: slightly battered, slightly boyish. nicely mature. The nose was broken and the jaw dislodged when he was playing rugby and soccer – and on one occasion a friend celebrated Jerome's eighteenth birthday by pushing his head through a plaster wall.

'I've had my nose fixed so I can breathe,' he says. 'But it always seems to get broken again.'

It does mean he can be cast in any rough-hewn role, though; whilst the dreamy, gentle smile which goes with the battered face endears him wonderfully well to women viewers.

He is a genuine athlete, too. He has run the London Marathon twice, worked in Sarajevo with the Red Cross and in Macedonia with a charitable theatre company called Rise, Phoenix, which aims at the rehabilitation of children harrowed by wars and fighting.

He is also right in character. Born in the Home Counties, in Ide Hill, near Sevenoaks in Kent, son of actor and singer Eric Flynn, and his then actress wife, Fern, he grew up in a home which was on the edge of the country.

JEROME FLYNN – PC Tom McCabe

Born: Kent, son of actor and singer Eric Flynn, with whom he has occasionally worked.

Career: Became an actor at seventeen years old after dropping out of school to work on stage in his father's production of *The Crucible*. Trained at the Central School of Speech and Drama. Credits include *London's Burning* (the original film), work at the RSC and five series of *Soldier, Soldier* in which he formed a partnership with Robson Green. Their recording of 'Unchained Melody' introduced the two men to a new career as singers, and they had three chart hits. Spent two years in Andrew Cohen's spiritual community, part of it in India, and still works with the Cohen organization.

'My mother really was the inspiration for my interest in animals, and hence in *Badger*,' he explains. 'She did not exactly run a sanctuary, but she was very much like a lot of women who do run them – the ones I keep meeting while I am working on the series.

'She was one of those people who was always taking in wildlife, and nursing it. If there was a damaged animal to be found on the road or in the fields, it would finish up in our kitchen, in a box next to the stove, being nursed better.

'We always had something there. There were at least two sets of fox cubs whose parents had been gassed, and who had been left helpless. She nursed them until they could look after themselves, and then they were sent off into the wild.

'For a time they would come back and play with us and the dogs – extraordinarily beautiful animals in the dusk – and then go off again. In the fullness of time, as they got wilder, they came back less often, and finally stopped coming altogether.'

As time went on, the fox cubs gave way to kestrels with injured wings, to stoats which had been hit by cars, to any damaged wild thing his mother could take in.

'I would come home from school, and go straight out into the field and the woods. I had a very happy childhood, but have to confess I did not know how lucky I was,' he says.

Now, he does. He is so devoted to wildlife that he regularly gets into a wet suit and goes swimming with a dolphin called Freddie at a harbour near Newcastle.

'I even persuaded my mother to celebrate her fiftieth birthday doing it,' he says.

Anybody who can enjoy – and persuade his mother to enjoy – a swim in the bitterly cold North Sea must have an evangelical and deep commitment to wildlife.

The *Badger* character is a big step for Jerome away from the roles he has played before. Since he plunged into the acting world, he has been a busy man. Roles in series such as *Boon, Between the Lines,* a major role in the pilot film version of *London's Burning* and *Bergerac* laid a firm basis for his success as professional soldier Paddy Garvey in the long-running *Soldier, Soldier*.

Soldier, Soldier also famously teamed him with Robson Green, who he says has become a part of his life now. The two men went on to record 'Unchained Melody' and 'I Believe', both of which topped the charts and shot them into the kind of income bracket most actors only dream of.

It brought them back together, too, for the period series *Ain't Misbehavin'* set in the shady club world of the Second World War.

Then came a period of re-assessment. Whereas Robson went on to become the highest paid actor on television with a multi-programme, multi-million-pound deal with ITV, Jerome decided to take a couple of years out to determine what he wanted to do with his life. The musical success, after all, had given him financial independence, and there is no point in having independence if you don't use it, so use it he did.

It was a remarkable gamble at a time when he could have named his price, but it has paid off in human terms. He spent a lot of his time away in the retreats organized by the spiritual teacher Andrew Cohen and says he benefited greatly from it. He is still involved with Cohen's group, and spends much of whatever spare time he has working with it.

The question was, when he eventually decided to return to London and acting, would the world be prepared to have him back? He need not have worried. As soon as he got back to this country, he was offered in quick succession a Ruth Rendell thriller called *Lake of Darkness*, which hit the screen in early 1999, and a role as football immortal Bobby Charlton in *Best*, a life of George Best.

Then the first script for *Badger* flopped through his letter-box and it was like a dream come true.

'Actually, I was a bit nervous of doing another series,' he says. 'But I was somehow just pulled into this one. It had a wonderful funny feel about it, a warm-heartedness which appealed to me, and, of course, it was set in Northumbria, with which I felt I already had a connection.'

Actors are always nervous about being too identified with a single role, and Jerome admits that when he was doing *Soldier, Soldier*, he became more and more restive.

'At the end of that, it was definitely time to go. Actually, at the beginning of each series I would decide this would be the last one, I would not do another, but the prospect of working with Rob again, and travelling to another far country, seduced me into it.'

His fondness for Robson Green continues. It can hardly be a coincidence that there is a dog in *Badger* Series II (a gift to Steph's son, Liam) which is called Robson, although the highest paid actor in television would probably rather it did not mess on the carpet.

At least Jerome can afford to get close to the dog. The same cannot be said of some of his other on-screen co-stars, though. When he is seen in close-up handing food to his captive badger, the hand which goes close to those razor-sharp teeth actually belongs to sanctuary-owner Kim Olson, and even then it is encased firmly in a thick hide glove.

Jerome must have found the 'no contact' rule quite reassuring when he was introduced to his animal co-stars for the very first episode of the first series, a pair of real alligators. This storyline was based on a Midlands newspaper article Kieran Prendiville saw several years ago about a council flat tenant who bought a six-inch baby alligator in the pub one night and was horrified by how fast it grew into a nine-foot monster – still in his council flat. By an alarming coincidence, a similar story surfaced in the newspapers at the end of Series I – this time in Derby.

The storyline involved McCabe and Steph the Vet in a raid on a Newcastle council house where Ray, an unemployed Geordie, was keeping his own pet alligator.

Filming the scene involved not one but two live alligators called George and Baby, and one replica. Baby, the supposedly 'trained' and gentle alligator, was chosen to do all the 'acting' which mainly involved lying on a bed and opening her mouth threateningly at the cameras as McCabe and Steph made their entrance.

'One of the handlers was telling me how easy-going and biddable Baby was,' recalls Phillippa Wilson. 'But when I asked him how he lost his finger, it turned out that Baby had bitten it off. Apparently, alligators are only comparatively trainable – George would probably have had his arm off at the elbow!'

PHILLIPPA WILSON – Steph Allen

Phillippa is one of the cast who was brought up in the area in which she is acting, and does not want to leave it. She says she once tried leaving to study at Manchester Polytechnic, but found herself so unhappy that she left after a year.

'It works for some and not for others, and I was one of the ones it did not work for,' she says. 'So I did a business course instead and hated that, too. Lovely people, but not what I wanted to do with my life.'

All that changed as soon as she landed the role of porcelain-and-white Gwendolyn Fairfax in a stage production of *The Importance of Being Ernest*. Phillippa, who is more on the dark and dramatic side, spent the whole three-month run of the Oscar Wilde classic covered in white make-up, but she adored the acting experience and never looked back.

PHILLIPPA WILSON – Steph Allen

Born: York, 14 April 1965. Moved to Newcastle at the age of five and regards herself as a bona fide Geordie.

Career: Persuaded to make the stage her life by her mother, who told her to follow her heart, no matter how unlikely its course. Long-time friend of Robson Green, with whom she trained at drama school. Starred with Robson in *Student Prince*. Also played Camilla Prince in *Emmerdale,* and appeared in *Heartbeat* as Penny Craddock, the starchy wife of sneaky Sergeant Craddock, the Welsh Lothario. Now lives in a flat in Tynemouth.

Her first decision, once she got the role in *Badger*, was to visit a sanctuary, and Phillippa instantly fell in love with the work her character does. She says that she would dearly have liked to work as a vet, and is now a regular visitor at one of the sanctuaries used as a model for the entirely fictional sanctuary created for the series. It is a characteristic of this series that the more episodes the actors put away in the can, the closer they grow to their screen roles. Phillippa maintains that Steph the Vet has many traits in common with her, except that Steph is cleverer.

'A lot of people think they love animals, but until you see what some people can do to animals, you do not realize exactly what the problem is,' she says with genuine distress in her voice.

'I wanted to see a person who runs a real-life animal sanctuary, because I wanted to see what it is like and get an idea of the character's true role.

'It was like having another layer applied to me. There are so many animals in the sanctuary which can never be released into the wild. There is an owl which was kept in a budgie cage in a back bedroom for ten years, who doesn't even realize it is an owl, and a deer called Hazel who blinded herself on barbed wire running away from poachers after her mother had been killed.

'And, of course, there is a badger which has been baited. How can people do these things?'

One of her first scenes was with a camera-hogging llama, so at least she learned straight away the meaning of the actors' motto: 'Never work with children or animals'.

Now, however, she finds herself acting with both, because Steph is more than just a vet with a sanctuary, she is also a single parent, bringing up a wayward son, Liam, played by young actor Scott Karalius. The two get on with genuine warmth and affection, and Phillippa describes her screen son unaffectedly as 'a dreamboat'.

Her character is also a woman who is in the process of falling in love all over again, a process which is subject to false starts and ups-and-downs just like any other romance, but with the additional problem of her relationship with her son to handle as well. It is not made easier by the reappearance in her life of her former husband, lawyer Ralph (Conor Mullen), who is everything that Tom McCabe is not.

'She and Tom have this fresh relationship, and one of the things I like about Steph is that she is irrational and experiences a lot of jealousy in her life, which is very much like me.'

McCabe and on-screen girlfriend, Steph the Vet (Phillippa Wilson).

Facing up to love scenes is always a major source of tension in an actor's life. The whole business of falling in love with someone you have only met minutes before can be difficult enough to fake, but with a busy film unit working just out of sight of the camera, it can become embarrassing as well.

'I loved Jerome as Paddy Garvey in *Soldier, Soldier*, where he had a lot of kissing to do, so I hoped I would be able to leave it to him, but he said it was just as awkward for him. So, in the end, we just set to.

'It turned out to be just fine. So now I go to work, and snog Jerome and get paid for it. Who's complaining? Can life offer more?'

Well, yes, it can. It can offer animals, and the unit has had to learn to live with the fact that at any given time of the day someone will be missing from the set because they have gone off to look at the goat, or the fox, or some other minor star.

Out of her vet's overall and away from the set, Phillippa is a devout warm-weather lover, which is very understandable after spending much of her time on set in winter conditions, wrapped up to the ears in fleece and thermal underwear.

'I love scuba diving, but the place I love doing it is in the Maldives,' she says. 'I have tried it here off the Northumberland coast, from St Abb's head, off the two piers at Tynemouth, and even on the Farne Islands with the seals, but the water is frighteningly cold, and you do get the impression after a while that your face is going to freeze right off.'

REBECCA LACEY – Claire Armitage

Rebecca Lacey is a professional actress from a professional acting family, and she handles her roles with a polish and expertise which can be frightening. Her credits cover every kind of acting from the broad comedy of *May to December* to the high drama of *Casualty* and *A Touch of Frost*. She has been in *Lovejoy, Hannay, The Darling Buds of May, The Bill* and many more.

It was pretty well inevitable that she and her sister, Ingrid, would end up on the stage. Her father, Ronald Lacey, starred in films such as *Raiders of the Lost Ark*, and her mother, Mela White, ran the bar in the television series *Bergerac* with great panache as Diamante Lil. Ronald, sadly, died in 1991 and Mela has now retired, leaving the family name to be carried on in the business by her daughters.

Rebecca at any rate is delighted by *Badger*. She likes Claire, the character she plays, because she says she has an affinity with strong, straightforward women. Well, strong ones anyway – Claire, in pursuit of something she wants, can be as devious as a hunting stoat, and is not above deliberately ruining McCabe's big date with her rival, Steph the Vet, out of mere naughtiness (Series I, Episode 3: 'The World According to Carp').

Rebecca says it is just the kind of thing a man would do to a mate, a kind of fit-up, and therefore perfectly in line with Claire, who is perfectly capable of crossing the divide between male and female.

'Though,' she adds hastily, 'it is not the kind of thing I would do myself.'

Rebecca tackled the role of unhappily married Claire – her screen husband is McCabe's boss – straight from a two-year stint as Dr George Woodman in the BBC's long-running hospital drama, *Casualty*. The role as a doctor in a busy emergency department was beginning to wear her down and after doing fifty episodes in two years, she says, she was overdue for a change.

She did not realize quite how much of a change it would be. Like other members of the cast, she regarded the idea of a series based on the work of a policeman who watched over wild animals as a bit 'off the wall', but changed her mind once she had read the script and met Paul Henery.

'At first I was inclined to be a bit dismissive,' she admits. 'But after talking to Paul, I was simply gobsmacked. I realized that if I made this show not only would I learn something new, but hopefully we would be telling the audience something new as well. It is certainly not just a cop show.'

She is quite right there, though Claire Armitage is a kind of copper herself. As Investigation Officer for the Royal Society for the Protection of Birds – which gets involved at the sharp end of all manner of bird and wild animal crime – she finds herself very much in the front line of the war against criminals who plunder our countryside.

Her opposite numbers in real life – such as Joan Childs, Investigation Officer for the RSPB – take very real risks in their job. Like the PWLOs they have to hide out in terrible conditions, watching protected nests to make sure that the eggs are not stolen, the chicks are not kidnapped and sold on the world market, or quite simply that rare birds which also happen to be birds of prey do not themselves become the prey of bigger two-legged raptors. It is a cold, often dirty job that can be very dangerous as well.

Added to the drama of her job, Claire Armitage has to address the fact that her marriage is going through a decidedly rough patch, and the temptation to throw herself on the mercy of the broad shoulders of Tom McCabe is very strong. The possibilities fascinate Rebecca.

Out of her costume and away from the *Badger* set she is a versatile character, a talented artist, and attends life-drawing classes to help develop her talent. Like most actors, she reads all the time, but, unlike a great many of them, she also writes for newspapers such as the *Guardian*, for which she did a feature explaining her reasons for leaving a sure-fire success like *Casualty* to gamble – successfully, as it turns out – on a newcomer like *Badger*. For the *Independent*, she has also reported on the Edinburgh Festival.

Born and brought up in the country, she enjoys a country lifestyle to this day, and can be very laid back about animals. Not only is she used to animals, she says, but she also finds it difficult to dislike a creature she knows something about, even bats, which can be a real dread for many people and in particular Julia (Jayne Charlton MacKenzie), landlady of the Goose and Gargle, who finds she has them in the attics of the pub (Series II, Episode 4: 'Cock o' the Walk').

'Actually, I find it impossible to hate anything I've had a really good look at and I have seen bats close up. They are actually the sweetest little things.'

If she has reservations about anything, she reckons it must be spiders. Even close up they look anything but cuddly. 'I cannot bring myself to trust anything that moves *that* fast,' she adds.

Her private life is pretty well set up for the countryside. She drives a small fast four-wheel drive which comes in for a good deal of scoffing from the cast and other professionals who throng the *Badger* set. They say it is too small to be rugged and too powerful for her home life in London. She points out smugly that it is easy to spot parking places in London because it seats her higher than other drivers, and is very useful when she visits her place in the South Wales countryside.

Like other people who spend much of their time in the real country as opposed to the manicured acres of the Home Counties, she knows that the real thing is often composed of cold winds, driving rain and thick sticky mud.

'My friends get very bothered about me wearing boots around the house, but I point out that mud is the reason all the floors are made of stone flags. They are far easier to clean.'

Unusually for a countrywoman, she is a vegetarian from conviction, and has been since the day she stood in a queue for lunch at the National Theatre and watched the blood run out of a huge steak the chef had just slapped on the griddle.

'It was the first time in my life I had ever thought of it as part of a real once-living animal. Previously, I had thought of it as just another form of food, but from that moment it became a piece of dead animal, and I could not bring myself to eat it ever again.'

She is certainly not an evangelistic vegetarian, she says firmly, and is perfectly ready to sit down while other people pile into steak and chips. And, anyway, she does not count fish in the same category as a formerly living animal. Just as well, since her favourite eating-place is a fish restaurant within easy reach of her previous home-from-home in Bristol, where *Casualty* is made.

REBECCA LACEY – Claire Armitage

Born: Surrey, 1968, daughter of Ronald Lacey and Mela White, and sister of actress Ingrid Lacey.

Career: Went almost immediately on to the stage and has a long list of television and stage credits to her name. Also three films: *The Romanovs, Second Victory* and *The Shooting Party*. Spent two years playing Dr George in the BBC smash-hit series *Casualty*, but quit because she thought she was becoming too identified with the role for her own good. Joined *Badger* because she was very impressed by the work of Paul Henery.

KEVIN DOYLE – David Armitage

Kevin Doyle is in the odd position of spending the first half of his life wanting to be a journalist and the second part doing anything but. Son and grandson of a professional soldier, he was put off joining the armed forces by his father who wanted him to have a different kind of life.

While he was still trying to break into the world of newspapers and broadcasting, he went along with a friend to audition for drama school and ended up accepting a place for himself.

A good deal of the reason, he says, was finance. A working-class lad originally born in Newcastle but brought up following his father from army posting to posting, he was in no position to keep travelling to London for interviews at £50 a time, plus the return fares to his home in the North, so when he was offered a place at drama school he grabbed it.

KEVIN DOYLE – David Armitage

Born: Newcastle, son of a professional soldier.

Education: Various places as his father was posted around the world.

Career: Entered acting by accident when he accompanied a friend to an audition, and thrives on the resulting career. Lives in London.

He has never had reason to regret his choice. His credits include some strong dramas, including *The Lakes*, *Silent Witness* and *At Home with the Braithwaites*, and now he finds himself handling the role of a police inspector with a subordinate who keeps disappearing to chase badger-baiters when he should be tracking down burglars, and a wife who spends more time watching birds' nests than lining his.

To a certain extent, he is responsible for making the character of David Armitage into a more likeable character than one might expect from his role as a boss who has little sympathy with Tom McCabe.

'I very much wanted him to be good at his job,' says Kevin. 'Not just someone who spends his time bossing people around, and I also wanted him to have a good sense of humour.'

Living with a wife who has quite such an obsession with birds might tax the sense of humour of almost anybody, but David Armitage even manages to get a laugh out of watching birds with his wife from time to time. The trouble is that Claire is obsessed with her job and David is becoming obsessed with having children.

'He is very keen on having children,' Kevin explains. 'He feels that everything is in place: they have a nice house and security, and have achieved whatever they wanted to achieve in terms of personal ambition. Now, as far as he is concerned, all that remains is for him to talk her into it.'

The trouble is that David turns out to have a low sperm count in a world in which everything else is reproducing like mad, and he finds that hard to accept. It is one of the strengths of the series that it is willing to tackle difficult subjects like this squarely, which other programmes might approach more tentatively.

'I can imagine it must be very difficult for a man to realize that he is not potent enough to have children; and it must be terrible for either of the couple to realize they are the one who cannot bring it about. You must feel that you are letting the other person down terribly. I can see how people can regard it as humiliating.'

ADRIAN BOWER – Jim Cassidy

Setting about the role of Jim Cassidy, Tom McCabe's gung-ho sidekick, was the challenge of a lifetime to Adrian Bower. He is a Cheshire man, born and raised in the lovely walled city of Chester and the Wirral peninsula.

He caught the acting bug at school where he says it made a change to enjoy a school lesson, so he devoted himself to acting for ever more. He went on after school to join a youth theatre, trained at the Guildhall School in London, and found himself doing a series of ever improving roles.

It was not a continuous process. Like many actors, he had to fill in the gaps between roles with odd jobs, and the resulting experience has given him a much richer view of life. He worked for a while on building sites, humping loads from one place to another, worked in bars, valeted cars, and even delivered ice-cream – a job which still, for some reason, fills him with joy.

He may look in frighteningly fit shape now, but he says there was a time when he had to work to put on weight. He trained in a gym every day and drank six pints of full-cream milk, an exercise which soon palled when he realized that with that much milk inside him, he had lost his capacity to go out for a beer with his friends in the evenings.

With Cassidy, he says, he found a certain rapport despite the fact that, unlike Cassidy, who likes animals only when edible, he loves pets and in particular cats. 'I always have pets and at the moment, those pets are cats,' he says.

ADRIAN BOWER – Jim Cassidy

Born: Chester, where he was also educated.

Career: Fell in love with the stage at school when he was dragooned into taking part in the school play and admits he was surprised to enjoy it. Trained at Guildhall School, London, but turned his hand to all kinds of manual work while looking for acting work. Recent roles include Dr Ross Freeman in *Dangerfield* and a part in *Gimme, Gimme, Gimme* before graduating to *Badger*. Now lives in London where he is delighted not to have to own a car.

'I suppose Jim Cassidy is partly me, though only partly,' he says. 'For one thing he is obsessed with his own appearance, a classy dresser and a careful one. Personally, I am a jeans and T-shirt man when I am not on set.

'Jim Cassidy also has a gift for being tactless – he will offend without intending to, and certainly without noticing – whereas I hope I am a little more thoughtful and aware of other people's feelings.

'Would I like him as a friend? Yeah, I suppose I might. He is certainly a likeable guy – a man I could go for a drink with – though I could not do his job in a million years. It's exciting enough, and has enough variety to keep me interested, but you should see the paperwork they have to do. It is terrifying.

They spend hours in the office filling in forms, and it prevents them getting out and getting on with the job.'

Like his colleagues, he threw himself into research for the role, and he is helped by the fact that the scenes of him working – and those of Jerome in the office – are actually filmed in a real police station: the magnificent Victorian police station at Blyth.

The real-life staff of the station were slightly bemused at first when the film crew descended on them, but they soon got used to the fake policemen who wandered in and out of the police station, and entered into the spirit of the thing. They are also a useful source of information about the procedure which is such a feature of all police-based drama.

Off screen, Adrian Bower is often to be found with his head in a book. He loves biography, real-life crime and detective thrillers in that order, though he admits that he is perfectly capable of simply grabbing the first book he comes to in a book shop and burying himself in that. It is the reading which really appeals to him.

Predictably, he likes his drama with plenty of action. He loves Westerns of all kinds, anything made by Sergio Leone or director Martin Scorsese, in particular *Raging Bull* and *Mean Streets,* plus *The Firm,* with Gary Oldman, and *The Godfather.*

Working on *Badger* has also given him the money to indulge his taste for travel. He particularly likes the capitals of Europe, the more spectacular the better, including the far from mean streets of Paris, and the beautiful medieval architecture of Prague.

There is also his music. He adores the Beatles, likes Motown, indulges himself in Sixties' hits and the whole Northern soul scene, and collects music by bands such as Stone Roses and the Fun Loving Criminals.

Blyth Police Station provides the setting for McCabe's office.

ALISON MAC – 'Wilf' Mannion

Alison says that like her, 'Wilf', Tom McCabe's previously unsuspected daughter, grew up a happy child in a happy family. It is not until the death of her parents that Wilf discovers the truth: that the man she always thought was her father was, in fact, a stepfather. Her mother, the former Mrs Tom McCabe, was pregnant when she left McCabe but never let him know.

Perhaps unfairly, Wilf blames McCabe for the break-up of the marriage, and treats him bitterly because she wrongly thinks that he left his wife and not, as is the truth, the other way round. It makes for an awkward relationship between the two of them in the first series, although in the second things seem to have improved a great deal, particularly when she begins to understand his devotion to his job and to the animals which are such an important part of it.

'She knows what she wants and she just goes for it, which is in some ways very similar to me,' says Alison, frankly. 'But I don't think I am nearly as tough as she is. If someone tells me I can't do something, I will probably accept that. If someone tells her the same thing, she would do it just to show them what's what!'

Like Wilf though, Alison swings a mean right hand. When she was required to slap her screen 'father' in the face in the first series (Episode 1: 'It's a Jungle Out There') she naturally enough pulled her punch to avoid hurting him in real life.

'Not realistic enough,' director Paul Harrison told her.

'What, the emotion, or the blow?' asked Alison, nervously.

'Neither,' said Paul. 'Hit him again – with feeling!'

Eager not to be caught out in the wrong again, Alison put her heart into it – and nearly took Jerome's head off!

'I could hear the whole unit go: "Ooooof!" and I went off to my trailer thinking I had done something unforgivable. Jerome was a bit shocked, not to mention stunned, but we discussed it afterwards and it came out all right.'

Wilf, of course, has her own problems, but to Alison's surprise, they turned out very like her own. 'She is stroppy with her Dad, but I suppose at her age most people are. At any age you have the same bickering, very loving relationship.

'Wilf thinks she is very grown up and does not want her father interfering with her life. But at the same time she wants him to be there for her when she needs him.

'Unfair, I know. But that's the way it is!' she says, sweetly.

One thing which distinguishes the two is that Wilf is a physical training coach, while Alison says just getting out of

ALISON MAC – Catherine 'Wilf' Mannion

Born: Newcastle, 11 April 1980, daughter of a stamp and coin dealer.

Education: School in Ripon followed by York University, studying film, television and literature. Continued her studies full-time whilst filming *Badger*.

Career: Alison developed a taste for acting at an early age. Her first film, *Speak Like a Child,* was acclaimed at the Venice Film Festival. Now lives in a village outside the city of Newcastle.

bed in her student digs is about as much energy as she wants to pump out at the beginning of any day.

When she realized she was going to have to spend a good deal of her performances in a leotard, and take part in a fun run (Series I, Episode 4: 'Setts, Lies and Videotape'), she decided that, at the very least, she had to learn how to look fit.

So she went to a gym and discovered, somewhat to her surprise, that very fit people even stand in a different posture from the run-of-the-mill student in the street. These days, she says, she can stand in the proper posture and not embarrass herself on a fun run – at least on screen.

Alison is unique among the cast because she played her role while still studying full time at university, and while otherwise living a normal student life. She lived in a student house, hung around in the common room with the rest, went out to the pictures or for a beer with her student boyfriend, and found the only real difference between her and her contemporaries was that, thanks to *Badger*, she didn't need a student loan, or a Saturday job to make some pocket money.

Otherwise, she says, the role has not changed her way of life. She has not even, despite her father's beseeching, replaced her rather crotchety black Fiat Cinquecento car with a more up-to-date model. She says, slightly guiltily, that her father has had the responsibility for keeping it on the road so far and, anyway, she loves it dearly. Alison's relationship with her own father has helped her to understand Wilf's feelings towards her screen father, even if it is not usually such a prickly relationship.

'My parents got used to me saying that I wanted to go on stage. When I was little, it was kind of cute, I suppose, and everybody could chuckle indulgently and wink at one another over my head. When I got older, it was a case of: "Oh, be quiet!" but when I got the part in *Speak Like a Child*, and it came out all right, they took me rather more seriously.

'It is hard when you are a teenager to get roles which are different. You are nearly always the rebel or the druggie. With the role of Wilf I can at least tell my grandparents and my old aunts to watch, and know they are not going to be embarrassed by me mouthing a string of foul language.'

Her taste runs to more elegant roles and her favourite film is the extremely stylish *Gone with the Wind*. She sees her future as being tied firmly to the English cinema.

PC PAUL HENERY – The Real Thing

The man who could tell them all about the pressures of the job in real life is Paul Henery, the police constable on whom the whole series is based.

Paul is a copper cut out to be a star, a fact which he finds disconcerting and embarrassing. Ask him about his work and he constantly reminds you that he is just one of the men and women working up and down the country catching the criminals who raid our countryside.

The son of a miner, he was determined that when he grew up he would not get caught in the trap of mine work which has seen so many communities broken up along with the British mining industry. He opted instead for becoming an artist, and still holds exhibitions of his work, mainly paintings of birds, and has won awards for his painting brilliance.

Life as a commercial artist in London, however, did not suit him and he opted instead for the hands-on experience of being a country park warden in Northumberland, which led to his present job as a Police Wildlife Liaison Officer. Before he set to work in the field, only about twenty wildlife crimes were logged per year. Within eighteen months he was logging more than 600 incidents annually, and the number was steadily climbing.

He is supported in Northumberland by more than thirty men and women giving up their spare time to do the job, and he runs training courses for other police officers following the same path. One of the reasons for the apparent increase in wildlife crime, he thinks, is that people simply did not know where and how to report it until recently, and now they do.

Until the invention of the PWLO in the early 1980s, harassed desk sergeants were inclined to pass on animal crime complaints to the local RSPCA and RSPB and their officers usually took cases of persecution and brutality to court themselves.

Flippant police officers were even known to mention the Flying Squad when anxious members of the public reported crimes on birds to them, an attitude which did not encourage concerned citizens to repeat the experience.

The arrival of the PWLO has put a stop to all that. Now, each force has at least one officer who knows which part of the law applies to criminal activities involving wildlife and the countryside, and how to apply it.

This can be a complex technical matter, and it is complicated further by the fact that the Wildlife and Countryside Act 1981, under which many wildlife crimes are prosecuted, has no in-built power of arrest. This means that as long as the suspected criminal can satisfactorily identify himself to the arresting officer – a driving licence will do – he cannot be detained. Instead, the arresting officer has to go to court to get a search warrant for his home and premises to collect evidence to back up the charges.

Some criminals – egg collectors are a good example (Series I, Episode 1: 'It's a Jungle Out There') – can get home and dispose of the evidence, and get together with friends and family to arrange a common alibi long before the outraged officer comes panting along with his search warrant.

The penalty for stealing eggs can be as much as £5000 and/or six months in prison for each offence. In one carefully co-ordinated campaign, Paul Henery gathered up 3500 illegally held birds' eggs. It included, in one single drawer, six clutches of the now extinct red-backed shrike – pretty well the entire breeding population for the year.

PAUL HENERY – Police Wildlife Liaison Officer

Born: Northumberland, 30 November 1963, son of a miner.

Education: Local school, where he stayed on to do A Levels and trained as an artist.

Career: Started work as an illustrator in London, but disliked city life. ('I am not a city kind of a person,' he explains.) Moved back to Northumberland first as a country park warden, then joined the local police force 'for security'. Became the local PWLO on the retirement of his predecessor, and took on the job full time on a one-year trial basis. Supported by a network of local part-time PWLOs, became the force's expert dealing with all wildlife crime.

But pinning the crime on the criminal is a different matter. 'Eggers', as they are called, are notoriously ingenious at hiding their collections where they cannot be found, sometimes in specially built hides in their own homes, but often tucked away out of sight in the homes of friends and relatives.

On one raid, famous to the PWLO community, the eggs had been hidden in the home of the grandmother of one of the collectors, but the local PWLO got wind of the trick and staged a simultaneous raid on Granny.

Unfortunately, the egger was one jump ahead of him. The eggs were gone, although under every bed and tucked away on the top of every wardrobe were boxes containing nests of hay and straw, some of which still contained shards of eggshell frustratingly too small for identification.

Granny was playing it for all she was worth in her role as a confused old lady who didn't know what they were talking about. 'Eggs?' she kept saying. 'I always get them from the milkman. Don't know anything about any other eggs, Constable…'

Eventually the exasperated officer snapped: 'So what are all these boxes of straw doing around the house, then?'

The 'little old lady' pose slipped for a moment, and her bright sharp little eyes suddenly turned stony: 'I collect straw, sonny,' she said in a flint-like voice. 'Wanna make something out of that?'

The PWLO knew when he was beat, but he also knew where his egger was hiding his eggs, and next time he knew where to look first.

NIGEL HESS – Music Composer

Pauline Cato provides the distinctive sound of the Northumbrian pipes.

The characteristic theme music for *Badger* was composed by award-winning musician Nigel Hess, the man who gave us, among many others, the music for *Wyciiffe, Hetty Wainthrop Investigates* and *Dangerfield*. He is, perhaps, the most practised composer in the field of television, and his work on *Badger* is no exception. Hess prides himself on catching the mood of the area in which the drama is set.

'In *Hetty Wainthrop*, for instance, I chose the sound of a brass band cornet because that is the instrument most associated with the North. With *Badger*, I wanted the kind of noise you get in folk-music sessions where little bands get together in a pub up there on the moors or in the towns and improvise for the evening.'

So, for the wild beautiful setting of Northumbria, he chose the sound of the Northumbrian pipes. It was a brave decision because the pipes are not familiar to many people outside the North East, and are easily mistaken for Irish pipes. But Nigel Hess knew how to make his little orchestra both characteristic and different.

He found piper Pauline Cato, whose technique on the pipes knows no equal, a folk fiddle, and a group of traditional backing musicians. He wrote several specific themes for the individual strands of storyline in the series, including a soft and tender one for the romance strand which runs through all the episodes.

In his fertile mind, each has its own title, although in the score and in the CD which contains twenty-seven of his themes, including *Badger*, none of them is identified by name. To ensure that each episode has its own fresh sound, and that the individual storyline themes of the episodes fit in seamlessly to the background, he makes sure the orchestra is assembled anew each time, and that the music is freshly recorded for each and every episode, instead of recording one background theme and making it fit every episode no matter how varied these may be.

His experience is impressive. He studied music at Cambridge, and, while still a student, was the Music Director of the Footlights Revue Company. In the 1980s, he spent some years as musical director and house composer for the Royal Shakespeare Company, and his scores for the Broadway productions of *Much Ado About Nothing* and *Cyrano de Bergerac* won awards in New York.

CHAPTER THREE

BEHIND THE SCENES

They had their writers, they had their stars, now the *Badger* team needed badgers – and by extension all kinds of other animals. 'It's a Jungle Out There' (Series I, Episode 1) seemed to have been written by Dr Dolittle and it was a cast joke that when they put together the fictitious sanctuary run by Steph the Vet it looked as though that, too, had been organized by Dr Dolittle

The script called for deer which were being poached, a badger for McCabe's back yard because he was supposed to be nursing one back to health after an unspecified accident, a peregrine falcon whose nest was the target of an egg thief, and two alligators.

Nobody who saw that first episode will have forgotten Baby and George, the alligators, although most people thought there was only one. Baby, as previously mentioned, was supposed to be a gentle, easy-to-handle, cuddly kind of an alligator who could be filmed close up pretending to be threatening, and George was a real villain who could be relied upon to trash the set on cue.

In the event both of them had to be goaded into action because the combination of a comfortable bed and the warmth of the studio lights turned them into happy contented alligators who only wanted to drop off to sleep and snooze the afternoon away.

Baby and George came from a firm called Amazing Animals, based at a zoological gardens in the Home Counties, and they are surprisingly popular film stars. The firm also sought out a leopard and two wolves for Series II, Episode 5: 'Predators'.

For the rest of the series, the man responsible for the animals was local handler John Cross, who runs a Newcastle firm called Dogstar, and is used to the demands of television. He cut his teeth on television commercials and Catherine Cookson epics, in which he provided dogs and horses to order. These days, if it appears on your television set, and moves on two or four legs, John Cross reckons he can provide it.

It is tempting to think that the men and women who provide the creatures for film and television actually live in a kind of domestic zoo, their homes crowded with animals from aardvarks to zebras, all hoping desperately for a job in show business and jumping every time the phone rings. But very few handlers actually own anything more exotic than a dog, cat or horse. The amount of time, money and talent required to train, feed, accommodate and handle any number of different species would be prohibitive to anyone but a professional zoo keeper. Amazing

JOHN CROSS – Animal handler

Born: North Wales, but raised at Abinger Hammer in Surrey.

Career: Moved to Northumberland to raise dogs and tomatoes, and for a time earned his living as a landscaping contractor with a boarding kennels on the side. Trained three Crufts champions and now judges at Crufts. Started finding animals first for commercials and then progressed to drama series. Has provided animals for *Coronation Street* (the dog that chased the fox and was given to Vera as a present by Jack), *Emmerdale* (the fox which discovered the body of one of *Emmerdale*'s many victims), *Our Friends in the North*, *Byker Grove* and now *Badger*. Lives in Newcastle.

Animals, which provided George and Baby, are among the very few people in Britain who provide zoo animals for films and television, and they have to run what is, in effect, a zoo to be able to do it.

But the secret of a good animal handler is a contact book the size of the Albert Hall, and an alert ear to hear of anybody with an unlikely pet.

John Cross, now in his mid-sixties, has been making contacts and finding the unlikely for the demanding, for decades. But his ears still prick up when he hears of a man who claims he has a trained bat which will settle on command, or an otter who will perform underwater without moving out of camera range.

The trouble is that even when he gets one, it is still, after all, a wild animal: 'And nobody knows exactly what a wild animal will do. Even domestic ones will give you a very nasty shock, and you can guarantee it will be at the worst possible moment,' he says.

John knows what he is talking about. His first expedition into the world of the camera was when he was required to provide a hundred trained dogs every day for a fortnight.

'It was for a dog food commercial and all the dogs had to race up a mountainside to get to their dog meat. It came out fifteen years ago and has been running pretty well ever since.

'They wanted one dog to leap over a gate in slow motion while the others ran underneath it, and I thought I had the perfect dog. He was a lovely looker, and went over that gate like the Spirit of Spring. We tried him out half-a-dozen times and he soared over it every time – until, that is, we brought on the other dogs. As soon as he saw them, he didn't want anything to do with that gate and wouldn't go anywhere near it! In the end we had to draft in another dog, a long-haired collie, who flew like Eddie the Eagle, but looked marvellous in slow motion.'

This hiccup didn't particularly surprise John, but then not very much does. As he says, 'When you work with wild animals for a living, you are only surprised when things go right.'

Starting with the fake 'sanctuary' built for Steph the Vet to work in, the animals in *Badger* have proved to be no less difficult than normal.

The director said he wanted to see all kinds of animals, and that is just what he got. They built the sanctuary in a field behind one of the buildings on the Matfen estate, and stocked it with anything they could lay their hands on. There were foxes and pot-bellied pigs, llamas and rheas, which are flightless birds about half the size of an ostrich and twice as bad tempered. Birds and animals of all descriptions.

CHILDREN AND ANIMALS...

John Cross says his worst nightmares occur with the commonest of animals, the domestic cat. It combines, he says, the unpredictability of a wild animal with the bloody-mindedness of a pampered pet. On one location for a Catherine Cookson drama, the script required a young girl to run out and rescue a cat from the path of a passing carriage. They chose a cat which always stayed put where it was once it had been pressed down gently but firmly on to its stomach. But they counted without the little girl who walked out on cue, leaned down to pick up the cat, panicked and pressed it down on to the road again before running away. The cat, true to its training, stayed put. John Cross had to rescue both cat and child before the coach arrived, filled with equally panic-stricken actors.

John's problems started immediately. They had to re-shoot one simple scene more than fifteen times because one of the llamas became camera-struck and hogged the lens every time the director shouted: 'Action!' No matter how hard they tried to shoot round it, that llama backed or pushed himself squarely into the frame, and they had to scrap the scene and try again. In the end they postponed shooting it altogether until the infuriating animal had been shuffled off away from the set.

The pot-bellied pigs behaved themselves beautifully but, as if to make up for it, the rheas became an unpleasant and dangerous double act. Every time the handlers tried to capture them and move them, they kicked like racehorses and a kick from a rhea can break a man's leg. When they were not kicking they were running around making everybody's life a misery.

Then there was the otter which starred in 'The World According to Carp' (Series I, Episode 3), who was exactly like a human film starlet from yesteryear. She was so pretty that the whole unit wanted to watch her working, and she was so enchanted with the human race that all she wanted was to make love to it. She snogged everyone she came across, starting with her owner, a lady from the Bristol area, and progressing with a cunning worthy of any human starlet to the director, Paul Harrison, and even the cameraman.

The trouble was that she could not act to save her life. Brought up from the West Country, and provided with her own hotel room – yes, really! – she steadfastly refused to perform even the simplest on-screen task without wandering off to smell the scenery, go for an unscheduled swim, or play hide and seek.

When is a llama not a llama? When it's a camera hog.

Required to swim ashore, run up the bank and into the trees which surround the lake at which they were filming, she swam ashore and decided to snuffle around in some foam, instead. She decorated herself with a delightful, luxuriant, white moustache, but never ran off into the woods.

Required to run up to the road, stop, sit up and look each way, then cross the road in such a way that McCabe's four-wheel-drive jeep could just miss her, she set off instead along the road away from the camera at high speed and vanished into the woods.

In the end they had to re-cast with not one but two replacement otters, before they could get the shots they wanted.

But not the otter. The otters native to Britain are European otters, which are large and may be authentic but are also a very cross-grained species who are considered impossible to train and are addicted to sinking their very considerable

Otter with a moustache: Beanie refuses to follow the script.

teeth into their co-stars. Film animal-handlers habitually use the more amenable, short-toed Asian otters, which are smaller, can be trained, and are in any case far more amiable and easy to live with. Despite adviser Paul Henery's pleas that the unit should use the European otter for the episode, they settled for an Asian one. And in the end, their patience was rewarded. In streaming icy winter rain the third otter they tried performed as scheduled.

They had trouble, too, with the badger McCabe kept in his back garden while it 'convalesced' and was then eventually (Series I, Episode 6) released into the wild, earning McCabe his first cuddle from his newly discovered daughter.

As the crew found out, there is no such thing as a trained wild animal. They will sometimes do what the camera wants them to do – but only as a coincidence or if it is something they would normally do. A squirrel may go through the most fascinating contortions to get at a packet of peanuts, but nobody can guarantee it will do the same thing twice in the same way. With wild animals, the experts say, you are best advised to go on the first take, because it is quite likely *that* is the only take you will be able to get.

The first badger to be seen on screen was Dusk, a badger taken into care by Kim Olson and her husband, who run the Sanctuary, a rescue and rehabilitation unit near Morpeth. Dusk was rescued, brain-damaged, after a road accident, and has been sheltered and nursed back to health.

Dusk, the badger, was fine when all the director needed to see was a quiet shy badger nestling in the straw, because that's all she wanted to do. But when the script required a more lively badger who would run off into the woods, two slightly more active ones had to be brought along to perform the task.

QUIET PLEASE... Deer figured largely in the first episode of the first series, and director Paul Harrison wanted to see them in natural wild countryside, rather than a deer park. John Cross negotiated the services of a number of the deer at Alnwick Castle, residence of the Duke of Northumberland, and painstakingly arranged to shepherd a herd of deer up the hillside and past the cameras at the correct moment. But just as the cameras started rolling, the frenzied barking of dogs made the deer explode in every direction except the one the unit wanted. It turned out that the Duke's chef, unaware of the arrangement, was giving the castle dogs a morning constitutional along a path through the woods. The whole scene had to be re-filmed the following day with just four deer left in the neighbourhood.

The badgers, which are incapable of looking after themselves in the wild, are never placed at risk of being lost in the undergrowth. They are filmed in pens made from carefully concealed fences, and the tunnels down which they disappear into their 'setts' are actually plastic pipes which lead them safely back to their dens.

Members of the public often worry about the fate of animals used in filming, but they would worry less if they saw the exquisite pains which are taken to ensure they are never mistreated, harmed or distressed in any way. This includes not allowing them to escape into the wild unless they came from the wild in the first place, and have not been so long in the world of human beings that they have lost their natural fear of man, a fear which helps keep them alive.

'Releasing an animal into the wild which has been kept as a pet,' says Jemima Parry Jones, MBE, an acknowledged authority on the subject, 'is a bit like telling someone who has been locked in a room for fifteen years to get out there and pull down an antelope for food. He simply could not. Releases into the wild have to be carefully managed and, in some cases, carried out by a licensed expert.'

Dusk becomes a TV star.

The Bridge on the Tyne, trademark of a remarkable city.

FINDING THE LOCATIONS

One of the major stars of *Badger* is, of course, Northumbria itself. The area, which includes Northumberland, County Durham, Tyne and Wear and the Tees Valley, spreads magnificently north along the east coast of Northern England, from the North Yorkshire Moors to Berwick-upon-Tweed and the river which divides England from Scotland. This, at one time, was England's first defence against the marauders from the North.

Northumbria is a collection of wonders. Along the coast are the age-old North Sea ports, once the beaches of access where the Northmen used to land their longships before spreading the Viking culture with longsword and battleaxe. They are still remembered in the prayer book of the Church of England in the words: 'Save us from the wrath of the North men.'

Some of the beaches have been swallowed up, now, by shipbuilding towns like Tyneside and Hartlepool, and some are the setting for fishing ports like Beadnel, where generations of fishermen can trace their family names back 500 years. But there are still plenty of great spreading strands along the North East coast, and the traditional design of the Viking longships still lives on in the high-prowed design of the Northumberland coble. This inshore fishing boat sits upright on the sand when the tide retreats, because, like the Viking ships, it has a flat bottom so that it can be beached without falling over on to its vulnerable sides.

There is the great spread of the Kielder Forest with its massive man-made lake, and the bird of prey centre from which some of the birds used in *Badger* are recruited, tucked behind the Northumberland National Park. There is the historic quay at Hartlepool, where the 1817 frigate *Trincomalee*, the oldest British warship still afloat, acts as a living museum.

There are the many castles such as the magnificent one at Alnwick, where the Duke of Northumberland spends his winters; Bamburgh on the coast; Chillingham with its herd of prehistoric white cattle; Dunstanburgh with its feet in the North Sea; Norham where Sir Walter Scott set his book, *Marmion*; Etal on the Border, keeping an eye on the predatory Scots, and many, many others. This is an embattled part of our country, and the architecture reflects it.

In 'Cock o' the Walk' (Series II, Episode 4) the illegal cock-fighting ring carry out their activities in a ruined pele (pronounced 'peel') tower. These tower houses are not uncommon in the Borders, on both sides, and were simple strongholds. The inhabitants put their animals in the ground floor and lived from the first floor upwards, accessing their living accommodation by a ladder which could be pulled up in emergencies. They must have smelled pretty strong, and if the invading enemies had enough time to lay a really good fire in the downstairs byre, they could very easily be turned from refuges into death-traps. They are a standing reminder of our violent past, and they make good temporary cattle and sheep pens.

Night-time filming can be a precarious business.

There are the beauties of the North Pennines, the wildness of the Cheviots, and running through it all, a physical reminder of our history, is the Wall the Roman emperor, Hadrian, built to keep out the Scots and define the northern limit of his reign. You can walk along the Wall to this day, visit the Roman forts which dot the countryside, inspect the temples, and see some of the reconstructions of the Roman look-out towers and mile castles.

The man who knows all this like his own backyard is Simon King, the location manager of the *Badger* unit, who found all the locations in which McCabe has his adventures.

Simon King says his wife is getting very fed up with his obsession for his job. It takes him two hours to cover the ten-minute trip to the shops and back, he says, because at every turning he sees a little alleyway he has not noticed before, a house which can double for a medieval tavern because it has no television aerial or satellite dish, or a stretch of open land which will be a perfect setting for *Byker Grove*.

Simon says he didn't so much choose his job as bump into it: 'I was building boats when I started work in television as a mini-bus driver on a student film,' he says. 'I heard they were

making a pilot film for a series called *Byker Grove,* signed on as a runner, and just kind of graduated to what I am doing now.'

Commercials keep him busy, but period dramas keep him happy. He has a list in his head of village streets without double yellow lines, historic buildings whose satellite dishes can be easily disguised, and front doors which can be replaced, however temporarily, with proper 'period' ones. He recognizes a good gable when he sees one, does Simon.

Simon knows where to find the pele tower used in the cock-fighting sequences, how to get up the valleys to Sweet Hope lake near Kirkwhelpington (Series I, Episode 3: 'The World According to Carp'), where one otter after another missed its cue, or how to find the spooky old vicarage in Co Durham where the 'bent' taxidermist plied his trade (Series I, Episode 2: 'I've Got Glue Under My Skin').

The old and the new: Hadrian's Wall and the Angel of the North.

It was Simon King who found the handsome Black Bull Inn at Matfen, which was transformed into the Goose and Gargle pub run by Julia (Jayne Charlton MacKenzie). The Armitages' house is almost next door in real life, though on screen it is carefully placed some distance away.

Simon King found the farm at which McCabe's stone-built 'cottage' is located, the site of Steph's Sanctuary, the moors on which the local lord's deer were poached (Series I, Episode 1, 'It's a Jungle Out There'), and the fields in which sheep were rustled (Series II, Episode 3: 'Holding On').

There are rules to finding locations. It is not enough just to find a house or a piece of scenery which fits the bill, any more than a casting director can rest on his or her laurels simply because they find an actor who looks right. A good location should have an atmosphere of its own. A spooky building can help enormously to build up atmosphere for a sinister storyline.

It must be roomy enough and in a large enough setting for filming to take place. There is no point in finding the perfect looking rickety cottage if the setting is too cramped to get a proper camera angle without also showing the awful modern conversion ten yards down the street.

It must have several other things, too. Adequate parking space either on site or within a reasonable distance, because location shooting involves an army of experts and their equipment. There has to be enough room for the make-up caravan and the costume van; room for the location headquarters and the actors' mobile dressing rooms. There has to be facilities for the catering van – location catering is one of the more arcane arts of television, because it is a principle of filming that a happy well-fed unit is a hard-working unit. There also has to be room for the converted bus which acts as a dining room and common room in bad weather.

If the project being filmed is a period piece, there will be specialized historical vehicles, too, which must be accommodated and kept safe. Horses to pull coaches arrive in horse boxes which have to be parked somewhere while the filming is in process. The wounded horse which is treated by Steph to win the trotting race in 'Holding On' (Series II, Episode 3) needed both accommodation and make-up.

Finding all this, whilst also holding in mind the needs of the script and the atmosphere of the piece, is extremely demanding, leaving Simon with no easy task.

CHAPTER FOUR

FIGHTING A CRUEL SPORT

t is easy to assume, seeing the high drama of Tom McCabe's life and work, that it all originated in the fertile brains of the writers who have brought the series to our screens. Sadly, considering the crimes he has to deal with, the series is very firmly based on the truth. Not all the cases McCabe deals with are taken directly from the case-books of the PWLOs, but every one of them is inspired by real-life cases and based on the truth. Deer poachers really do slaughter animals by the dozen overnight (Series I, Episode 1: 'It's a Jungle Out There'); grown men really do dig badgers out of their setts and set dogs on them (Series I, Episode 4: 'Setts, Lies and Videotape'), and there really is a thriving trade in plundering the nests of rare birds in order to sell them abroad.

The producers consult the real-life professionals constantly. PC Paul Henery is always on hand to steer the case back to solid ground if it looks like wandering into questionable turf, and he and Jerome Flynn regularly talk together about their mutual interest in animals and wildlife.

'I like Jerome. He is genuinely interested in wildlife and we get on together very easily,' says Paul. 'I think the series is a good thing for the PWLO network as well.'

So how did this network of very special policemen come to exist in the first place?

Terry Rands, who first suggested a specialized wildlife crime force.

If any one man can be said to have started the idea going, it is Terry Rands, the now retired former Assistant Chief Constable of Essex. When he was a superintendent, in 1980, he wrote what was, at the time, a controversial article in *The Police Review*. It was a reasoned and informed article that stated that despite a list of legislation from the Protection of Birds Act of 1954–67, Deer Act of 1963, Conservation of Seals Act of 1970, the Badgers Act 1973 and the Conservation of Wild Creatures and Wild Plants Act 1975 – or maybe *because* of this plethora of related but not identical Acts – not many policemen had a clear idea of wildlife legislation, and their responsibilities under the Acts.

The result was that organizations such as the RSPCA and the RSPB had to take upon themselves the responsibility of bringing cases to court, as well as dealing with people who complained to their local police station and were often referred to these voluntary organizations.

This led to mixed feelings. Not unsurprisingly, there was some resentment among the officials of these non-governmental organizations about the amount of time and money they were expected to lay out on what was basically a police job. On the other hand, dedicated men and women such as the investigations officers of the RSPB decidedly wanted to be in at the kill, when people like birds' eggers, falcon thieves and bird-of-prey persecutors, and badger-baiters, came to court.

An added complication, even twenty years ago, was the increasing pressure on police forces to cut their budgets, and show better results in a list of priority crimes despite their diminishing staff levels.

Taking birds' eggs, for instance, which many people associated with schoolboys' activities, rather like using a catapult and climbing trees, naturally came much lower down the scale than burglary. And, even when the RSPCA or RSPB managed to get a case that far – and proving a wildlife crime was often so difficult as to make a court case impossible – the penalties were so weak that the police began to wonder whether getting their man into the dock was worth the effort and money.

The first sign of a breakthrough was in Kirby Lonsdale in 1979 when a man found guilty of taking three peregrine eggs was fined £900. This was hardly a fortune, considering he could have netted at least £3000 – probably more if he sold the birds on the international market – but it was a step in the right direction.

Terry Rands suggested that there should be one police officer in each force with a special responsibility to study the law relating to wildlife, and that this officer should be available to advise arresting officers where they stood.

'Good idea,' said his superiors. 'You're it!'

And there the matter might have rested, if it had not been for the enthusiasm of Rands and his colleague, the then-Superintendent Mick Brewer of Harlow, and others, combined with Rands's talent for nagging people along what he considered to be the right lines.

The 'weapon' which fell immediately into the hands of the police was the Wildlife and Countryside Act of 1981, which covered everything from greater crested newts to magic mushrooms.

Acting Chief Constable Mick Brewer, a founding member of the PWLOs.

One force after another took up the idea of having one concerned officer who could study the wildlife legislation and advise colleagues on its provisions. Thus, the network of the PWLO was formed.

It held its first national conference in 1989, and the following year Rands was able to say: 'Now we have a Wildlife Liaison Officer in virtually every police force...'

Ten years later, there are more than 650 PWLOs and the number is growing all the time. The man most concerned with the health and expansion of the PWLO movement now is that same Mick Brewer, who, at the time of writing, is Acting Chief Constable of Warwickshire.

The PWLOs are desperately needed. When Paul Henery was appointed as Northumbria's first full-time PWLO, on the retirement of the previous incumbent (who was only a part-time PWLO), Paul was not even sure if there would be enough work to keep him busy. Within months, however, he was already overworked. Not

Safely underground,
these badgers eye the
camera with suspicion.

because the amount of wildlife crime was rising so fast – although subsequent research has shown that it was – but because people had a focus for their suspicions and their complaints. They had somewhere to go and complain.

Recorded wildlife crime in the Northumbria area went up from twenty or so cases a year to more than 600 a year.

There are roughly three areas of wildlife crime, though these areas include almost as many sub-divisions as there are animals and plants to abuse.

'Anyway, so far as I am concerned, we have three main areas of crime, these days,' says Paul Henery. 'Badger-baiting comes top with me because of its inherent cruelty and the type of offender. Research shows that the men who bait badgers are also involved in other areas of violent crime, like armed robbery, bank raiding and the like. They are people we should want to watch and catch anyway.

'The second is animal poaching for profit. I am not talking about the old guy who goes out after a couple of rabbits for the pot. The men I am after are the ones who make a business of it – the ones who steal pheasants, deer, salmon and sea trout on a commercial scale. And the third is rare bird persecution.'

He could also have added plant stealing, which is now taking a terrible toll on our countryside, but more of that later.

BADGER-BAITING

Badgers are universally loved by the British public. They are regarded with affection by almost everyone who has seen one episode of *Brockside* or *Badger Watch,* and by a lot of people who have never actually set eyes on a badger.

BADGERS AND THE LAW

The Protection of Badgers Act, 1992, makes it an offence to:
- Wilfully kill or injure a badger or attempt to take a badger from the wild
- Possess the body or any remains of a dead badger
- Possess, sell, or offer for sale a living badger
- Cruelly ill-treat any badger
- Use badger 'tongs' in any attempt to kill or take a badger from the wild
- Dig for any badger, for whatever reason
- Use a firearm to kill a badger
- Interfere with a badger sett by obstructing the entrance, destroying the sett, or encouraging a dog to enter the sett or in any way disturbing the occupant.

There is, however, a down-side to badgers, and it has to be recognized. Badgers are large aggressive carnivores, universally respected by the people who are legally required to deal with them. PWLOs regard them as 'thirty-pound ferrets', and they are justified in doing so. Badgers are big, fast moving, and can be both aggressive and as destructive as a fox.

They also carry tuberculosis, which is infectious to both humans and cattle. They have been blamed for the spread of TB into cow herds, and the Ministry of Agriculture, Fisheries and Food is currently carrying out an experiment to find out just how widespread the contagion is.

Badgers certainly do have TB. When they range widely on their nightly expeditions, they urinate as they go, and cattle which eat the grass on which a badger has urinated can and do develop bovine TB. This can contaminate their milk, which then, if not checked, can pass into the human food chain.

Since the policy of 'clean ring' culling (killing infected badgers in an infected area until a ring of uninfected setts is reached) was abandoned in the mid 1980s, apparently due to pressure from badger groups, the incidence of TB in milk herds has risen by 700 per cent.

Whatever the scientific findings from the cull-and-clear policy, which although controversial seems to be scientifically unassailable, the police's standing advice for officers is not to handle even the corpse of a road-killed badger without wearing disposable gloves.

So, however lovable and cuddly Brock may look on television, he has an effect on other animals which does not endear him to the agricultural community.

One woman, living in Sussex, recently reported that her hen-run had been raided time after time by what she assumed was an unusually strong fox. Too late she discovered that the culprit was a local badger which tore the protective netting off the hen-house windows, broke glass from the frames and even tore up floor boards in order to get at the succulent hens.

Badgers are very strong and, as two police officers on patrol in a rural area discovered, can be very destructive. Having found a badger which had been hit by a car, they conscientiously put it in the boot of their car and took it back to their headquarters where it was locked in an empty office while a vet was called to check on how it had been killed.

In the interim, however, the badger, which had only been stunned by the collision, came to, presumably with a sore head and a ferocious temper, and completely trashed the office.

Badgers must therefore be handled with great care. It can be very difficult to get a badger off your leg, and their bites are extremely painful.

During the making of *Badger* the crew were called to a farm where a young badger had been found hiding out in straw at the back of a barn. It had clearly been baited: it had a spade mark across its face and bite marks on its back. How it had got away was not clear, but it was taken immediately to a sanctuary where it was treated and later allowed back into the wild.

Badgers are not only baited in their own home setts. As shown in *Badger* (Series I, Episode 4: 'Setts, Lies and Videotape'), there is a brisk interest in blood sports in cities. The badger is taken off to a location where a 'pit' is constructed with fences and hay bales, and a select group of spectators and backers are invited to watch the proceedings and bet on the outcome – rather in the style of a bare knuckle fight, a cock-fight or a dog-fight. Indeed, the men concerned will probably be the same men who attend those kinds of events.

In the *Badger* story, the badger was supplied by a building-site worker who was encouraged to dig out a sett which was interfering with the development of a building site.

It is not unusual for a developer to find that there is an established badger sett, right in the middle of his proposed site for a luscious little development of executive-style homes. Most builders, of course, observe the law strictly, but for some men who have shareholders and bank managers pressurizing them, there is temptation. If the sett were not there the

BADGER-BAITING – A CRUEL SPORT

Because people don't often see badgers, now protected by the Protection of Badgers Act 1992, they assume they are rare and threatened. But this is no longer true. Distinguished by their black-and-white striped faces and bumbling gait, they live underground in social groups, are unobtrusive and go abroad mainly at night. They are very strong and aggressive when cornered, and criminals and law-enforcers alike know better than to come within snapping distance of a badger. When a badger bites, it bites to the bone and it takes a crowbar to prise its jaws off a leg.

Criminals handle them with huge iron tongs with which they grab the animal round the neck to move it from one place to another. They prize the animal for its aggression, and the ones they prize in particular are pregnant or nursing females, which will fight with even greater ferocity in defence of their young. Criminals will go to inordinate lengths to get their hands on such an animal.

Most badger digging is done in broad daylight at a sett which is conveniently out of sight of most of the public. The first move is to fit a terrier with a radio location-finder, a perfectly legitimate instrument when used for ferreting in wild rabbit burrows. The terrier is then sent down the sett to isolate one of the occupants, and the signal is monitored from the surface. When the signal stops moving, the men move in to do what is known as 'crowning down'. In order to 'crown down', they dig a large pit which can go down ten feet or so. This is occasionally enlarged to form an extempore badger-baiting pit into which the dogs can be dropped.

Some badger-baiting is performed just for 'fun', but it is usual for the baiters to make side bets on which dog will inflict the first wounds, which will inflict the most bites, which will eventually kill the badger, etc. The largest bet known so far is said to be £40,000 on a single London 'bait', so this is serious criminal business.

Of course, most badgers are stronger and more aggressive and dangerous than the dogs which are set on them, so it is necessary for a 'caring' dog-owner to give his animal more of a chance by brutally wounding the badger. Breaking the jaw or a leg is the usual method, but it is not unknown for a badger to be blinded, or have its back broken.

A badger may be caged and taken hundreds of miles to be 'baited'.

INSPECTOR STEVE KOURIK – PWLO of Hertfordshire

Born: London, son of an Austrian who left wartime Austria one jump ahead of the Gestapo, and spent the Second World War making gun-sights.

Education: Aloysius College in Highgate, North London.

Career: Trained as forensic chemist at Brunel University, but opted for a career in the police instead. Joined the force in 1973 and worked his way up. Now supported by twenty-seven divisional PWLOs.

work would not be held up, possibly for weeks or months. How easy it would be to ignore the sett, run a couple of bulldozers over the site and apologize later.

This is a mistake: under the Protection of Badgers Act, the penalty for killing a badger or interfering with a sett is £5000 and/or a six-month jail sentence *for each and every offence*. If a developer needs to move a sett, he must apply to English Nature for a licence. He will not be allowed to dig, even by hand, within ten metres of a sett entrance, use light digging machinery within 20 metres or heavy plant within 30 metres (Series I, Episode 4: 'Setts, Lies and Videotape'). Drawing maps which exaggerate distances to make it appear that the machinery is a legal distance away, at least on paper, is likely to get the developer into even more trouble.

Baiting carried out in the countryside can take place in the open air on a fine winter's morning before everyone goes home for a good roast lunch, and a family day by the fire. It is an indication of the character of the people who indulge in such a pursuit that they regard this as a proper way to spend their time on a fine Sunday morning.

Blocking a sett so that the badger is either trapped within it, or permanently deprived of access to it, is also an offence. Proving such a case, however, can be complicated, because servants of fox hunts who hold a licence for blocking the earths of foxes or setts of badgers are allowed to block a sett to prevent a pursued fox from taking refuge in it.

The law, however, is very specific about which materials can be used for such a purpose, and how strongly the sett can be blocked. It is perfectly legal to stuff a sett with tightly wadded hay or loose soil. This makes it impossible for a hard-pressed fox to disappear down it, but allows an irritated badger to scoop it out at his leisure.

What is not legal is for a sett to be blocked with, for instance, heavy lumps of wet clay well stamped down, or for the sides and surroundings to be dug out, and packed down the hole. In 1998, in the Queen's Bench, Lord Justice Rose and Mr Justice Sullivan decided that when you are packing a sett entrance, 'loose soil' means what it says – not clods of clay well stamped down (*Lovett v Bussey*, 3 April 1998).

Local badger groups – and there will certainly be one within your area – are a valuable extra surveillance tool in preventing all kinds of badger crime. When they see something they do not like, they shout their heads off. Inspector Steve Kourik, PWLO of Hertfordshire, says that working closely with badger groups within his police area has caused the illegal digging of badger setts to plummet.

'The public has now become aware of where badger setts are, and if, while walking their dogs, they see someone behaving oddly, they will report it straight away,' he says.

THE PENALTIES

The courts have started – not before time, in the opinion of the PWLOs – to hand down stiff custodial sentences to wildlife criminals. Four men trapped by DNA tests and convicted of digging badgers in 1996 were sentenced to five months' imprisonment each and had their dogs confiscated. A gamekeeper who had been trapping and snaring badgers in the most horrendous circumstances in Cumbria was sent to jail for three months in 1999 after the RSPCA brought a case against him.

A badger is dug out from its sett.

CHAPTER FIVE

ILLEGAL HARE-COURSING

Badger-baiting is not the only pursuit of the violent criminal. Another, often pursued by the same people, is illegal hare-coursing. Some crimes are very territorial, and illegal hare-coursing is one of them. Coursers need large open tracts of even-surfaced land without cover for the hares, on which their dogs can reach top running speed. North Hertfordshire, within the territory of Inspector Steve Kourik, and Thames Valley, the bailiwick of DC Sheila Wright, based at Wokingham, are favourite targets, as are the flat fields of Cambridgeshire.

PWLOs who have large open fields in their territory invariably make the acquaintance of illegal hare courses. The modern motorway is not just a benefit to the law-abiding traveller – it is also a boon to the wildlife criminal. Not only can he use the transport network to carry his live loot around the countryside, he can also drive quickly to other parts of the country to carry out his crimes, and then return home to sleep in his own bed.

Two groups of people in particular find this easy, fast travelling a great blessing on a Sunday morning: the illegal hare-coursers and professional poachers.

Illegal hare-coursers are notoriously hard to catch and bring to book, despite the fact that they are easily spotted and usually make no secret of what they are doing. Police officers look out for groups of vehicles, usually vans or four-wheel drives, parked on grass verges, in lay-bys or farm tracks for no apparent reason. Nearby they expect to see the usual line of men with dogs walking across large open fields.

'If they see you, they will either keep walking away from you or turn round and walk back to you proclaiming they are only out walking the dogs,' says the standard police officers' guide on the subject, published by and for *Countrywatch,* which PC Hale, its founder, calls 'Neighbourhood Watch for the Countryside', and which is backed by the Thames Valley Police.

However, PC Hale also warns that a single police officer, unsupported by a number of colleagues, should treat such a situation with extreme caution.

'Never put yourself at risk searching vehicles – only do it if you have somebody with you,' he says.

An even more dangerous phenomenon, he says, is the Convoy, consisting of transit-type vans, front and back, with a number of expensive cars in between. The cars contain criminals on their way to a gambling event, which can involve anything from badger-baiting to hare-coursing to cock-fighting. The vans contain their minders.

The illegal hare-coursing groups traditionally operate on Sunday mornings in the autumn and winter after the standing crops have been cut. These days, though,

HARES AND THE LAW

Hare-coursing is illegal when it is carried out:
- on land without the owner's consent
- after the hours of darkness without consent
- on an ecclesiastical holiday, such as Christmas Day, or on a Sunday.

There are three main laws related to illegal coursing:
- The Night Poaching Act, 1828.
- The Game Act, 1831.
- The Poaching Prevention Act, 1862.

because the police are more aware of their activities, they are perfectly capable of making their arrangements on any other day of the week.

Hare-coursing – and there is a legal form of this sport (see box, right) – originated in prehistoric times.

The legal form of coursing is strictly regulated, and carried out under the supervision of a mounted judge and 'slippers' whose job it is to 'let slip' the dogs. They are licensed by the National Coursing Club.

The course begins when beaters start a hare which runs across an open, mown space. Pairs of dogs, usually greyhounds, whippets or salukis, wearing coloured collars for identification, are released to chase the hare, and the competition is based on their technique, turn of speed, skill at 'turning' the hare and their dexterity in the chase.

The hare in legal coursing is rarely killed because the National Coursing Club goes to great lengths to try and ensure it survives the chase, and an escape band of un-mown undergrowth surrounds the coursing area.

Illegal coursers have no such considerations. They simply drive to their chosen ground in fleets of vehicles which often

LEGAL HARE-COURSING

This sport was known to the Ancient Greeks, and a Roman writer, remarking on it in AD 116, pointed out that true coursers were delighted when the hare escaped. Today's legal coursers maintain stoutly that they are, too, and claim that while fewer than 300 hares are killed annually during legal coursing events, more than 400,000 are shot in game-control programmes.

In this country, bringing down hares and rabbits with dogs goes with the harvest, and was originally carried out to provide meat for the pot. Typically, it would to happen when a big field was being mown, and locals with their dogs would gather round and wait for the rabbits and hares which lived in the crop to run for it as the reapers got closer to them. Hares are classified as game and are, therefore, the property of the land owner. Rabbits are not. Then, the dogs would be slipped and any rabbits caught would belong to the owner of the dog.

GREYHOUNDS

It is thought that the name 'greyhound' derives from the original name 'gazehound' because greyhounds hunt by sight rather than smell. If they cannot see their prey, they almost invariably lose it, whereas hounds would be able to track it by smell.

Greyhounds are prized for coursing and racing because of their speed, which can be in excess of 40mph.

contain whole families and several dogs. This is not an exclusively male crime, either. Large numbers of women take part and there are frequently children present, being trained up to become the next generation of coursers. The vehicles often simply crash through gates and fences, and the participants with the dogs form a line stretching across the field and start walking in a vast sweep across it.

If a hare gets up and starts to run, one or several dogs are released, and the course continues until the hare is killed. The winning dog is the one which kills the hare. This continues until the field has been thoroughly depopulated, and the coursers then move on to the next field to repeat the process.

The coursing is either done purely for fun, or in order to bet on the relative performances of the dogs. Bets can run to thousands of pounds, and the dogs, which are 'lurchers' or cross-bred greyhounds, are highly prized and often change hands for large sums of money.

As mentioned before, the people who indulge in this form of sport are often violent, and will react aggressively to any attempt to interrupt them. One young

Above: the hare poised to run.

Left: The dogs are 'slipped' in the legal form of hare-coursing.

DC SHEILA WRIGHT – PWLO for Thames Valley

Born: London, daughter of a civil servant.

Career: Herself a civil servant in her first job, Sheila joined the police twenty-two years ago and worked first as a uniformed officer, moved to the Regional Crime Squad, then on to the Drugs Squad. Applied for the job of PWLO when it became a full-time appointment, and took on responsibility for training other PWLOs.

police officer who found himself following a convoy of would-be coursers down a narrow lane was trapped when the vehicle directly in front of him stopped suddenly, and five men climbed out with pick-axe handles and told him to make himself scarce.

Alone and unarmed, he had little chance of summoning back-up in time to make any difference to the course of events. Also, since it is necessary when bringing a case to provide eye-witness evidence backed up by several witnesses, it would have been pointless for him to continue.

The tactic used against these illegal hare-coursers in DC Sheila Wright's area is to 'soak' the area with policemen – either regular officers or regulars supported by specially recruited 'specials' – and simply cause so much hassle that the coursers eventually get the message and stay away.

'It was very successful, and, hopefully, we did not just move them out of the area, but made them go away altogether,' she comments.

Even when caught red-handed (sometimes literally) the coursers brazenly claim that they were innocently walking their pets when a hare jumped up in front of them and the dog was away after it before anybody could do anything to prevent it.

Hare-coursers have an enviable knowledge of the countryside, and know the letter of the law applying to their pursuit. This means they know, if they are to be charged, a witness must be found who will swear that he or she saw a specific individual let loose a specific dog and that the plain intention was to run down a specific hare.

In the confused circumstances, it is difficult for anyone to be certain of the facts, particularly when defence witnesses will swear to almost anything, including the fact that the accused does not own a dog and was, in any case, at home in another county at the time of the offence.

Today, because of the growing use of DNA evidence in wildlife cases, those who break the law rarely actually handle the dead animals, or put them into their vehicles where bloodstains might be found.

What hare-coursers enjoy is the thrill of the chase, and the animals they watch being chased do not figure in their list of priorities at all. If they can't find a hare and a deer happens to be occupying the nearest field, they are perfectly prepared to course that, instead. It is not unknown for them to throw their dogs out of the window of a speeding vehicle to chase a quarry. Dead game is often left where it falls.

CHAPTER SIX

POACHING FOR PROFIT

nother crime which is more common in some areas than others is poaching. This was the subject of more than one episode of *Badger*, including the very first episode in Series I: 'It's a Jungle Out There'. Some areas, including Northumbria, the North Yorkshire moors and the glorious countryside of Cumbria, as well as obvious areas such as Scotland, are particular targets for deer-poachers.

Forget any ideas you may have about poachers simply being out for something for the pot, dressed in a ragged tweed jacket with a pocketful of snares, a shotgun disguised as a walking stick, and a sack with string round its neck for storing the booty. Today's poachers are much more likely to be hard, brutal criminals with a nose for profit and, of course, no qualms about the law on the handling and killing of the animals they steal. In 'It's a Jungle Out There', McCabe has to ambush deer-poachers to catch them in the act of raiding a local herd.

The most common and violent form of deer-poaching is called 'lamping'. Poachers, like other wildlife criminals, are knowledgeable about their prey. They may be local men who put their local knowledge to use, or gangs from other parts of the country who cruise the area during daylight, working out where the deer like to sleep at night, and where the largest herds congregate.

They then return at night, often in some force, crash through gates and drive among the deer. The quarry is picked out by the 'lamper' with a powerful searchlight, paralysing it with fear.

The dogs – usually 'long dogs' or lurchers – are sent down the beam of light to pull down the deer, until the poachers catch up with it, and either slit its throat or shoot it. Or the poachers may drive up to the deer and shoot it with a rifle (shotguns of less than 12-bore calibre are unreliable against large animals such as deer unless specialized ammunition is used) or even a crossbow. Modern crossbows are powerful, accurate weapons that are perfect for a poacher as they have the added bonus of being silent as well as deadly.

DEER-POACHING

Under the Deer Act 1991, it is an offence to enter land without permission in search or pursuit of any deer with intent to take, kill or injure it. It is also an offence while on land to take, kill or injure any deer or try to do so, or to search for or pursue any deer or to remove the carcass.

During the close seasons, it is an offence to kill any deer.

The permitted firearms used to kill deer have to be high-velocity rifles of not less than .240 calibre, and most professionals will not use any rifle of less than .376 calibre. A shotgun may only be legally used by the occupier on his own land, using a rifled slug, fired from a 12-bore shotgun, and even then he has to prove that the deer were causing serious damage.

If the poaching ground is far enough away from witnesses, the deer are often cleaned and butchered on the spot, their entrails (known as 'gralloch') and hooves left in a pile for the gamekeeper to find.

If there is a gamekeeper in the vicinity, or likely to be one, the carcasses will be taken away to somewhere quiet or butchered in the van, although this could be used as evidence against the poachers because it will be irreversibly contaminated with DNA.

With venison valued at around £5 per pound on the legitimate market, and possibly £3 per pound at the back door of a none-too-particular hotel or restaurant, a forty-pound deer carcass can be worth anything up to £120 on the illegal market. A well-organized gang can easily take a dozen deer in a single night, so that would not be a bad return on an investment of a few gallons of petrol, some bullets and a bit of time.

Deer are not the only target for poachers, of course, although pound-for-pound, they represent the best value. Obviously, the bigger the deer, the better the profit, and only a few need to be sought. Once butchered, venison is anonymous, save that poached venison is rarely properly 'hung' and may be tainted because it was not immediately drained of its blood. Blood left to stagnate in a carcass thrown into the back of a van can develop toxins which can taint the meat and be dangerous to the eater.

None of this deters poachers.

Ian Grindy, a former gamekeeper now working as an estate manager for North West Water, recalls one nightmare time when he was working for a private estate in the North West, which was taking punishing losses of its game.

The estate was losing hundreds of birds on a weekly basis, and, try as they might, the two gamekeepers never managed to track down the poachers or discover how they were managing to take their hauls away.

They worked out that the weight of the game would have made it impossible for the thieves to carry their booty away by hand, but never managed to catch the poachers in the act.

After a while, however, the poachers became careless and the gamekeepers found pick-up truck tyre marks in lay-bys on the roads bordering the estate. They then discovered tyre marks within the estate, leading to the roosts from which birds were being taken. Strangely, though, the tyre marks were single track, and Ian Grindy,

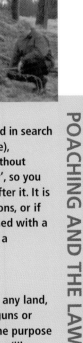

POACHING AND THE LAW

BY DAY:
It is an offence unlawfully to enter land or be on any land in search or pursuit of game (hares, partridges, pheasant or grouse), woodcock, snipe or rabbits. Sending a dog on to land without actually stepping on that land yourself is 'unlawful entry', so you can't shoot a hare from the road and send your dog in after it. It is a greater offence to be in a group of five or more persons, or if five or more threaten violence, or if one of them is armed with a firearm. During the day, only a police officer can arrest a suspected poacher and seize his equipment.

BY NIGHT:
It is an offence to take or destroy game and rabbits on any land, open or closed, any highway or road, with or without guns or snares. It is an offence to enter or be on any land for the purpose of destroying game with a net, gun, trap or other device (like a lamp). If more than three people trespass on any land at night and one is armed with a gun, crossbow, bludgeon or other offensive weapon, all are equally guilty. During the night, the landowner, their gamekeeper or other employees have the authority to hold someone until the police arrive.

Fallow deer were introduced to this country by the Normans.

suspecting that the poachers were using motor cycles, could not understand why he and his colleague never heard one. Given the regularity of the thefts, it was

A poacher at work in the shadows is hard to spot, even with a night-sight.

obvious that a regular market had been established and that the poachers were supplying a continuing demand.

By mounting a round-the-clock watch – which meant that both gamekeepers did a full day's work and then took it in turns to spend the night on patrol – and calling in the local police, he eventually nabbed his poachers, who, it turned out, were using not motor cycles but wheelbarrows to transport their booty.

Taken to court, the poachers were charged with 280 specimen offences, and fined the modest sum of £250 each. But trust a crook to be too dim to keep his mouth shut – one of them gave himself and his colleagues away. Outside the court, the ringleader jeered at the policeman who had brought the case.

'What's £250?' he shouted. 'I'll make it back next week. Last year I made £20,000!'

Instead of looking put out, the policeman merely looked thoughtful and made a note. His very next phone call was to the Inland Revenue, to report the poachers for undisclosed income. The Inland Revenue 'ghost busters' moved in and the fines were enormous, proving there is more than one way to skin a poacher.

The police also suspected that this operation was only a part of a much bigger operation, involving the taking of deer from Northern parks and salmon from rivers in the West Country.

The damage that poaching does in terms of animals and humans spreads outwards in ever increasing circles. Gamekeepers say that there is a vast difference between daytime poachers and night-time ones. The anonymity afforded by darkness, which is almost total inside a game park, can encourage the violence which is implicit in poaching. Nervous, keyed-up men, out at night carrying firearms, are a volatile mixture.

Keepers are also aware that if a gang turns nasty their families and homes are also at risk. There are several instances of gangs besieging a gamekeeper and his family in their homes, and tragedy has been averted only by luck and the timely arrival of the police.

Then there is the cost of the crimes to the entire rural community. Many estates, both large and small, depend on shooting for their survival and it is not unusual for a well-stocked shoot to put down 6000 birds at the beginning of the season. Sportsmen from the Continent and the US will happily pay up to £5000 for a day's shooting for a small party, and for that kind of money the clients expect good lively birds – and lots of them.

A sustained raid on a game estate can halve the number of birds, and probably involve the appointment of a new head gamekeeper. Two bad seasons on a medium or small shoot, and there will not be a gamekeeper at all, because there will be no clients. Gamekeepers are aware of this and conscious of the fine line they tread between guarding the game and guarding their own and their family's lives not only against violence, but against animosity in their local communities.

Not a born angler, McCabe on the trail of a counterfeiter.

In *Badger* Series I, Episode 6: 'Low Fidelity', Kieran Prendiville touches on this dilemma when Dominic McGuire, the innocent gamekeeper on a local shoot, is accused of killing hen harriers, and is suspended from his job. Under pressure and disapproval of her classmates, his daughter Teresa also turns against him.

Without the shooting, a number of local people will be out of work, starting with the owner of the shoot and working outwards through local hotels and inns, to the tradespeople and country workers who depend on casual work like beating.

Game fish, too, are targets for the poacher. Salmon or sea trout are a delicacy, and these days, with refrigerated vans and open roads, salmon poached in South West England can be on a Scottish hotel table within twelve hours.

The poachers sometimes use two small boats – robust inflatable dinghies will do nicely – with a long fine net strung between them. If the salmon are running, they can expect to pick up forty to fifty in a night. In some tidal waters, all the thieves have to do is check the pools left by the receding tide and scoop out the fish trapped there.

Another system is to poison the water with a substance which de-oxygenates it. Anything living within the stream will then die of lack of oxygen, and can be scooped out and sold. Since the creature did not ingest the poison, they are safe to eat.

Fish poaching is particularly profitable in the North of England and Scotland where salmon is also traditionally farmed. There, with each rod paying money which often runs into the thousands for the rent of fishing streams, the water is so valuable that some owners hire ex-SAS men to protect their investments.

The fish do not, in themselves, have to be all that valuable, either. In 'The World According to Carp' (Series I, Episode 3), the business of the poachers was to steal prize carp from one competition lake in the Midlands to seed a pond in Northumbria so that a fishing competition could be held there. This rarely works well, however, because top fishermen are as knowledgeable about the fish they catch as they are about one another: a really top rod is even able to recognize individual fish by sight.

CHAPTER SEVEN

A BIRD IN THE HAND...

For some reason, birds are a special target for several classes of wildlife criminals. Since even the largest of birds are vulnerable, criminals hit rare species particularly hard. Sometimes, too, the birds' ways of life make them particularly vulnerable. Hen harriers, for example, which featured in *Badger* (Series I, Episode 6: 'Low Fidelity'), are ground-nesting birds which hunt by patrolling in long low sweeps. Their nests are easy to wipe out simply by stamping on them, and the adults are particularly easy to shoot because they are within short range of the guns.

Bird persecution falls into three main groups: egg collecting, falcon stealing, and poisoning, shooting or nest destruction by people who see them as a threat to their livelihood.

Claire and McCabe keep watch to catch a rare bird 'egger'.

The first kind of bird criminal is the birds' egg collector, seen in *Badger* (Series 1, Episode 1: 'It's a Jungle Out There'). In this story, the criminal targeted the nest of a peregrine falcon which was being watched by RSPB Investigations Officer Claire Armitage (Rebecca Lacey), only to find that another raider had already been there.

All real-life PWLOs have an unwelcome familiarity with egg collectors, probably because of the eggers' exasperating insistence that they are not doing anything wrong. PC Paul Henery maintains that one egg collector in his area is so cocky about his obsession that the policeman regularly arranges for him to go on television, because nothing the police can say or do can damage the man as much as he can damage himself.

That particular egger is even arrogant enough to be training a younger collector to take over from him when he is too old to go climbing for himself.

'He says he loves wildlife and loves the countryside, but nevertheless, he goes out and destroys whole families of birds by stealing their eggs,' says Henery. 'And he argues all the time that he is doing nothing wrong.

'One time he was on television telling about the nest of a passerine which he raided regularly. He took one clutch of eggs, and the bird re-laid, so he took that one as well, and she re-laid again. In all, he took five clutches of eggs

The egg poacher in the first episode, unaware he's eating poisoned venison.

off her and when the poor bird re-laid for the sixth time, he generously let her keep that clutch.

'The way he was telling it, he obviously thought he was doing the bird a favour but everyone watching was thinking: "You bastard!" The fact that he was doing wrong completely passed him by.'

Another PWLO admits that he has made friends with a former egg-collector and now regularly goes with him on field trips – which, of course, have absolutely nothing to do with bird egging.

'I only met the man because I prosecuted him,' he says. 'But we became friends, and, since he gave up collecting eggs, I have been out on many a trip with him. His knowledge about birds is enormous. He argues that he only ever took one egg from a nest – but a bird often deserts a clutch of eggs when one has been taken, so he may have killed the clutch as surely as if he had taken the lot.'

It is more usual for eggers to take the whole clutch, and occasionally the nest in which they were laid. The more rare the bird, the more valuable the clutch to a collector, so the last clutch laid by the last surviving breeding mother in the country is by definition the most desirable.

The eggs are rarely marketed, so there is usually no monetary gain, although there is growing evidence of a thriving international exchange of illegal birds' eggs through the Internet.

Generally, though, eggers are like the collectors who fuel international art thieves. They want the egg or clutch simply because they hunger to own it, even if they cannot ever show it to anybody else other than trusted co-enthusiasts.

'They will argue that when they take a clutch, the bird will re-lay,' says Paul Henery. 'But something like an osprey, one of this country's most rare birds, cannot re-lay. Take its eggs, and that is the end of the osprey for that year.'

Luckily, the obsessive nature of the egg-collector can help the prosecuting officer to make an arrest.

Egg-collectors usually keep a diary in which the story of each egg, where it was found, and how and when it was taken, is painstakingly noted, right down to the details of how the collector avoided suspicion by the authorities. This, plus their attempts to fool the police, can lead to some give-away contradictions. One collector whose illicit haul of eggs was reckoned to be 3000, attempted to cover up where, when and how he came by the eggs by keeping a huge library of record cards. On examination, though, this subterfuge proved useless for his defence because on several occasions the cards claimed that he had collected eggs in two different counties at the same time on the same day.

JOAN CHILDS – RSPB Investigations Officer

Born: York, daughter of a teacher.

Educated: Scarborough, Manchester University and Cranfield College in Bedfordshire.

Career: Her parents first sparked her interest in wildlife because of their fascination with the wild birds in their own back garden. It led to Joan studying natural history at school and going on to do a zoology degree at university, followed by a five-year post-graduate period of research which left her with an MPhil in the subject. Joined RSPB straight from university and became project manager in youth unit. Worked her way up through the ranks to the special investigations unit.

Joan Childs, the Investigations Officer for the RSPB, who is the real-life equivalent of Claire Armitage in *Badger*, says that finding the collection can be just the beginning of the problem for her.

'They keep them in a lock-up garage rented under a false name, or with the girlfriend at her house, or in the loft, or behind a panel over the stairs,' she says. 'The really amateur ones simply put them in trays on top of the wardrobe, so those are easy to find.'

But even being confronted with the evidence does not faze some of the more arrogant eggers. 'We were present at an informal interview with one egger who completely denied any knowledge of the collection,' she says. 'He had never seen it before, had no knowledge of it, didn't know where it had come from, and had no idea why anyone should think it was anything to do with him.

'It was a strange defence, because we found it in his garage. But he simply went on denying all knowledge of it until we came to the fingerprints. We said: "If we took your fingerprints, they would not appear on the drawers of the cabinet, then?"

'He said: "No!", but he suddenly went very quiet, and as soon as we left the interview room, he walked over to the cabinet, which was standing outside, and very deliberately pressed his hands all over the glass of the trays, which we all found very amusing.

'The magistrates thought it was a bit of a giggle, too. They found him guilty and fined him.'

Until recently, bird egger offences were rarely taken seriously by the courts, or indeed by most senior policemen, as cases were always hard to prove and the penalties awarded by the courts, almost laughable. However, in recent years one or two large fines have suggested that the authorities are developing a less tolerant attitude to the offence

Wildlife experts, however, are uncertain whether even the most salutary of fines will actually deter the really obsessional collectors, and want to see custodial sentences passed.

They quote the case in 1999 of Wayne Short, one of the country's most persistent offenders, who was fined £3500 in a Coventry court for the theft of eggs of protected species, including those of the extremely rare white-tailed eagle. It was his sixth conviction. On at least one occasion in the past he was fined £5000 and almost immediately offended again.

EGG-STEALING PENALTIES

Fines for collecting birds' eggs are usually linked with charges of disturbing the birds, robbing the nests and so forth. They can range at the top level from £1000 to £5000 per offence in the case of specially protected species, although top-rate fines are rarely imposed. The biggest fines ever were imposed in 1997 on two brothers, Lee McLaren and Jamie MacLaren (although brothers they spell their names differently) who were fined a total of £90,000 for egg stealing. On appeal the fines were reduced to £6000 and £4000. Since one brother was a taxi driver and the other unemployed, the fines were, in any case, devastating.

Joan Childs says that birds' eggers are so obsessive that only custodial sentences will affect them. 'Under the present Act, the fines are means-adjusted which means that, although in theory a person could be fined the highest amount for each offence and the top fine could amount to millions, in practice they are usually fined only a few hundred pounds.

'When heavy fines are imposed they are invariably overturned on appeal, so the magistrates are loath to impose them.

'In practice, what deters the eggers more is the loss of their collection, which is mandatory. However, some of them are so obsessive that they just go out and start a new collection.

'There was a suggestion in the Queen's Speech of 1999 that a new Countryside Act is on the way, and if that is so custodial sentences may be embodied in it.'

The law on egg collecting is complex. All egg collecting has been an offence under the law since the Wild Birds Protection Act of 1954. There are exceptions to cover collections of rare eggs already in the possession of collectors before this date, but the exceptions are few and far between.

The Wildlife and Countryside Act of 1981, under which much wildlife crime is prosecuted, strengthened the Wild Birds Protection Act by making the keeping of birds' eggs an offence of which the offender must prove himself innocent, rather than the law prove him guilty. In short, if you have a bird's egg in your possession, you will need an iron-clad excuse for it, or risk being fined and have the egg forfeited as well.

Joan Childs cannot help but be impressed by the expertise of eggers. 'They are experts in their field. They know a great deal about the habits of the birds, and where they like to nest. They read through the literature and, with only the slightest of hints, can work out where nests are no matter how hard we try to conceal them.

'They are expert climbers and very impressive abseilers, since the only way to get to some nests is to climb a mountain and abseil down a cliff face to reach them from above.

'For most of them, the expert knowledge is concentrated around the eggs which they are after: the times the birds mate, the gestation time, and the dates when they are most likely to lay.'

Sometimes, the eggers are even more accurate about those dates than the people who are keeping surveillance on the nests. Tales abound of bird enthusiasts who keep careful watch over a treasured nest to prevent it being raided, only to find that the raiders out-guessed them and sneaked in first.

Really sneaky raiders conceal their thefts by replacing the stolen eggs with others, so that even the bird sitting on the nest does not realize it has been hoodwinked. There are tales of eggers carefully climbing mountains and making dangerous abseils to nest sites only to discover that the eggs they have risked so much to steal are ordinary hen's eggs, left there by an earlier, cheekier robber.

Not all the people who climb mountains to prey on birds want to steal their eggs for a collection. Some of them want to steal eggs in order to pass them off as captive-bred birds which can be legitimately sold on the open market. Some want to steal chicks for the same reason.

A very few are after adult birds which can be used as breeding stock. But trying to capture an adult peregrine, which can have a wingspan over a metre across, plus a very bad temper, is very specialized work indeed. Ospreys, red kites, buzzards and honey buzzards can be one and a half times as big, and nobody in their right mind would tackle a golden eagle, all talons, beak and two clear metres of wingspan. No, what the despoilers want is a pocket full of eggs or chicks and a fast getaway, preferably out of the country.

The most desirable birds of prey are the hunting raptors which in the right market can be worth dizzying prices. Peregrines, the world's fastest birds of prey, are particularly prized in the Arab world, where hawking is a passion, and the possession of a particularly fine bird is a matter of pride.

But the Arab states are by no means the only home of falconry. There are many respectable falconers in this country, as well as a number of illegal falconers – particularly, for some reason, in the Northumbria region. The European Continent is also home to a lot of falcon buyers, legal and illegal, with Germany being a particularly good market.

Many cases of illegal trade in stolen birds of prey pass across the cluttered desk of Andy Fisher, the PWLO for the London area, based at Scotland Yard. Fisher is almost unique in the PWLO world because he is not a policeman, but a civil servant with specialist knowledge in his area, who co-ordinates the efforts of the ten divisional police officers in the Metropolitan area.

Like Joan Childs, he is frustrated that under the 1981 Wildlife and Countryside Act there are no custodial sentences, and that although the fines can be punishing, they are rarely used with full effect. There are provisions, however, for such sentences under another set of regulations called the COTES (Control of Trade In Endangered Species) Enforcement Regulations, of 1997.

'The trade in endangered species like peregrines attracts a fine up to £5000, plus up to two years in prison for each offence,' says Fisher.

The rewards of the trade are, however, too tempting to deter the raiders.

There is a perfectly legitimate trade in captive-bred birds which change hands for around £700 each, and are eagerly sought by falconers in Britain, the Continent and the Arab states. However, on the legitimate market in this country, a bird must have a sealed ring on its leg which could only have been put on as soon as it was hatched, and supporting documentation containing the bird's registration number and details of its parentage. And it is for this reason that dishonest traders will pay high prices for unhatched eggs which can then be hatched by their own certificated captive pairs.

An osprey, once extinct in the UK, shows off his five-foot wingspan.

Breeding birds in captivity is a long and painstaking process. The success rate of captive-bred birds is not high, and there are always more customers than there are young falcons for sale. So the temptation to steal or buy in wild birds and pass them off as captive-bred under cover of a legitimate breeding programme is high, and so are the rewards.

One salutary case is that of Derek Canning, an established bird-of-prey breeder in Northumbria, who in 1995 was sentenced in Newcastle Crown Court to eighteen months' imprisonment for stealing and selling protected rare birds. The court was told that he had a breeding pair of peregrine falcons, but that he was stealing wild chicks from their nesting sites, and illegally selling them on as the progeny of his captive – and legitimately held – birds.

DNA: THE KEY TO THE TRUTH

The success rate of PWLOs and their colleagues in the RSPB and RSPCA is being boosted very successfully with the advances in DNA testing pioneered at Nottingham University. At one time, DNA testing was long winded, expensive and difficult to do because it involved taking blood samples from a live bird. Because of the rules of evidence, this had to be done on the spot when the bird was often in a distressed state anyway. Sticking a needle into it to take a sample might well be fatal to the creature, and had to be done by a qualified person, usually a vet, who could be relied upon not to slaughter the evidence. Now, thanks to the work of the University team, identity can be established with as little as a single feather.

The authorities began to suspect all was not well when he seemed to have a remarkable record of successful breeding from his peregrines. They started to check on him and caught him one day with a pair of peregrine falcon chicks in his car only twenty-four hours after two were reported missing from a nest in Kielder Forest. An inspection of his premises showed a map on which ten nesting sites were identified.

Although his crimes were proved by DNA testing, he has always protested his innocence and continues to do so even after serving part of his sentence and despite the fact that his appeal was dismissed.

In 1995, Peter Gurr, a falcon breeder who earned his living as a storeman, was sent to prison for four months and banned from keeping falcons for five years after he was found guilty of buying stolen eggs for £150 per egg and selling the hatched chicks as captive-bred ones, complete with the proper documentation, for £550 on the legitimate market.

He was thought to have sold more than twenty birds in Britain, Italy and Spain. He, too, attracted the attention of the authorities with what seemed on the face of it to be a remarkably successful breeding programme in which he was apparently getting seventy-five per cent success, against the recognized normal success rate of twenty-five per cent.

Once again, DNA testing proved that the birds which he claimed had been bred from captive parents could not in scientific fact be related to them.

However, even the Peter Gurr case does not seem to have had any effect on criminals who regard it as their right to loot the environment. In July 1999 another three peregrine chicks vanished from their nest in the Pentland Hills of Scotland, and there can be little doubt that they are now abroad.

The criminals are remarkably sophisticated. They plan their operations with fine attention to detail, and treat the birds they steal with great care. A dead peregrine is just feathers, a live one is money in the bank.

First the thieves find the sites of a breeding pair of wild falcons. This takes time and knowledge, so it is a trade which invites habitual criminals to repeat their crimes time and time again.

The three difficulties for the criminal are: catching his birds, which involves a dizzying level of expertise in rock climbing and abseiling merely to get at the nest. Since many nests are under surveillance, he needs to watch the watchers as carefully as he watches his quarry, and this, too, takes time and application.

Then he has to transport his birds or eggs carefully. In the case of eggs which are nearing the point of hatching, this is slightly easier because all he has to do is keep them warm and avoid breaking them. A specially converted vacuum flask with sockets for the eggs in an insulated bed is enough to get them down from the nest.

THE PEREGRINE FALCON

Said to be the fastest bird in the world, reaching speeds of over 150 mph when it swoops on its prey (although recently a gyrfalcon was clocked at this speed in flight). Its prey is generally smaller birds such as pheasant or red grouse, which makes it unpopular with gamekeepers.

The peregrine is identifiable by its dark plumage fading to light barred colouring on the underside. It was once reduced to 360 pairs in the British Isles, but is estimated to have recovered to around 1200 pairs. Smuggled peregrines are said to be selling as high as £5000 for a particularly fine mature bird in Europe and the Arab states.

Live chicks are more difficult, but specialized containers can be made, which also serve to conceal the chicks f the raider should fall foul of the law. Birds have been found in car door panels, hollow spare wheels, and specially made containers in car boots and the like. During the holiday season, camping trailers and caravans make ideal transports for smuggling goods, and wherever you are in the British Isles, you are within easy reach of a ferry port.

Once aboard the ferry, the raider is safe; once on the Continent, the birds are lost. But there are exceptions. Recently, some falcons sent abroad as eggs were returned to this country as fledged birds to be released into the wild, following an international operation against illegal trade in falcons.

There are men, too, who like to keep large birds of prey as an expression of their machismo just as others like to be seen walking half-trained savage dogs. Luckily, PWLOs are often tipped off that this or that villain was in a bar last night with a golden eagle on his arm. Since the villain is often found to be keeping the bird illegally or in unsuitable conditions, he can easily be parted from it. One PWLO reports finding an eagle owl, largest of the owls, being kept in a cage designed for a budgerigar and only let out from time to time to fly around the room 'to let him get a bit of exercise'.

Birds of prey are not the only targets for criminals: any form of bird life attracts persecution. Some years ago, it was the songbirds who suffered most because, since historic times, there has been a tradition of trapping small birds in places as far apart as East London and the mining areas of North Yorkshire.

As in many other areas of wildlife crime, detection is made harder because there is already a thriving and perfectly legitimate trade in captive-bred songbirds such as goldfinches, chaffinches and bullfinches.

British songbirds are particularly valued because of the quality of their song, and they are exported in large numbers, particularly to the Mediterranean and Malta, where many households have as many as half-a-dozen in the same cage.

The trouble once again is that breeding these birds in captivity requires expertise, dedication and a lot of patience, whereas capturing them from the wild is a comparatively simple affair.

They are often caught in cage traps – beautifully crafted little wooden cages separated into two or more compartments. The bird fancier puts a captive songbird in a locked compartment in one end of the trap, and leaves the entrance to the other compartment open and primed with a rubber band. Passing wild birds hear the song from the captive one and approach it, entering the open end of the trap which promptly snaps shut. Some traps are constructed with a series of catching compartments, each of which will imprison a single bird.

Some breeders use the trapped wild birds to enrich their breeding stock, and then release them again; some trade, selling them for anything up to £80 a pair.

A thriving market for this illegal trade is Malta, where they are prized like budgerigars – but there is also a darker side to the trade. Songbirds are a food delicacy in some Mediterranean countries, where greenfinches, tits and linnets are eaten as kebabs, in pâté or stews. Naturally, the recipes for these delicacies require large numbers of the tiny birds and few such birds are left along the coast of Italy and in Malta. During the annual migration when the birds fly north from Africa across the Mediterranean, they are eagerly awaited by shooting club sportsmen, who, armed with repeating shotguns with laser sights and infra-red night scopes, use them for target practice on an horrendous scale. In Malta alone the annual death toll is put at over six million, including species such as robins, swallows, finches, ospreys, kestrels and herons.

Birds taken for this kind of trade can be caught with the same kind of 'mist' nets used by professional bird-ringers, who string the nets in the trees where the birds gather to roost at night; or on 'bird-limed' sticks which, having been coated with sticky fluid, are like giant fly-papers, and are set out in the trees in a back garden.

In mid-1999, RSPCA inspectors caught a bird trader with more than 400 finches ready to be sent abroad; and during a pet shop raid more than 800 British wild birds were discovered being prepared for export. The Society says that some birders are regularly netting birds in the open countryside, or even urban parks, to feed the trade.

A peregrine falcon, said to be the fastest bird in the world.

CHAPTER EIGHT

SPLIT LOYALTIES

ronically, the people who are most feared by conservationists and wildlife officers are the only ones who have an excuse for their persecution of rare birds of prey. They are the men and women who live and make their living in the countryside, who genuinely fear that birds of prey will damage their stocks.

Raptor persecution (killing birds of prey) was tackled in *Badger* – Series I, Episode 6: 'Low Fidelity' – in a particularly moving way. In a lecture to a school class, McCabe gave a warning about people, including unscrupulous gamekeepers, who kill birds of prey to protect their game birds.

When some birds are discovered to have been killed, McCabe's well-meant piece of advice leads to the bullying of a young girl whose father is a local gamekeeper, and the episode illustrates how easily wildlife concern can lead to misunderstandings and family troubles.

A kestrel in captivity is a very unhappy creature.

In one scene, Graham Newman, the Estate Manager on a local shooting moor, has to defend himself from McCabe's suspicions, and in doing so shifts the blame to his innocent gamekeeper, Dominic McGuire. McCabe points out that in the last three years, out of fifty eggs laid by birds of prey on this particular estate, not one has survived – and isn't that rather suspicious? Birds of prey thriving all around, but not on this piece of moorland?

The gamekeepers in the series react angrily: they breed game birds, not birds of prey. It is the business of gamekeepers to keep game, not feed predators.

The viewer accepts quite readily that people who kill endangered species are evil, and should be caught and punished for it, at least by losing their jobs. And the law agrees with them. But it is only fair to say that hen harriers and other predators do live on game and they cannot distinguish between specially bred game birds which belong to particular shoots and wild birds simply breeding on moorland.

A peregrine is as likely to swoop on a carrier pigeon on an errand of mercy as it is on a passing wood-pigeon, and pigeon-fanciers know that. In one case in Wales, a succession of poisoned cats and, eventually, a poisoned dog, led the police to a pigeon-fancier who was deliberately trying to poison birds of prey which attacked his prize pigeons. The fact that he was also poisoning animals did not appear to bother him one whit.

There are shooting estates in the North of England where the foraging of birds of prey has significantly affected the populations of game birds. However, the law takes a very grim view of anybody – gamekeeper, farmer, or fisherman – who takes the law, gun or can of poison into his own hands to protect his stock. If he uses the latter to deal with predators, he may also threaten other forms of life which happen to cross his land,

Claire comforts the daughter of a wrongly accused gamekeeper.

including his own stock, pets, dogs and even small children who may unconsciously contaminate their hands or boots and transfer the contamination to their mouths.

Gamekeepers, say the PWLOs, are predominantly decent but, as in all walks of life, there are some unscrupulous individuals among them. And they are not always acting on their own. Their employers may distance themselves and take up a moral stance if their keeper is caught out, but all too often they are aware of what is going on.

The position is further complicated by the fact that some carefully circumscribed traps and trapping is permitted by the law. For instance, with the exception of the Larsen trap, almost all decoy traps are illegal. Like the much smaller and strictly illegal linnet trap, the Larsen is a cage divided into two sections, and its design is minutely laid down by law. It is designed to trap corvids (birds of the crow family) which prey on new-born lambs and other creatures, often pecking out the eyes and causing the death of the victims.

The savage jaws of a gin trap, now illegal.

A decoy bird, which *must* be a member of the crow family, is put into the closed end of the trap, and the other end left open. It is designed in such a way that any bird entering springs the trap, and is securely locked inside. Corvids are extremely territorial, so local crows, seeing another crow on their turf as it were, will fly down to attack it, trapping themselves in the process.

The trap *must* have food and water inside, and room for both decoy and decoyed to flap their wings. The trap *must* be checked every day and its contents disposed of humanely. Neither the decoy bird nor the intended target must be left to suffer.

It is, of course, illegal to use Larsen traps to catch birds of prey, but traps are usually put in out-of-the-way places, and the temptation to teach a marauding bird of prey a sharp lesson can be strong. These days, however, as a result of a case brought by the RSPB, the practice of using pigeons as bait in traps has been outlawed.

Joan Childs of the RSPB recalls the occasion when she had to hide to catch one misbehaving gamekeeper. 'If someone puts a pigeon in a trap,' she argues, 'you can be sure they are after birds of prey. On this particular occasion, someone who had been walking a dog reported to us that he had seen a Larsen trap with a pigeon inside it. Now, usually if you go to the farmer or gamekeeper and say: "What about this trap on your land?" he will hotly deny all knowledge of it.

'So you have to catch them attending to it. The police do not have the time for long surveillance in cases like this, so we try to video the man attending the trap, so he cannot claim it is not his.'

Accordingly, along with a male colleague who was working the video camera, Joan hid herself in deep frost under a bush on the track approaching the trap so that she could get the registration number of the man's vehicle when he came to check on the trap.

'Gamekeepers get up early, so we had to be there in the small hours. Just as it was starting to get light, I heard a vehicle coming up the track, and got my binoculars ready but, to my horror, it was a little quad bike with no registration number and a dog on the back.

'The dog smelled me straight off, of course, and hopped off the bike and ran over to my hiding place, barking and sniffing around the undergrowth. Fortunately, he was a Labrador, so I wasn't going to get eaten, but when the gamekeeper stopped the bike I was sure he had spotted me.

'Luckily, he was cold and fed up as well, so he just slapped the dog across the nose, pushed it back on the quad and drove on to the clearing where we got some very good video of him checking his trap.'

The ambush led to a prosecution, and the prosecution led to a change in the law that made it illegal to use pigeons as bait in Larsen traps, which in its turn enabled Paul Henery, in Northumbria, to prosecute another wildlife criminal who was doing just that. The cruelty of this case appalled Henery, but it also provided him with an addition to his list of the worst excuses in the world.

'I got a call on New Year's Day, 1997, from a dog-walker who warned us that there was a pigeon in a Larsen trap in a field,' he recalls. 'The conditions were horrendous that winter. We were getting temperatures of minus fifteen and twenty degrees, and there was this pigeon trapped out in the open.

'The man's defence when I got to his house was that he had come across this racing pigeon which was tired from a race, and put it in his Larsen trap to tend it, providing food and water! He claimed he did not know the trap was set. The fact that it was minus twenty degrees in the field didn't seem to matter to him in the slightest!'

The gamekeeper was charged with attempting to trap goshawks and fined a couple of hundred pounds.

'But what really hurt him was that his shotgun certificate was revoked for a while. For a gamekeeper, that can be very inconvenient.'

PWLOs particularly hate the device called a pole trap. This takes advantage of the hunting habits of certain birds of prey, such as owls and kestrels, which like to rest on the top of fence posts, telegraph poles and even dead trees while hunting. The gamekeeper selects obvious posts in vulnerable positions near his breeding pens, and nails what is known as a Fenn trap to the top.

Fenn traps are a traditional trap, like the now illegal gin trap, which when set lie like an open mouth that snaps closed when the prey steps into it. Gin traps had serrated jaws which acted like a bite from a fierce animal. Fenn traps differ in that they do not have teeth but, on brittle bones like those of an alighting bird, they are just as devastating.

The hunting owl or kestrel does not see the trap, and, unsuspectingly, lands on the post. The trap snaps closed, breaking the bird's legs. In dreadful pain, the bird often flaps around, dislodging the trap which then falls off the top of the pole leaving the bird suspended by its broken legs until the setter of the trap returns to release it, which can be as long as twenty-four hours later. By this time the bird is usually, but not always, dead from its suffering.

RSPB investigator Duncan McNiven exposed the use of such traps in North Wales where a gamekeeper in charge of 25,000 young pheasants was convicted of setting post traps to guard thirteen pheasant pens in the woods. When police called at his home, he had similar traps hanging on the wall. His defence: a trespasser had set them while his back was turned. The magistrates did not believe him and fined him £400.

The cases go on and on. A farmer in Oxfordshire was fined £13,500 for shooting a red kite and committing three offences of possessing poison and traps; an Ulster farmer was convicted of shooting two choughs – birds on the protected list; youths in the Thames Valley 'baited' a swan to get it to reach its head up to them on a bridge, then cut its throat as it did so. Their explanation: they did it to protect the fish.

Then there are anglers who shoot cormorants to protect their fishing, as in 'The World According to Carp' (Series I, Episode 3). Some anglers' magazines even support the call for a cull of cormorants which they call 'the black plague'.

Over-dramatic maybe, but, as fishing enthusiasts and fish farmers will point out, it is also true that cormorants can eat a dozen fish at a time, and that they find the rich pickings in fish farms and protected water irresistible.

Another scourge for the PWLO and indeed everybody concerned with wildlife, is poison, which also appears in *Badger* Series I, Episode 3, where it is used to get rid of an otter which the estate manager fears is threatening his fishing.

Poisons are generally used to rid an area of a particular kind of vermin – for instance, anti-coagulants are commonly used as rat poison. In permitted use, poisons are laid down in boxes which can be entered only by the vermin at which they are aimed, or used in established rat runs or mouse holes, which will keep domestic animals from eating them. However, some farmers are not as careful as others, and accidental poisoning is not uncommon.

Dr Ed Blane of the Farming and Rural Research Conservation Agency, who advised on poisons in the *Badger* episode, says: 'The most common type of small chemical spill in which we become involved with PWLOs is by slug pellets which will kill anything.

'There is a regulation that people using this kind of poison must carefully observe the conditions for use, but poisons are expensive and the farmers tend to hang on to residues long after the container has finished being safe. We hear of cases where the sack has been moved, leaving a pile of pellets where a passing animal can pick it up. Often, it is the farmer's own dog. Slug pellets are a regular cause of accidental poisoning.

'They are metaldehyde based and a shiny blue colour to look at. They are distributed on to fields during the early spring, and if the trailer containing them hits a bump, they may come out in a clump. The next animal along stops for a nibble and dies. The most common victims of this kind of poisoning are badgers, foxes and domestic dogs out for a walk, but rooks, which will eat almost anything, are also often victims.

'The dogs, of course, are taken by their owners to the vets, so we know what poisoned them. But creatures like badgers and foxes are far more likely to crawl away under a bush and die, so you never see their corpses, or at any rate not in time to analyse what killed them.

'But one sure sign of a poisoning incident is a ring of dead birds some distance away. Some poisons take time to work, and the creatures get a uniform distance away before falling.'

CORMORANTS Large dark seabird which can grow up to a metre long and feeds voraciously on small fish. Has webbed feet and can swim on the surface or under water in its pursuit of fish or eels. Its plumage lacks waterproofing so it is often seen sitting on a post near the water, holding its wings out to dry. Prefers sea fishing, but is seen in estuaries, reservoirs and rivers, particularly in the winter. Often mistaken for a shag which is smaller, a much more noticeable greenish colour, and tends to stick to sea fishing despite rough weather. Dives for long periods.

The agency detected one poisoning outbreak because of the number of pigeons which were raining down on roads in the vicinity and tracked the cause to a man spreading a poison called Temik 10G which is mixed with seed when it is drilled. Minute quantities of the poison, which is distributed in small black grains which look uncannily like seed and is aimed at controlling soil-dwelling pests, were lying on the surface of the field mixed in with the scattered seed, and the birds were picking it up along with seeds.

Although Temik 10G is a deadly nerve poison, the pigeons were not eating enough of it to kill them on the spot, and managed to fly a uniform distance away before they became affected, lost control of their bodies, and fell into the road where they were hit by passing cars.

To the horror of the tractor driver who had merely been doing his job without a suspicion of the carnage his innocent activity was causing, an inspection of the surrounding countryside revealed a broad band of dying and dead birds.

When a farmer or gamekeeper puts out poison bait, he probably does not intend to kill anything but a particularly evasive fox which is preying on his chickens.

There are a number of poisons available for the control of vermin, but the use of such substances is strictly regulated because a number of birds and animals will regularly scavenge on dead meat and at times, like the depths of winter, will eat almost anything.

PLANT-RAIDERS

Birds and animals are not the only targets of wildlife criminals. Plants may be less dramatic as victims, but they are even more vulnerable because they cannot fly or run away.

The man who achieved immortality by bringing the first plant-raiders to book in court for a particularly devastating raid is PC Garth Coupland who operates in East Anglia. Like McCabe in *Badger*, PC Coupland is a PWLO as well as a hard-working rural policeman, so his spare time tends to be spent on long walks with the family, with every member keeping their eyes open for evidence of marauders.

Out on such a walk one afternoon, PC Coupland noticed a van parked near a local waterway. It is the business of policemen to be nosy and suspicious, so he took a quick peep through the rear windows. Inside the van were a collection of plastic bags, several garden rakes and forks. On his way back later that day, he saw the van again and re-checked it. The bags were now full, and further investigation revealed that they contained £3500 worth of a unique water flower called the water soldier, which submerges during the winter and surfaces to take the air, as it were, during the summer. The two men driving the van, who were from a water garden centre in the Midlands, did some plea bargaining, and admitted the theft of the plants. They were fined £200 which incensed PC Coupland, who knew they would have been more heavily punished under the Wildlife and Countryside Act of 1981.

PC GARTH COUPLAND – PWLO

Career: Garth Coupland is a typical PWLO. A rural patrol officer, covering virtually the whole of the Norfolk Broads, he gets no extra pay for his wildlife activities, but is allowed extra time to do it in. A lifelong natural historian of note, he also writes authoritative articles for nature magazines. His countryside cartoons – *Splat! An Adult's View of the British Countryside* was just one of his titles – are much admired, as are his black-and-white drawings of wildlife.

'What really got me mad was that the crime was so pointless. Every single one of those plants died,' says PC Coupland. 'But it was an important case because it was the first prosecution ever on plants.'

Not by any means the last, though. Wild plant stealing is another of those expanding criminal industries, it is so easy and so quickly executed. Inspector Steve Kourik reports on a similar raid on a hillside in Hertfordshire which denuded the entire hillside of wild bluebells. The thieves wanted them to sell at car boot sales. 'Two men working hard can steal literally thousands of bulbs in a few hours,' he says, 'and that hillside may never sprout another bluebell.'

According to the police, there are at least three professional wild-flower stealing gangs operating in Cambridgeshire at the moment, with more springing up every day.

CHAPTER NINE

COCK-FIGHTING

You do not need a special stadium for cock-fighting, as Tom McCabe discovers in *Badger* (Series II, Episode 4: 'Cock o' the Walk'). Any front room in a suburban semi will do, as the RSPCA Special Operations Unit found out when it started watching some video tapes that had been seized during a police raid on suspected animal abusers.

The video clearly showed a group of men standing around on a blood-stained carpet in a semi-detached house in a city suburb. On the carpet, hemmed in by a fence of legs which formed the cock-fighting ring, two fighting cocks were battling to the death. The only trouble was that because the camera man was concentrating on the birds, the RSPCA could only see the spectators from the chest down.

Most 'sports' which involve the abuse of animals come from darker periods of history, and cock-fighting is no exception. The adherents of this particular 'sport' can point to a long and dishonourable history, not all of it restricted to this country. In places such as Asia and Indonesia, and even as close as the Lille district of France, cock-fighting is a legal pursuit, where people openly cheer on one or other of the fighting cocks and bet on the outcome of the fights. Thousands of pounds change hands in bets and in prices paid for fighting birds, which are carefully groomed and pampered for their appearances in the ring. Phrases like 'Battle Stags' abound.

Cockerels naturally grow frighteningly long bone 'spurs' on the back of their legs which they use to fight other birds, but cock-fighting professionals like to make their 'sport' even more bloody by attaching false metal spurs over the bird's natural protuberances. These spurs are made by specialists and there is even an international market in them available through the Internet.

Like badger-baiters and other bird-abusers, cock-fighters are notoriously hard to prosecute successfully in this country, even when they are caught in the act. This is because the birds' own natural aggression keeps them fighting even when their owners have run off, swearing they know nothing about it, guv.

The 'sport' is based on the cockerels' natural inclination to fight, sometimes to the death, and the preferred birds for fighting are big Shamo and Malay cockerels which can grow to weights like 12–13 pounds, and are much prized for their fighting spirit. Even for a trained and expert man, they are hard birds to handle and some people cannot handle them at all.

Chief Inspector Mike Butcher, head of the RSPCA's Special Operations Unit, having been called upon to investigate so many allegations of this kind of animal abuse – most recently at the unlikely location of Bexleyheath, near London – has become something of a specialist on cock- and dog-fighting.

'There are two forms of cock-fighting,' says Chief Inspector Butcher. 'In one they retain their natural spurs, which are sharpened, or wear metal spurs or "gaffes" which are attached to a strip of linen or chamois leather and tied over the natural spur

McCabe and Claire find a
sharpened steel spur in
'Cock o' the Walk'.

The cocks are shown off,
prior to the fight.

The audience in this cock-fighting scene receive their brief.

with a length of twine. In the other – a form of sparring – they are "tried out" without spurs to see what they will be like as fighters.'

In the more formal meetings, the cock-fighters make a fighting ring with straw bales or hurdles, and post 'rules of the ring' which must be adhered to, and which have not changed significantly in over a thousand years.

The spectators gather round as the owners groom the fighting cocks, then present them in the ring to show them off. Sometimes the birds are pushed against each other to get their fighting blood up, and stimulate their natural instincts, and this serves to give the spectators a preview of what kind of a performance the cockerels are likely to put up in the ring.

Drugs are sometimes used to raise the birds' pain barrier in order to keep them fighting when, badly hurt, they would be inclined to break off. The cock-fighters can sometimes be identified by the insanitary 'medical' kits they carry with them, filled with encrusted hypodermic needles, small bottles of unidentifiable potions, and needles for stitching up the birds' wounds. Their sanitary standards are usually revolting, proving once again that knowledge about animals does not always equate with compassion for them.

In *Badger* Series II, Episode 4: 'Cock o' the Walk', a young girl is seriously poisoned by a drug left at the site of an illegal cock fight. Any small child, pricked by a filthy needle for instance, could develop all kinds of infections, quite apart from the effect of the actual drug.

Once the birds have been prepared and the spectators have had a chance to assess them, it is time for the real business of the meeting.

Bets are placed on which bird will draw blood first, which is expected to win, and on whether a bird is 'brave' enough (the professionals greatly value a persistent fighter which they call a 'game bird'). The birds are then released and allowed to fight until one or other owner cries 'enough', one of the birds has been downed three times in two minutes, or one of the birds kills the other.

The latter happens often because the needle-sharp metal spurs are over an inch long, and the cockerels are heavy and strong. The spurs regularly become stuck in the opponent's chest, and are torn out only when the attacking bird flaps and struggles enough to wrench them out, dealing terrible damage to the wounded bird.

When a bird goes down, the remaining cock will leap into the air and drive its spurs into the head and brain of the prostrate loser. The owner of the losing bird can call 'enough' in time to save his bird, but the referee never intervenes.

Cock-fighters, like dog-fighters and badger-baiters, know their rights under the laws with great exactitude. They must be caught actually taking part in a cock fight, or be caught in possession of cock-fighting equipment which bears traces of having

RULES OF THE PIT

(As laid down for one cock-fighting session in Bexley, see above.)
1. As soon as the birds are in the pit, the fight is on, unless otherwise stated.
2. The two-minute rule applies: the bird that goes down three times in two minutes is deemed the loser.
3. Once a bird is down, no bird in the pit will be touched unless both parties agree.
4. Any person who does not wish to obey these rules must state this before pitting his bird.

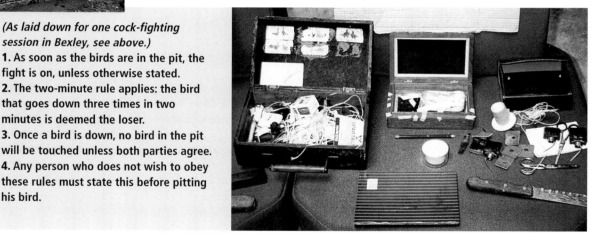

The real thing: rules for the fight and equipment seized in a police raid.

been used. DNA, for instance, can be used to establish if the spurs are tainted with blood and if so what kind of blood it is. If there is no blood, the owner cannot be accused of an offence.

In a desperate attempt to find some excuse on which his client could be acquitted, one barrister asked the expert witness if there was any other kind of blood which showed significant similarities to that of fighting cocks, and might be mistaken for it.

'Certainly, sir.'

'And what kind of animal might that be? And did you make allowances for the similarity of blood type?'

A video seized by police shows two cocks shaping up for the fight.

'A sperm whale, sir. But since no sperm whale was found at the site, I dismissed it from my calculations!'

Like most criminals, cock-fighters know a number of ways to get round the law, and regularly rely on these. On open-air sites, for instance, the spectators merely mark a circle on the ground, and stand around it with their feet on the line and their legs forming the enclosure in which the fight is to take place. (The same method that was used in the semi-detached house fight mentioned earlier.)

If they are in the open, and a stranger, or member of the authorities, such as an RSPCA man or a police officer, approaches, they simply turn their backs and walk away. 'Cock fighting, officer?' they say with amazement. 'No, I heard a bit of a kerfuffle, and saw some people standing so I came over to see what was happening. Wouldn't you?'

Nobody who ever ran across a school playground in response to the shout: 'Fight! Fight!' would argue with them. After all, what was it that attracted the police officer in the first place?

One way round this is to make covert videos of the fight taking place, and try to get the faces of the audience on the tape. But since the criminals know this, they regard any stranger with open suspicion.

The police can bring charges only if they find the spectators in possession of cock-fighting equipment, and no cock-fighter is going to be daft enough to be caught with spurs in his pocket. At the first sound of interference, he drops them and swears he has never seen them or their like before.

Luckily, cock-fighters like to film the fights for further enjoyment later. And it is often these videos, seized during a police raid, which lead the RSPCA and the PWLO to cock-fighting rings, and convict the criminals.

COCK-FIGHTING AND THE LAW

Cock-fighting is prosecuted under two pieces of legislation: the Protection of Animals Act of 1911 and the Cock-Fighting Act of 1952 which also makes it an offence to have in possession the spurs or other paraphernalia of cock-fighting with the intention of cock-fighting.

The problem is that some people have a genuine interest in cock-fighting as an historical practice, and the prosecution has to prove that the cock-fighting equipment they find is actually being used and not merely held as a curio.

The 1911 Act also makes it an offence to put any kind of animals together for the purposes of fighting, so it covers dog-fighting as well. If the animals are also wounded and not taken to a vet for treatment – and a cock with characteristic cock-fighting injuries will not be taken to a vet who would immediately report it – the owner can be prosecuted under the Act and face a penalty of £5000, or six months in prison, or both.

Even being confronted with their own picture on screen does not make some criminals confess. In a recent case, where a joint RSPCA and PWLO raid on a major cock-fighting ring in Kent netted multiple offenders, each man stood up in court and vigorously denied he had been anywhere near the site, even after the magistrates had seen the evidence with their own eyes.

Like most animal-abusers, cock-fighters can be extremely violent people, and it is an axiom that if the police and RSPCA inspectors are to make a raid on a cock-fighting event, the police will need as many officers as there are likely to be cock-fighters.

Nobody expects the cock-fighters to stay where they are and say: 'It's a fair cop!' They are going to have to be chased, tackled and brought down. The police authorities are careful about the life and safety of their officers, so they will not risk

The stage is set and the excitement rises in this scene from the series.

Dog-fighting is another brutal 'sport' that draws the betting crowds.

their task force being outnumbered and perhaps badly injured. The cock-fighters know this, and schedule their major events for Sundays and football days when pressure on the police manpower is at its greatest. A traditional favourite is New Year's Day, when the police are busy bringing charges against revellers recovering from a hectic twenty-four hours.

A further complication is that the slightest thing may lead to a cock fight being cancelled, and the most elaborate preparations, involving paying police officers overtime and arranging for people to come in on their day off, may suddenly come to nothing. For example, one major operation came to nought because one of the cocks developed a cough, and other owners would not risk their birds in the same place where they might become infected. They were perfectly prepared for their champion birds to be hacked to death, but would not risk them developing a sickness which might impair their fighting ability.

There are times, though, when providence delivers their enemies into their hands. The RSPCA Special Operations Unit recalls one raid on a dog fight in a private house in which both the incoming RSPCA and police task force, and the dog-fighters were videoing the event.

'The man with the camera actually videoed us coming through the door,' says Mike Butcher. 'You hear him say: "Oh, shit! It's the police!" and then he drops the camera, which goes on running. The next thing you hear is a policeman say: "Hello, what's this?" as he picks the camera up.

'They showed the film in court and the man got four months in prison. There was no argument about it. He might have claimed they were not doing anything, but there they are, on their own video, dog-fighting. It was an open-and-shut case.'

In the tough complex world of the PWLO there are very few cases as clear as this one. Some magistrates, for instance, may not take the offence as seriously as the law would like. To the frustration of the PWLO and RSPCA man who knows that the person in court is telling a pack of lies, they may choose to believe what sounds like a reasonable excuse.

Even when a conviction does result, the fine may be ridiculously low or impossible to collect because the miscreant has no fixed abode and takes to the road to avoid the consequences of his crime.

For the unfortunate bird, of course, the consequences are always the same: mutilation or death.

CHAPTER TEN

THE SANCTUARIES

Without the work of people, like Steph Allen, who run animal sanctuaries, almost invariably at their own expense in both money and time, the animal world would be in a very bad state indeed.

The police are in a difficult position. Always short of money and manpower, they nevertheless have a legal duty to look after the animal victims of the crimes they are prosecuting. The animals are, in themselves, evidence, and they have to be kept in secure and humane conditions until the case comes to court.

When it is over, the animals will have to be given a home or returned to the wild. Returning an animal to the wild is in itself a difficult specialized job, and in many cases, such as barn owls for instance, requires a licence. People who want to release wild animals cannot just open the door and shoo them out to fend for themselves, particularly when animals have been kept in close proximity to human beings. Familiarity breeds a lack of fear which can be dangerous to both humans and animals. A large aggressive animal, for example, which has lost its fear of humans can never be trusted, and a small vulnerable one which has lost its reflex action to flee at the approach of man can never be safe.

A wild animal, such as a badger which has been maltreated and then allowed to recover in a sanctuary, cannot simply be taken to the nearest patch of woodland and eased out of the car to find its own way in life. Badgers are highly territorial and the ground may already be the territory of an existing sett which will certainly attack the incomer and possibly kill it, so the poor badger will be in a worse situation than it was before.

The same is true of wild birds. Birds in a familiar setting know where to feed and where to take shelter from natural predators, so releasing them elsewhere is the equivalent of sending a hospitalized patient into the roughest part of town and telling them to find their own place in a community which will regard them as a welcome new source of nourishment!

Paul Henery is very careful when he releases animals to do it in a setting which at least resembles their previous habitat, even if he cannot be certain that it is the original.

For all these reasons, the sanctuaries, like the fictional one in *Badger* which is run by Steph the Vet, are absolutely essential. Yet they struggle day in, day out, for their very existence.

Steph the Vet's sanctuary, created for the series.

THE SANCTUARY

Steph's Sanctuary is based on a number of local sanctuaries, but most firmly on the Sanctuary which is run in Morpeth by Kim Olson and Allan Petterson. The ironic thing is that, like most sanctuary supervisors, they never intended to start a sanctuary in the first place. Kim was a journalist who fell in love with a Swedish postal official, and moved to Sweden where she lectured in English. They sold their two homes and BMW and moved to Tanzania to work with animals.

'It was Allan who initially had the interest in wildlife, and because of this we had a dream of going to East Africa to work with wildlife. We did a course on wildlife, and, while there, worked as volunteers in a game sanctuary where I caught the wildlife dream as well. It all went well, although we were living on our savings, which were obviously not going to last for ever.

Kim Olson and Allan Petterson outside their real Sanctuary.

'Then Allan was offered the job of managing the sanctuary and we thought our problems were over. But it is very hard for an outsider to get a work permit in Tanzania, and eventually we were forced to leave and come home to Britain.'

Barn owls, now sadly rare, take shelter at the Sanctuary.

They were disappointed to leave Tanzania but, without a source of income, it was clear they would soon be broke. On their return to Northumberland, they had no intention of opening a sanctuary, but fate had other ideas. Their reputation as people involved with wildlife had come before them.

'It all started about seven years ago with a sea disaster. There was a major oil spill and a lot of oiled-up seabirds. The vets started ringing and asking if we could take in a few oiled-up guillemots and other birds. The Press heard about this and it simply escalated from there.

'The first animal we took in was actually a seagull with a broken wing, which we released. Then came the oiled-up seabirds, several of which we managed to release back to the wild. After that it just grew. At first we were taking about fifty animals a year, but now we treat around 700 animals a year.'

Their first problem was premises: animals require room, the clean air of the countryside plus a healthy distance between them and their neighbours for the sake of both parties.

Kim and Allan were living in a rented farm which had outbuildings into which they could put their patients and accommodate those which became, through their inability to cope with life outside, residents. Four years later, unable to renew their lease, they and their charges were homeless.

KIM OLSON – Sanctuary owner

Born: Gateshead, daughter of an oil company worker.

Education: Followed her father around the Middle East until she was sent to boarding school in Britain.

Career: Started life as a journalist, working for the *Scotsman* newspaper. Worked in Tanzania before returning to this country, around seven years ago, and started running the Sanctuary almost straight away.

'We had to buy a place, and, three years ago, found this derelict farm with derelict outbuildings. It was winter, there was no heating, no lighting, and no running water except when it rained.

'Our only options were to take it or close down, and, as closing down was not an option, we moved in. That first winter was terrible – we froze. We were continually wet and muddy, and conditions were so bad that one day I just walked outside, sat down and cried. I was cold, wet, covered in mud, and I had no way of washing. We were also up to our eyes in debt because of the enormous mortgage on the premises.'

But like most sanctuary people, they did not really consider closing down. They soldiered on, supported by a growing army of volunteers who work, unpaid, sometimes around the clock to keep the place going.

Their collection of animals grows almost by the day. From starting with a few oiled-up unhappy seabirds, they now have badgers, owls, kestrels, hedgehogs, donkeys and even goats. They boast that they never turn an animal away.

Over the years they have learned a lot about animals, but one lesson is paramount. They are not vets and, although they can do basic first aid and provide the appropriate therapy for recovering animals, they leave the medical treatment and drugs to people who, like Steph, know what they are about.

The vets and police officers, desperate for somewhere which will look after the animals, after the initial treatment, are only too happy to leave them in the care of the Sanctuary.

Their most pressing problem is money. They run two shops, one in Alnwick and the other in Morpeth, whose income keeps them alive and the mortgage serviced, but for the day-to-day running costs of the Sanctuary, they rely on sparse but welcome sponsorship and voluntary contributions, and the voluntary support of their growing army of helpers.

'They come from all over. We have police helpers, carpenters, young people – people from all walks of life. We rely on thirty to fifty of them, but it is a hard, dirty job and not everyone is suited to it.

'People see a nice fluffy bunny programme on television, and think they would like to help out, but they forget that it has to be done seven days a week, 365 days a year, including Christmas Day, Boxing Day and New Year, even if you are a bit hung over.

'Some young people come along to get hands-on experience, but do not last two days; others really take to it. And we are here the whole time. Allan and I used to like going down to the pub for a drink, but we simply can't do that now.'

Their transport is a van sponsored by a local motor trader called Jennings.

'One Sunday we had to rescue a swan, a greylag goose and a heron in the back of an ordinary Toyota car, and I thought: "This is getting ludicrous!" I contacted Jennings and they offered to sponsor a van for us, which was wonderful. We also get sponsorship from BA and Barclays Bank, and Safeway give us their waste produce which is a blessing. But the hardest thing remains the day-to-day running of the Sanctuary. We need £12,000 to £15,000 a year – and neither of us takes a salary out of it.'

They do not operate in a vacuum, either. There are several others in the area which act as rescue organizations for specialized groups, such as domestic pets, mistreated and unwanted horses and the like. But the Sanctuary is one of the very few which will deal with *all* kinds of animals.

If Britain seems to be full of people who spend their time maltreating animals, both wild and domestic, it is also full of people who care desperately about animals' welfare and who are prepared to put time and money into their concerns. If we have a great deal of animal crime, we also have a great many campaigners against it.

The Animal Rescue Directory, compiled by Tracy L'Epine, lists nearly 1000 United Kingdom animal-rescue centres for wildlife, domestic and farm animals, from the British Chelonia Group in Bristol, which specializes in tortoises and terrapins, to the Raptor and Ferret centre in Bow, East London.

Most specialize, but some, like Kim Olson, will take any animal in trouble and do their best.

WILDLIFE RESCUE CENTRE

Caroline Gould, who runs the Vale Wildlife Rescue Centre in Gloucestershire, and whose daily routine has been the subject of a Radio 4 series, says that even being in close proximity to human beings is refined torture for many animals. Like Kim, Caroline has no formal qualifications for running a sanctuary, and never set out to run one in the first place. On the contrary, despite an interest in wildlife, she and her former husband used to keep and fly birds of prey.

Caroline Gould tends a patient at the Vale Wildlife Rescue Centre.

'I worked as a vet's nurse for a couple of months which was as close as I got to training,' she says. 'The sanctuary started with one single owl with a broken wing which a vet asked us to look after because he knew of our birds of prey. Not knowing anything about wildlife then, I agreed to do it. But if I had known what I know now, I would not have entertained the idea. I had no idea how the owl would cope with captivity or how it might behave.

'I know now that birds of prey in particular suffer dreadfully in captivity. For a bird that has always flown and cannot now fly, there is no quality of life. It is in captivity, and it sees human beings every day at close quarters. That is refined torture for a wild animal or a bird.'

For a creature reared in captivity, she says, it is a totally different matter. Each case which turns up at the Vale has to be judged on its merits.

In 1984, the couple had to face the question of whether or not to turn their occasional refuge for animals into a fully fledged sanctuary. But as their 30 x 150 ft back garden slowly filled up with aviaries and pens – and their house with children – the decision had to be made. They became a registered charity in 1990, and moved to their present six-and-a-half-acre site in 1992. These days they take in animals from Herefordshire, Worcestershire, Gloucestershire and a lot of the West Midlands and South Wales. Their intake is around 4800 animals per year, and a fair proportion of these stay on as residents.

Over the years, the marriage broke up, and various emergencies, such as recruiting suitable volunteers to help keep patients clean and fed, and finding financial backing for various enterprises, have fallen heavily on Caroline's shoulders. She has a robust jokey relationship with the local RSPCA, and a more guarded one with the animal-loving public.

'To a certain extent, people are our biggest problem,' she says. 'Often, they find what they think are orphaned babies, but they are not. People pick up a fox cub because they cannot see the mother around, but she may be under the nearest bush, too frightened to come out. Or they pick up a day-old fawn, whose mother may be only a few yards away. We tell them the best thing is to leave the animal where it is,

Tame foxes are shouted at to make them lose their trust of man.

but they think we don't want to get involved, and bring it in anyway. It's nobody's fault. Before I started working with animals full time, I would have found it just as difficult to leave them where they were. But people must accept that I do know what I am talking about.'

She has her own way of treating the thirty or forty fox cubs she rescues per year – and which she tries very hard to return to the wild. They are kept away from human contact in case they 'imprint' or begin to accept humans as friends; and the ones which have been reared by well-meaning people before they get to her have to be alienated.

'Once they are big enough to go outside, we put them in pens. Someone cleans them out and feeds them once a day. You can tell the ones which have been hand-reared before they came to us, because they come running up with their tails wagging. We have to respond to this by shouting and banging things to make them run away when they see us.'

In *Badger* (Series II, Episode 3: 'Holding On'), Ray, Steph the Vet's new helper, demonstrates this technique.

Like many sanctuary owners, she treats badgers with the greatest respect. 'We get about fifty or sixty badgers a year, mostly with road-accident injuries or territorial fighting wounds. They will fight viciously for territory, and the old ones have to defend their territory against younger ones who want to take it over. The injuries can be horrendous, and while the fight sometimes ends with one of them – usually the old one – giving in and running away, usually by that time it is literally torn to pieces, has nowhere to lie up and nowhere to hunt, so they die of their injuries or from starvation.'

Occasionally, though, they get brought to her, in which case she has to make up her mind whether they are likely to recover. Handling them is extremely dangerous, she says. They have a vicious bite and their jaws 'lock' into position.

'Calling them a thirty-pound ferret is accurate, I suppose, but it does not really give you an idea of how dangerous they can be. They are definitely the worst animal that we deal with. And if you get bitten by one, you will never forget it.'

Seventy-five per cent of her cases – about 3600 casualties a year – involve birds. She has a scar over her eye where she learned the hard way not to handle a heron without first securing its beak, which is as sharp as a stiletto and as deadly accurate as a crossbow.

'They always peck at the eyes, but I didn't know that at the time,' she explains. The RSPCA man who brought her the bird – it had a broken wing – swears to this day that he thought she knew what she was doing and didn't want to interfere because he didn't want his head bitten off. From his expression you realize that Caroline is respected almost as much for her strong will as for her daunting and hard-won expertise.

Her patients, though, are not always as set on regaining their freedom as Caroline is. A small percentage simply refuse to leave, no matter how hard she tries. A heron, which was treated for a broken wing, has haunted the back entrance to the treatment room for years. Every time they try to put him back in the wild, he circles and arrives back, elegantly demanding food and attention. Each time, they say, he takes just a little longer to come back, and one day they hope to see the back of him for good.

A growing number of the animals brought to them are iguanas, which are currently enjoying popularity as pets, only to escape or be abandoned in the wild because they are becoming a handful to live with. Caroline says iguanas can be worryingly aggressive, and though they look attractively off-beat as babies, they grow quickly into extremely large, ugly and dangerous reptiles. The bite of an iguana,

IGUANAS

They are known in the Caribbean as 'tree chickens' because one can, when cooked, feed a family of four – an indication of how big that attractively off-beat little lizard is going to be when mature. They can grow from a beautiful emerald green ten-inch creature into a six-foot-six-inch dragon trailing a formidable spiked-whip tail which it will use to lash out at anything it finds threatening. This can hurt an adult and cause severe injury to a child.

Iguanas take a long time to tame, sometimes with little success, and require a huge vivarium which has to be specially built and warmly heated. They have to be handled with long thick gloves, and approached with great care.

as McCabe discovers in *Badger* (Series II, Episode 5: 'Predators'), can be very nasty and the lizard can also draw blood by lashing people with its scaly spiny tail.

In that episode, McCabe has to track down a private collection of animals which have just been abandoned into the wild by an eccentric collector who finds them too expensive to keep.

The release of any alien species into the wild in this country is an offence. The results of the uncontrolled flooding of Britain's countryside with animals who have no place in it, and which have no natural predators, has caused terrible suffering to home-grown wildlife in the past and is continuing to do so now.

In some cases, the extremity of Britain's climate automatically controls the escape of some species such as venomous insects and spiders, because they do not breed below a certain temperature. But others, such as coypu (an aquatic South American rodent that resembles a small beaver with a rat-like tail) and mink (a semi-aquatic mammal), can thrive with dreadful side-effects on wildlife which has no defence against them.

Coypu, which escaped into the Norfolk Broads in the 1950s, did tremendous damage to the banks of the waterways, and it was years before the authorities were stirred to hunt them down, at a cost running into millions. The effect on other wildlife which depended on the banks they destroyed was terrible.

Even in the 1990s we were paying a price for the brief popularity of cinema's Teenage Mutant Ninja Turtles. In the wake of the film there was a fashion for buying terrapins which, as babies, looked like cute little versions of the film and television stars. But, like everything else which has had a brief period of popularity, the terrapins got bigger and more difficult to look after, and eventually too many owners 'set them free' by lobbing them like living hand-grenades into the nearest pond.

Hand-grenades, indeed. The terrapins waxed luxuriously large and greedy, and ate their way through all the other pond wildlife. In the end the people who 'set them free', besides devastating the lives and freedom of other local animals, condemned their terrapins to death from starvation because all that was left for them to eat were other terrapins.

THE SPECIALIST

'The dogs don't bite, but Mrs Parry Jones does,' says the sign outside the National Birds of Prey Centre, Newent, Gloucestershire, which is a fair warning about the off-beat personality who runs it.

Jemima Parry Jones, mentioned earlier, is the country's – and probably the world's – top authority on birds of prey and their breeding in captivity. In what she laughingly calls her spare time from the full-time job of running the country's biggest bird-of-prey sanctuary, she travels the world lecturing and advising upon the treatment and the art of coping with other people's birds of prey.

When they had trouble with vultures in Bombay, they called her in to advise them. The Philippine Eag e Foundation solicited her help with the Philippine eagle situation, and the Japanese have also sought her help. She lectures in South Africa, California and Australia.

She came to the business of running a sanctuary at a very early age because her great uncle started a family tradition of interest in the art of hawking, and her father started the Birds of Prey Centre with twelve birds. She now has more than 300 and her success at breeding notoriously difficult species in captivity is second to none. It was for her contribution to bird conservation that she was made an MBE.

Jemima is an eccentric person, as she would be the first to admit. Spectacularly undomesticated – her former husband once threatened to buy her an oxy-acetylene torch so that she could spoil food faster – and determinedly off-beat, she once made a television film in which she took a pig out for tea in a local country house hotel.

The pig, Jemima said, behaved impeccably. She wanted to take him to the Ritz, but was prevented not because of the pig but because the Top People's hotel does not allow filming in its public rooms.

Her Centre is a model which has often been copied, but never equalled. It is both a facility for keeping and breeding rare birds, and a centre for publicizing them and educating the public.

She says that if by educating the public she can dissuade one teenager from taking a pot-shot with his airgun at a hovering hawk, she has achieved her object, but she clearly achieves a great deal more than that.

In her Centre, the birds are kept in scrupulously clean, open-fronted aviaries where each has enough room to spread its wings and exercise. 'It's so clean I think the birds are afraid to sh**!' said one overawed visiting sanctuary builder. The large staff took this as a compliment.

Jemima has twelve full-time staff and six part-timers who come in during the busy season. They have a daily flying demonstration with what she calls 'The Flying Team' which ranges from a golden eagle to a little owl.

Her feed bill alone for a year is £22,000, her wages bill £140,000 and she reckons to spend £10,000 to £15,000 on vets' bills. The Centre has become her waking and sleeping life. The staff are devoted to her, and the birds come to her call.

It is not much of a surprise to find she is prepared to die for them. When an outbreak of a virulent form of fowl pest was sweeping through the district and the authorities threatened to extend the official slaughter policy to her birds, she simply told them: 'You are not slaughtering one single bird in this place unless you slaughter me first!'

It is a measure of the respect in which she is held that they had second thoughts. Jemima and her staff meticulously caught up their charges and inoculated each of them, to make sure they were safe.

She has every kind of bird of prey from the smallest of owls in the area known as the Hawk Walk, to a potty condor which is in love with her and refuses to fly. 'It loves me,' she admits. 'But it does not love the rest of the world. It would eat anyone else who came near.'

Indeed, she swears she is going to leave her body to be fed to the condor, in a final campaign to publicize the Centre.

'Can't you just see it in the papers?' she says. '"At three o'clock, Mrs Parry Jones's left leg will be fed to the condor?" The queues would stretch from here to Gloucester!'

Just for a moment, she looks almost as though she might be serious.

The centre has an unrivalled success rate in breeding captive birds.

But then to Jemima, no less than to Caroline Gould at the Vale and Kim Olson at the Sanctuary, conservation is a very serious issue.

PWLOs like Paul Henery bring her the birds they are going to use in court as evidence against offenders for her to look after. The RSPB and the RSPCA are also regular callers, with damaged birds or with boarders who will be needed later for this or that case.

The McCabes of the police world are regular guests on her training courses. She has a regular two-day course in which policemen, in the short term at least, are turned into bird-of-prey experts.

There is at least one ex-policeman on her staff, which also includes university graduates and one man who came for work experience and stayed as a full-time worker. She takes in 200 birds a year, many of which are returned to the wild when they have been treated and cared for.

THE HEDGEHOG LADY

A very different kind of specialist from Jemima Parry Jones, is Elaine Drewery, the sub-postmistress at the tiny village of Authorpe, near Louth in Lincolnshire. She specializes in that most down-to-earth of animals: the hedgehog.

Seventeen years ago, someone brought Elaine an injured hedgehog. She was known in the village for her love of animals of all kinds and her almost uncanny knack of mending broken creatures. She treated the hedgehog, and word got around. Elaine enjoyed it. She always welcomed a new interest in what was already a packed and busy life.

Opposite: Jemima Parry Jones, a world authority on birds of prey.

If she took in about ten of them at any one time, Elaine reckoned, she would be able to cope, and the hedgehogs would probably benefit. As the mother of four growing children, she had little spare time, but a ready working force and, above all, a lasting liking for hedgehogs.

But Elaine had not reckoned with how large a demand there was for someone to care for these little creatures. Sick, hurt and lame, the prickly probelms flooded in and within twelve years, she had 240 of them in and around the house each summer, and rarely has fewer than fifty even in winter.

At one time, she had fifty in her living-room alone, rustling around giving the hedgehog's characteristic little grunt, and luxuriating in the warmth of the fire which burned there twenty-four hours a day.

They live in little cages and cardboard boxes in the back of her sofa bed, balled up in discarded woollies or simply cuddled into a cosy corner. The room itself is plastered with hedgehogabilia, pictures and stuffed toys, T-shirts and sweat shirts. In fact, apart from hedgehogs there is only space for a chair, a television and her bed, which is in itself covered in hedgehog toys, including one that is three feet tall.

HEDGEHOGS

One of Britain's most easily recognized mammals, found all over the British Isles with the exception of certain Scottish offshore islands, and as much at home in an urban garden setting as in open countryside. Will come to food laid in garden, but should not be offered bread and cows' milk because it cannot digest it. The hedgehog itself does not know this and will eat it if offered, often giving itself severe and, in the case of a weakling immature animal, fatal stomach problems.

Hibernates by choice in the winter. Particularly vulnerable to road accidents and in garden settings to strimmer, lawnmower, rake and bonfire damage.

The whole place smells strongly of hedgehogs, because fifty little stomachs on the go night and day on a diet of cat-food and goats' milk can raise quite a strong odour.

'I suppose I have been taken over by hedgehogs,' says Elaine in what must rank as one of the understatements of all time. 'And there's bound to be a bit of a honk.'

Outside, where there were once stables, there are now convalescent wards for hedgehogs, though she does not draw the line very strictly: there are also runs for injured foxes, pens for ducks and geese, and a series of cats and a group of dogs.

She has a hospital where her kitchen used to be, which is even equipped with an incubator to help the really poorly inmates, and a used-clothes business called Hogsfam in what used to be the four bedrooms. This raises money for the hedgehogs and, incidentally, also clothes Elaine, who has long since been unable to afford shop-bought clothes.

Her children put up with the prickles and the smells for as long as they could, but, in the end, they gave up and one by one moved out to find a hedgehog-free environment. These days, she has one helper, a former postman called Nigel who left his job to help out, and stayed to become indispensable.

Ken Livingstone, the politician, is a firm supporter, and several rehabilitated hedgehogs have been liberated in his garden.

The common British hedgehog receives some very uncommon care.

Elaine Drewery in her hedgehog road show.

CHAPTER ELEVEN

DO BIG CATS LIVE HERE?

ewspaper headline writers and television newsreaders are fond of mocking big-cat stories. Every time somebody reports being chased by a large animal, catching sight of a large cat eating a sheep, or seeing a spitting shape slinking away into the dark in a country lane, the hoots of derision from the news media are deafening. However, despite the risk of being publicly mocked, a surprising number of PWLOs take these reports seriously, and so did the writers Nick Hicks-Beach and Shelley Miller when they set to work on *Badger* (Series II, Episode 5: 'Predators').

In this storyline a private collector of exotic animals becomes seriously worried about running costs, and persuades an accomplice to stage a fake raid on his home during which his collection can be killed off.

The 'raider', however, loses his nerve at the last moment and, instead of killing the animals, he turns them loose. So McCabe and Cassidy are presented with the problem of staging a big-game hunt in the English countryside for a racoon, an iguana, two wolves and a leopard.

This is the kind of situation Quentin Rose, Europe's only professional dangerous-animal trapper and consultant, handles on a regular basis, and the *Badger* character is based on him and his work.

Could cats like this be prowling in our woods?

Perhaps the last place in the world you might expect to find the only registered dangerous-animal trapper in England is in the narrow winding streets of a pretty Gloucester town which boasts the largest abbey tower the Normans ever built. In this part of Gloucestershire, Mr Pickwick stopped at the local coaching inn for dinner; and in the churchyard you can find the effigy of a knight who fought in and survived the Battle of Poitiers with the Black Prince in 1356.

Quentin Rose is a bit of a surprise. A big-game hunter is usually represented as looking like Stewart Granger in *King Solomon's Mines* – big, macho and sun-tanned. Rose, by contrast, is a compact, quiet and perceptive man with a tonsure of dark hair and quick intelligent eyes.

He has made it his work to track down any big cats at large in the British countryside, and, after spending years at it, has one of the most complete maps of large cat sightings in Britain. He now has a thriving practice as a tracker of escaped animals and the monitor of the unseen; and, he says, a progressively more dangerous population of large alien carnivores.

A former zoo keeper, who spent fifteen years in that job, Rose learned to track animals when he spent a period with Chipewayan and Cree Indians in Northern Canada, and subsequently applied this skill to his chosen calling when he returned to this country.

'When I went back to work in zoos, I was usually instrumental in tracking down any animals which escaped,' he explains. 'In some cases when they were too dangerous to

QUENTIN ROSE – Professional dangerous-animal trapper

Born: Son of an army officer.

Education: Cardiff University where he studied zoology.

Career: Worked at Windsor Safari Park, Port Lympne and a number of other zoos, then spent time in Northern Canada living in the wilderness. Learned tracking with a group of Indians, making him the natural choice to track down escaped zoo animals when he returned to this country. Now lives in Gloucestershire, where he has devoted himself to the full-time study and pursuit of large wild animals.

recapture, I was forced to shoot them. But I always hate shooting escaped animals. I would much rather "dart" and recover them without harming them.'

Over the course of the next few years he found – and either captured or helped to capture – an elephant, tiger, caracal lynx, wolf, four wild boar, which had to be shot, three deer, a beaver, ten baboons and numerous others.

Then the increasing number of reports of big cat sightings began to concern him. He already knew from his experience of zoo escapes that it is possible for a large carnivore to be in a district without the human population being aware of it, so he took reports of the sightings more seriously than most people.

The large cat phenomenon started in the 1970s, when there was no restriction on owning large cats, and a rather foolish fashion came into being for having pumas and leopards as pets.

'Some people kept lions in their garden sheds,' Quentin Rose says. 'And black leopards – another name for the panther – accompanied many a rangy model down the aptly named cat walk.'

The fashion, a truly silly fad, became a dangerous stupidity one day when a leopard being taken for a walk down a London street attacked a child. The Government, in a knee-jerk reaction for which all governments are famous, rushed through the Dangerous Wild Animals Act of 1976 and overnight the owners of these animals found themselves faced with a dilemma.

The Act made it illegal to keep a dangerous animal without properly prepared quarters, a vet's inspection and a licence, the cost of which varied from one district to another, but which could cost thousands of pounds. (To this day, the cost of a licence varies from one authority to another. Some are as much as £2000 to £3000; others can be as little as £45, including the mandatory veterinary inspection.) Under the new Act, people who already owned such animals had to apply for a licence, offer their pets to a properly equipped establishment, or have them put down.

Zoos were inundated with offers of unwanted cats, for which they had no room, and as a result many were destroyed. Some licences were issued, but a large number of people, unwilling to have their expensive pets destroyed, drove them into the countryside and turned them loose. In certain locations, enough animals were released to form a viable breeding population.

It is the progeny of these expensive status symbols, claims Quentin Rose, which now stalk our woods and wild places. 'Make no mistake,' he says, 'they are there and they are multiplying.'

The PWLO network agrees with him. He has now collected sighting reports which indicate twenty-eight areas in which there have been regular and reliable sightings of black leopards, thirty-two for pumas, fourteen for lynx and six for jungle cats, leopard cats and ocelot.

The 'road kill' statistics – reports of animals killed on the roads – back him up. A jungle cat was run over near Ludlow, another found dead in woods nearby. An ocelot has been shot near Chester, a leopard cat (like a leopard but smaller) found dead in the Borders. In 1986, a Scottish farmer, near Inverness, actually caught a puma in a wooden cage in his own farmyard after he became exasperated over the stock he was losing. Its stuffed remains, known affectionately as 'Felicity', are to be seen in the local museum.

Since a caracal lynx can be as big as a border collie, and a European lynx the size of a labrador, we are talking about significantly large carnivores, says Quentin Rose.

'Mostly, of course, they avoid humans, and since at the moment they appear to have a range as large as 250 square miles, they are rarely seen.

'Another factor is that sightings are often not reported because people are afraid of being laughed at. I found one village where twenty per cent of the residents had seen a big cat, but nobody mentioned it because they were afraid of being mocked.'

Many sightings, of course, can be dismissed as genuine mistakes – or, surprisingly rarely, deliberate hoaxes. The mistakes are usually easy to establish and often turn out to be a fleeting glimpse of a labrador dog, an unusually big domestic cat or some other harmless animal.

One lady, hearing reports of a big cat in the area, excitedly rang the police and subsequently, when Quentin Rose was called in, described the animal with efficient accuracy. 'It was a mink,' says Rose. 'She had never seen a mink or a puma, so when she saw an animal she didn't recognize, she put two and two together and made five!'

The most far-fetched sighting so far turned out to be a black plastic bag. However, some sightings are not domestic toms, minks or plastic bags. Some sightings are dangerous cats.

'I know of eight attacks or aggressive encounters with humans, usually – although not invariably – when the animal has been surprised or cornered by accident. In the Mendips, two women out walking with their children were attacked by a leopard as they got back into their car. The leopard then chased the car as they drove off.

'A man fishing at night on the North Devon coast was apparently jumped on from behind by a leopard which tried to bite his neck. Luckily, he had a head-band torch on, and the cat only bit the battery pack which was hanging from the back of his head. When he turned the torch on, the cat ran off.'

But, just as McCabe and Cassidy discover, the big cat at large may not be the only danger in the district. Over-excited 'white hunters', with firearms and itchy trigger fingers, can pose a far more deadly threat.

Terry Moor of the Cat Survival Trust in Welwyn, Hertfordshire, says that he saw a female puma skulking around a farm where he goes to buy dead chickens for his own collection of cats. Terry, who is certainly qualified to recognize a big cat when he sees one because he lives with them every day of his life, says he believes there are several within his area, and he has heard of others further afield.

Towards the end of 1999 Quentin Rose was called in to confirm the identity of a puma filmed on a security camera on an industrial estate in Telford, Shropshire, but, he said, that was a large domestic cat. The RSPCA agrees with him.

PWLO Inspector Steve Kourik, of Hertfordshire, says that he gets a lot of calls on the big cat issue. In the past few years more than seventy alleged sightings have landed on his desk, and while a proportion of them can be written off as honest

THE VIGILANTE

Quentin Rose tells a story of a former soldier who decided to shoot a big cat he had heard was at large in a West Country village and had gone to ground in the local cemetery. He armed himself, baited the cemetery, and was poking around one night when he actually trod on the cat in long grass. It knocked him down, clawed his wife and disappeared into the darkness before he had a chance to use his gun. Both the ex-soldier and his wife were terrified, and she was painfully wounded. In any case, it would hardly delight the police if they had to call on him to explain why he was proposing to spray bullets around the high street of a peaceful English country village.

Leopards almost always go for the person they think is attacking them, and, without specialized ammunition, shotguns are pretty useless against a big cat. A farmer with a load of birdshot will invite attack if he wounds one. Worse, by wounding it and letting it escape he makes the animal into a danger to everyone it comes across until it dies.

Wolves have also been released from private collections into the wild.

mistakes, he is convinced that some are genuine sightings of very worrying animals.

Given that several police districts have confirmed reports of such animals being killed on the roads, it is obvious that there are a number of these creatures still at large in this country. It is also axiomatic in the world of wildlife that if you have what are called 'road kills' – note the plural – there must be a population of such animals. If lots of dead hedgehogs mean the existence of lots more live ones which are not killed by a car, then a few dead caracal lynxes can mean there are other, live caracal lynxes which are not killed.

Quentin Rose has amassed some convincing figures in his quest to confirm the existence of big cats. There are, he says, at least 130 reported incidents of dangerous exotic mammals escaping captivity or being deliberately released into the countryside between 1970 and 1988; and, according to figures issued by the Ministry of Agriculture, Fisheries and Food, a further twenty-two incidents since then. Some of the animals in these incidents remain at large, and it is quite possible that they have managed to breed.

Most escaped animals are recaptured quickly, but some remain at large and their instincts are frightening. Rose recaptured two escaped lynxes which had already killed four sheep and were suspected of killing a further six.

'They were females and they had never hunted in their lives,' says Rose. 'But they killed the sheep perfectly. Cats don't need to be taught to kill.'

There is, of course, no argument about wild boar being at large in the countryside, because it is known that they have escaped from farms where they were being raised as a cash crop. The worry is that, as in France where they are natives, they may start inter-breeding with domesticated pigs being organically raised in the open. This, quite apart from spreading diseases between pig farms, could produce a dangerously volatile hybrid animal. Wild boars can be as dangerous as a bear and they are strong and fiendishly destructive animals.

Rose is concerned that because reports of large wild cats are almost always dismissed – mocked – as poppycock, the public are failing to take them seriously and, sooner or later, someone will be killed.

'Nobody took the coypu seriously until it had established itself so strongly that it was significantly damaging the Norfolk Broads. Then it cost millions to cut down the population,' he says. 'Coypu are stupid animals which are dead easy to catch; cats are dangerous, intelligent and very hard to catch. If they are hurt or hungry, they turn to the most stupid and defenceless prey they can find – *us*.'

A puma in its natural setting, very far from the British countryside.

CHAPTER TWELVE

THE ANIMAL CO-STARS

Actors dread working with children or animals. Actors are supposed to be able to act: children and animals are not. So a child 'actor' or performing animal looks twice as clever as an adult actor. Children also look cute – most adults do not. Children make the audience go: 'Ahhh!' – actors normally do not. Shirley Temple was a top Hollywood star in her heyday, yet her acting abilities were mediocre and her storylines often stomach-churning. Lassie, who was not one but a succession of different sheepdogs, was a star, but who can name the human actors who appeared in the Lassie films?

Animals are stars just by being physically present on the screen. Actors have to work for it – they do not have appealing liquid eyes and a glossy coat to make them look cuddly. A human actor swimming in a lake has to be careful his costume stays on, remember to hit the right mark for the camera, recite his lines with appropriate passion on cue, and try not to drown, at least while on camera. An otter, however, swimming in a lake only has to do what comes naturally and he or she is a star.

What makes this all the more infuriating for actors is that every animal star has to be coaxed, cajoled, implored and cuddled into the simplest thing – and, even then, for take after take after take, does not always get it right. Then, when they do, usually by accident, the enchanted audience says: 'Ahhh, isn't it *clever*?'

And the trouble is, the audience is right. Domestic animals can, given a trainer's patience, experience and expertise, be trained to do simple things. Wild animals – even wild animals born and raised in captivity – remain totally unpredictable. Ask anybody who has ever put a ferret down a rabbit hole, or any falconer who has watched his favourite bird of prey go off on an expedition of its own.

For an animal handler who provides animals to star in films or television, there is another problem: the film unit is quite rightly concerned only with getting the right animal to behave as the team wishes it to on the day. But the true skill in filming with animals is to let the animals' natural behaviour fit the demands of the script. A badger, for example, which would naturally dive for the nearest hole in the ground needs to be fitted into a sequence that shows a badger making for its sett, and so on. If a wild badger – and it is a maxim of wildlife filming that there is no such thing as a trained badger – really was allowed to dive down a real sett, with its network of entrances, exits and underground chambers, it would just disappear, never to be seen again.

Since it is against the law to interfere with a truly wild badger, any that are seen on *Badger* have to have been reared in captivity or have been rescued and imprinted so closely with their carers that, for their own safety, they can no longer be allowed back into the wild.

A vet is always present on a film set to make sure that no animal, wild or tame, is ever distressed in any way; and no animal, of course, is ever hurt during filming.

The badger-baiting scene (Series I, Episode 4: 'Setts, Lies and Videotape') in *Badger* did not contain one single live badger. Only a stuffed badger was ever present in the warehouse with the terriers.

For the scene in which McCabe released his badger into the wild (Series I, Episode 6: 'Low Fidelity'), a simple enough scene on screen, some elaborate preparation was needed. First, the animal team had to construct a special enclosure which could not be seen by the camera. The netting sides were dug into the ground because, while badgers may look slow and shuffling on screen, in real life they are capable of moving like lightning, and dig faster than a terrier. Take your eyes off a badger who wants out for a split second and he will be under the fence and away.

The 'sett' entrance down which the badger had to disappear was, in fact, a hole leading into a plastic tube and back into the enclosure, so that no matter how fast the badger went off, he always ended up safely in the same place.

If a badger, which has adapted to life in captivity and therefore to the presence of human beings, were to be put back into the wild, he would be in danger in several different ways. Badgers, as mentioned, are extremely territorial. A strange badger is not welcomed by his compatriots: he is the target for every badger in the vicinity.

Another danger is human brutality, especially that of badger-baiters. Not all of these use the formal ring-and-terrier release ritual. Some simply set a lurcher dog on to any badger they come across in the open, and while a badger will put up a spirited fight against a terrier, even a powerful pit bull terrier, he has little chance against a lurcher which is fast and has the advantage of height, particularly if the badger is already injured in the first place.

A badger injured in a fight and driven to flight has no home to head for. Badgers, like most wild animals, have only one course to pursue when badly wounded. They find a hole, crawl in and lay up until they either get better or die. A badger in strange countryside, however, is effectively in the same position as a displaced human being. He needs food and shelter, but he has no natural familiar hunting ground to live off, and if he tries to move in on somebody else's hunting ground he will find himself in conflict for territory.

People who are qualified and licensed to handle badgers know all this and make elaborate arrangements for their release, sometimes going as far as constructing an artificial sett for the badger to inhabit, well away from known badger haunts. This is the procedure followed when, for one reason or another, a licence is issued to move badgers from a site which is to be developed.

The otter sequences in *Badger* (Series I, Episode 3: 'The World According to Carp') were particularly problematic to film because the otter had quite a complex role in this story about counterfeit money hidden in the banks of a lake scheduled for a fishing competition.

Some actors can't be directed: Beanie makes up her own script.

Beanie, the otter starlet introduced earlier, was required to come out of the lake, run up the bank and sit up at the edge of the road, where McCabe's four-wheel-drive car would whisk past it.

The crew had a clever device to make it sit up on cue: a piece of fishy bait was attached to the end of a rod and dangled over the otter's head as it arrived at the roadside. In the next shot, which would be inter-spliced with a shot of the vehicle on the same stretch of road, the otter was supposed to cross the road and disappear into the woods on the other side. Simple? Well, actually, no.

The otter showed no interest in following the script. Instead of posing prettily for the camera, it ran off into the woods. It also refused point blank to cross the road as required.

John Cross, the veteran animal handler for the series, takes up the story.

'Of course, everybody wanted to see the otter do its stuff, so they all congregated behind the camera, out of shot, to watch. The whole cast, camera crew, sound team, everybody, were behind the camera on the side of the road they wanted the otter to come to. And, of course, it would not go anywhere near them. The way to get the shot was to remove the team so that they would not frighten the animal, and have only one person on the far side of the road to pick the otter up.'

Further into the story, the otter was required to dig counterfeit money out of its holt in the bank, thereby exposing the plot laid by the crooked restaurateur, Moncur.

Once again the otter showed little enthusiasm for the requirements of the script. To try to make it behave according to plan, the owner collected its droppings – known in the otter trade as 'spraints' – and pushed them into the hole along with the counterfeit money, in the hope that the otter, recognizing its own smell, would burrow through the money to get at it. The spraints of an otter have a strong odour, and these were liberally spread all over the notes. This did not make the handling of otter-tainted cash popular with the crew.

One way or another, the otter became universally admired for its looks, but was reckoned to be a dead loss as an actor.

Dogs which are used in films and on television are more amenable, and several take to the requirements of the screen with gusto. One, for instance, was the magnificent labrador dog which had been cast as one of Steph the Vet's first patients. Phillippa Wilson recalls the scene clearly:

'I was supposed to give him an injection which made him lose consciousness. Naturally I could not give a real animal a real injection, so we had a labrador who had been trained to pass out as a trick. All you had to do was touch his side, and down he would go, boom. It was his trick and he loved it, so each time he did it he wagged his tail furiously and waited to be made a fuss of. I was trying to remember my lines while just out of sight of the camera there was this huge tail wagging like a fan – and right under my nose were these huge brown eyes gazing up at me, waiting to be told he was a good dog.'

Since Phillippa is cast as a vet, she naturally has to deal with animals more than anybody else in the cast, including McCabe himself. Which also means she runs into more snags.

First of all for instance, there was the troublesome llama, mentioned earlier as having a veritable talent for hogging the shot. However, it was a talent that spelt the end of this particular llama's television career, as eventually the crew had to reschedule the shot and film it without the llama appearing at all.

They had entirely the opposite problem with an injured barn owl in Series I, Episode 2: 'I've Got Glue Under My Skin', when Steph had to have a prickly conversation with Claire (Rebecca Lacey) in the sanctuary.

'We were supposed to be talking either side of this owl's perch, and it was supposed to be in shot between us,' says Phillippa. 'But as soon as the camera started turning, the owl shuffled off out of shot. No matter how we shifted the perch or re-aligned the camera, off he went, out of shot every time.'

Steph and Claire –
without the elusive owl.

Snugly tucked into the eaves of the Goose and Gargle pub.

Owls seem prone to fits of temperament when they are taken to the sanctuary. Like the Little Owl in Series II, Episode 2: 'The Price of a Daughter', which was supposed to have been found in the street by Ray the Alligator Man (Brendan P. Healy) with a broken wing, and taken to Steph to have it fixed.

All went well until the owl arrived at the sanctuary, where, just as it was announced that it had a broken wing, the contrary bird rose up and flapped both its wings like an industrial fan. You can't train owls much, either.

One animal which is a nightmare for everybody is the humble British bat. There are fifteen species of bat found in the British Isles, from the small and relatively common pipistrelle to the rare and endangered greater horseshoe bat, and they have one thing in common: they terrify most women.

Julia (Jayne Charlton MacKenzie) who runs the Goose and Gargle pub, is no exception, so when she discovers in Series II, Episode 4: 'Cock o' the Walk' that there are bats in her attic, the poor girl is panic stricken.

Working with bats is also a nightmare for cameramen. For one thing bats fly only in the dusk and at night when they forage for the insects which are their sole nourishment. For another, they are virtually impossible to train.

There are, however, bat experts who know ways round these difficulties, and John Cross found just such an expert when he went looking.

John came across a devout bat-fan cameraman who specializes in filming bats for nature films. This man was able to provide long-eared and Daubenton's bats, and knew the perfect time to film bats within a house.

The bats, which were released by one of their keepers, flew through the loft of the set and out of the trapdoor at the other end, where they were met by their carer and safely put away. They may look as though they are acting on cue, but they were only doing what bats do naturally.

The scene lasts just a few seconds on screen, but took hours to set up and film, an indication of the care that goes into making the series as authentic as possible.

Bat fans point out that, although there are fifteen different types of bat in this country, very few people actually know much about them. As the only flying mammal in the British Isles, they are also subject to a lot of undeserved hostile prejudice.

No British bat is harmful in any way to anything except the insects they live on, and a pipistrelle can eat 3500 insects in one night. Many of the insects that bats eat are crop pests. So, in many ways, bats are a boon to farmers and owners of old houses and buildings in which the insects might otherwise become a danger to health.

Because by nature they are woodland dwellers, bats spend most of their lives in the open, making their roosts in holes in trees, caves and tunnels, and during the last hundred years in derelict farm buildings, and occasionally occupied buildings as well. They roost in roof spaces, behind hanging tiles and very occasionally within houses.

Because they are vulnerable to disturbance the law goes out of its way to make sure they are not disturbed in any way, and people who try to make them move on, merely by making noises and waving things, are committing an offence under the Wildlife and Countryside Act of 1981. You are not even allowed to block the entrance to a roost when the bats are all away during the winter.

People who are distressed by the presence of bats, who want to make repairs to the loft the bats are using as a roost, or who want to extend their homes which would mean disturbing the bats, are obliged to consult their local English Nature office, or call in bat experts from the Bat Conservation Trust who can recommend a licensed bat man to help with the problem.

In fact, bat experts are convinced that people who are terrified of bats would not be if only they could learn something about the creatures. Psychiatrists, for instance, think women particularly are terrified of bats because they fear they will get caught in their hair. They forget that while they can only see the bat fleetingly, the bat can see them at all times and will easily be able to avoid them.

Contrary to popular belief, bats are not blind – they have quite good eyesight. They do, however, navigate in the dark by sonar, emitting high-pitched squeaks, some of which can – with difficulty – be caught by a human ear.

Bats are protected under the Wildlife and Countryside Act of 1981.
It is an offence to:
■ **Kill a bat or injure it in any way**
■ **Handle a bat**
■ **Disturb roosting bats**
■ **Destroy or damage a bat roost**
■ **Block access to a bat roost**
■ **Keep bats in captivity**
■ **Sell or trade any bats alive or dead.**
The only exceptions to these rules are people who are licensed to handle bats, usually contacted through English Nature or through one of the ninety bat groups throughout the United Kingdom.

BATS AND THE LAW

If they are roosting in a house they will not, contrary to some people's belief, gnaw through electric wires, rot woodwork or brickwork, or attack domestic pets. Their droppings, which are dark in colour, turn to dust in dry conditions; but if the bats are roosting in a leaky loft, they may smell in the damp. The easiest way to stop the smell is to repair the roof, and thank your lucky stars that the smell of the bats alerted you to the fact that you had a damp problem.

Dogs, which are inclined to do what their trainer wants them to do just to please him, are easier than most animals to train. John Cross is particularly proud of a German shepherd dog he uses which has starred in a number of television

productions as a ferocious beast, although it is in fact a friendly fun-loving dog which prefers playing and bouncing around to growling and attacking people.

'This dog was a former prison guard dog, which was retired because he was too playful. He was trained to a simple ball, which he would chase endlessly and enthusiastically wherever you happened to put it,' John explains.

'In one television series, a number of children were supposed to be raiding an orchard and be trapped in a tree by this ferocious animal, and the dog put on a great performance, barking his head off and jumping endlessly at them as they cringed in the branches of their tree. In fact he was not in the slightest interested in the children. Just before the scene started, he saw us throw his ball to the children, and he was after that!'

He was also used to simulate attacks on adults.

'You only had to show him the ball and pretend to hide it in someone's collar and he would jump up at them barking and apparently going for their throat. Sometimes it was not even necessary to put the ball there – as long as he thought you had.'

The same trick worked with a dog-fox raised in captivity and trained to respond to a bar of chocolate. Show him the chocolate and he would snuffle around and worry until he found it.

'We used this fox to make a scene for *Emmerdale*, where there was a body in the woods and a fox was supposed to find it and be seen sniffing at it,' says John Cross. 'Filming that scene demonstrated how important it is to prepare the set properly. They could not see why it was necessary to build a special pen to stop the fox from running off, and against my better judgement I agreed to do the scene without it. We put the block of chocolate in the actor's armpit, and the fox came trotting up, right on cue, burrowed into his armpit and pulled out the chocolate. Then he ran off over the horizon and we didn't see him again for three days, when he came back and found his keeper.

'That taught me a lesson, though. I never again did a scene without the fence in place. The poor fox must have been terrified out in the dark by himself.'

You might think that all of the above does not apply to alligators. They are scaly, not cuddly; they are not lovable – they eat people. Above all, they are not pretty.

Only a mother alligator could find one even remotely appealing. But you would be wrong about their lack of popularity.

'For some reason, people like to star alligators in their scripts,' says Jim Club of Amazing Animals who provided the alligators for the first scenes of the very first episode of *Badger*. 'Some ask for crocodiles, but we try to talk them out of that because crocodiles are much more aggressive than alligators, and the only difference as far as the public is concerned is that they have a narrower snout and are a slightly different colour.'

The alligator in 'It's a Jungle Out There', Kieran Prendiville's first script for *Badger*, was in fact played by three alligators – two real ones, Baby and George, mentioned earlier, and one animatronic dummy which would roll its eyes, open its mouth and could be relied upon not to eat its co-stars.

The story required McCabe and Steph the Vet to mount a raid on a council house occupied by Ray (Brendan P. Healy) and his pet alligator, Patsy. Patsy was covered by the Dangerous Animals Act and the bedroom of a council house in Newcastle could not be considered a fit place to keep a dangerous animal, so Patsy had to go to a proper zoological garden. However, it is one thing to decide to move an alligator, and quite another to actually do it.

On screen, McCabe and Steph entered the bedroom, snared the by now irritated Patsy with a noose around her snout and then proceeded to keep her trap closed with a good wrapping of tape, in the course of which operation, Patsy trashed the

Baby the alligator has to be encouraged to snap her jaws at the camera.

bedroom. In reality, however, not one of the three actors was present on the set when a live alligator was there.

Baby, the first alligator, was put on the bed by her handlers, and told to give her finest performance. All she had to do was open her mouth wide and roar at the camera in a menacing manner. Since any alligator with its mouth open cannot look anything but menacing, this was hardly a demanding role. All the same, Baby nearly blew it because she was too comfortable on the bed and, under the heat of the lights, settled down to go to sleep. Only a succession of prods with a broom handle could persuade her to wake up, roar and do her menacing stuff.

Once she had, she was carried away, and George, her colleague, was brought in. George is a stroppy alligator, a tough guy from the swamps who will trash a hotel room without raising a sweat, and eat a film set for breakfast. But George, too, took one look around, made himself comfortable and settled down for an afternoon's snooze until spurred into action with a broom handle, at which he obediently threw himself off the bed and proceeded to eat the furniture, the bedding and anything else within range.

The scenes in which Ray spent time in bed with Patsy, and the scenes in which Steph and McCabe subdued the alligator were all made using the animatronic alligator. 'And even that was a bit frightening, once the alligator got going,' says Phillippa. 'It looked fine until it started blinking at you, and then suddenly you wanted to be absolutely sure they were using the fake!'

Curiously, both Phillippa and Jerome were prepared to do their stuff with live alligators, and even the fact that one of the handlers had lost a finger did not put them off. It did, however, put off Murray Ferguson, the producer of the first series. He shuddered at the idea of £500,000 per episode being gambled on the proposition that actors can move quicker than a hungry alligator, and shut his stars away from danger until it had gone home.

The different shots were then spliced together using camera magic to put the human actors right in there with the animals. It was so successful that several members of the public complained that the actors had been put in danger for the scene.

Jim Club is used to this reaction. Animals are his life, and the firm he works for provides creatures such as leopards, wolves (Series II, Episode 5: 'Predators'), venomous snakes and even big reptiles. The golden rule with dangerous animals, he says, is to be careful never to startle them. 'You have to remember that these are wild animals. No matter how well you think you know them, a wild animal will turn on you in a split second without any apparent reason. And if you startle or surprise them, they will definitely bite you.'

In the case of a poodle, a startled snap of the jaws may ruin your socks, but if you startle an alligator, a leopard or a wolf, it can ruin your whole life. The rule is: stay away.

CHAPTER THIRTEEN

THE ART OF TAXIDERMY

The art of preserving animals in what looks like a natural state in order to keep them after death dates back about 350 years, and was used to great effect by the great travelling naturalists of the eighteenth century who brought home not just notes and sketches of the animals they found, but the very bodies, bones and skins, mounted as in life.

The enemies of a naturalist in those years were time and temperature. It could take them two years, for example, to get to the remoter shores of South America by boat, and another two years to penetrate the interior on foot, often fighting off angry locals along the way.

Their way of collecting the wonderful creatures they saw was to shoot one, dissect it before it had a chance to decay – a matter of hours in high temperatures and high humidity – and bring back the tanned skin and the bones intact to study them at leisure in Britain.

In order to show others what these animals looked like in real life, the craft for rebuilding the body and stitching back the skin developed, so that the creature could be re-created to look as it did when alive. For millions of people who could not travel, the only way they would ever see a tiger, a lion or a South American tree sloth would be stuffed in a museum or a travelling curiosity show. Scientists used the stuffed animals to lecture from, to study, to draw conclusions – not always accurate – and form theories.

Just as there is art in sculpture, there is art in re-creating living characteristics in the dead. Good taxidermists are much prized for their skills, and their work is sometimes awesome in its realism.

Naturally enough, the most prized stuffed creatures are the most rare. The rarer they become, the higher price they command, so it was inevitable that unscrupulous people should turn to the blackest of black markets to make their profits. Just as unscrupulous egg-collectors collect the eggs of the most endangered of birds, these people make a business of providing stuffed examples of endangered species.

Badger, Series I, Episode 2: 'I've Got Glue Under My Skin', focused on a taxidermist, who had been struck off the register of the Guild of Taxidermists for preserving illegally killed protected animals, imported or slaughtered in this country, to feed a market in rare creatures.

The script was reminiscent of a 1996 real-life case in Chester Crown Court when Dutch dealer Nicolaas Peters, operating out of Gwent, was prosecuted for running a thriving business supplying protected creatures and their body parts to two businesses in America.

In court, the RSPCA Inspector said that: 'Walking into his house was like walking into a dead zoo.'

The collection in Peters's premises at the time included the skull of a Philippine eagle, one of the rarest birds in the world, the skull of a threatened Siberian tiger, and

A 'dead zoo', McCabe looks unimpressed by the taxidermists' work.

the skulls and skins of forty-two other protected species. 'The damage done,' said the prosecuting counsel, 'cannot be expressed in financial terms.'

There were more than 500 specimens crammed into the building, some of them still in the process of being worked on. Customs officers – involved because the haul constituted several offences under the Convention on International Trade in Endangered Species (CITES) – joined with RSPCA Inspectors, RSPB official Guy Shorrock and Investigations Officer Joan Childs, and the World Wildlife Fund representatives in the case.

Peters, the dealer, got a two-year sentence.

The case sickened Kim McDonald, the chairman of the Guild of Taxidermists, for two reasons. The first is that he is a genuine wildlife lover. The second is that with more than 300 members, he is well aware that one dishonest taxidermist taints the public perception of all the honest ones. Just as the vast majority of policemen are honest and loathe a 'bent' colleague for the damage he does to them, so the vast majority of taxidermists are honest, skilled craftsmen who hate the tiny number of highly publicized 'bent' colleagues.

'Trophies have always been mounted for sportsmen who want a permanent memorial to their skill as hunters,' he points out. 'But taxidermy has also always provided specimens for education, for museums and zoos which need animals that can be examined and experienced close-up without the danger that they might eat you.

'Naturalists used their skill to bring specimens home. They might be two years' trek away from a harbour where they could rejoin their ship, and the specimens they collected could then be two or more years in the hold of the ship taking them home. The chance of bringing home a live animal was almost nil.'

Originally, the trade had to make its own body forms which were either carved from wood, and added to usable bones such as skulls and leg bones, or built up by winding wool and twine on to an armature and literally stuffing the skins. These days the technique is far more advanced. There are highly specialized firms which make eyes for each distinct type of animal, including human beings, body shapes in two-part foam, and face masks for large animals such as tigers.

The realistic and dramatic effect of an animal is, however, still dependent on the skill of the taxidermist.

'What happens when a carcass is delivered to the taxidermist is that you skin it out. In the case of something like a bird, where you need the head shape, you leave

Jim Cassidy inspects the only safe tiger he is liable to meet.

Carried away with their job: McCabe and Cassidy impound a stuffed panther as evidence.

KIM McDONALD – Taxidermist

Born: East Anglia, 20 June 1947, son of a stockbroker.

Career: Wanted to become a vet, but could not afford to support himself through a five-year training course. Followed his father into the stockbroking business and spent twenty years in the City. Eventually decided to set himself up in business as a dealer in taxidermy exhibits, and then decided it was more profitable to deal first, directly with the taxidermists and, secondly, to become one himself. Now Chairman of the Guild of Taxidermists.

in the skull. The rest you throw away, or, in some cases, such as pheasant, grouse or salmon, eat.'

There are several established firms which specialize in fish trophies, and do not touch anything else. Others make a speciality of mounted shooting trophies.

Many of the creatures which arrive on the taxidermist's work bench are road-accident kills. Birds with their high speeds and light bones are particularly vulnerable to impact, and when a spectacular bird of prey flies into something at top speed, death is inevitable, from shock if not from the impact.

Some birds are notoriously regular road-kill victims. Barn owls, for instance, hunt in the evening by patrolling road verges and sitting on fence posts. Since they are often only a few feet off the ground, and a motorist naturally does not expect a large white bird to suddenly appear out of the dusk, they are frequently struck by cars. A motorist with a beautiful bird on his bonnet may well want to preserve it as an exhibit in his home, and the process of preservation is remarkably quick.

'Assuming it is not too badly damaged, and assuming I got it at 9.00 in the morning, I could have it skinned out by half-past, and washed, tanned and finished by noon,' says Kim McDonald.

Foxes – also notorious road-kill victims and very popular as taxidermy subjects – take a day and a half.

'I make an incision along the animal's back and lift the carcass out, leaving the skin. There is a firm which makes three different sized body shapes for foxes, for instance. Of course, ninety per cent of foxes are not a standard size, so you have to adjust the body form, but after a lot of practice you know exactly what to do.'

The matter of tanning the skin so that it remains wholesome and pliable enough to be draped and then stitched over the form is a skilled matter. In Victorian times when taxidermy reached the peak of its expertise, almost all animals were preserved with arsenic. In large quantities, of course, arsenic is poisonous and the reason that many Victorian exhibits were preserved in glass cases was as much for the protection of the public as for the protection of the animal.

Kim McDonald says that there is some evidence that the small quantities of arsenic the taxidermists absorbed through their skins acted as a tonic and helped to keep them healthy. He cites a study done in Nottingham at the time which showed the average age of local taxidermists at death was seventy-six years old, a phenomenally good age in a century when people commonly died much younger than they do now.

These days the chemicals borax and camphor, which have the advantage of not poisoning the public, are much more commonly used.

Taxidermy, of course, is carefully controlled by law. All but a handful of animals are protected species, and taxidermists need a licence to treat them. There are two kinds of licence: one is called a general licence and is issued under the Wildlife and Countryside Act of 1981. This covers the treatment of common British birds such as blackbirds, robins, black-headed gulls and the like. Taxidermists are obliged to notify the DETR (Department of the Environment, Transport and the Regions) when they sell a specimen.

The second kind of licence, which is far more difficult to come by, is the Article Ten licence which is required by the Convention on International Trade in Endangered Species. It covers threatened and protected species from Siberian tigers to sparrow hawks, buzzards and birds of prey.

The average taxidermist would come into contact with such an animal only on rare occasions. Established firms are occasionally approached by zoos or private collectors who want a dead animal, such as a tiger, to be preserved, but the sheer volume of such a large body would give any but the most expert of taxidermist problems.

Kim McDonald says the largest animal he has ever done was a tiger. 'In such a case there is no question of opening the body along the backbone and lifting the animal out of its skin. The sheer weight of the tiger would kill you. It has to be opened along the belly and the inside of the legs, then the skin is tanned, draped over the body form, and sewn into place with very tiny stitches. The hard part is getting it to look right.

'With a common British mammal, such as a stoat, for instance, the punter probably thinks a stoat is a stoat, is a stoat, and he would not know if it looked natural or not. But most people have a very firm idea of what they think a tiger should look like. Anybody paying £2000 or so, which is what it would cost to stuff and mount a tiger, knows what he wants it to look like when it is finished.'

Like all 'straight' taxidermists, McDonald is used to occasional approaches from shifty individuals who 'just happen' to have come across a man in a pub with a dead puma for sale, who are wondering how much it would cost to have it stuffed and mounted for sale. He is well aware that there is an international trade in carcasses which have been killed to order for the illegal trade, and of the penalties which would be imposed if he wanted – which he does not – to engage in such a deal.

'Hopefully, people like that run up against a brick wall wherever they go,' he says. 'Or, even better, the taxidermist takes all his details, and makes a quick call to the local PWLO with a name, address and a tale of woe.'

CHAPTER FOURTEEN

THE GLOBAL THREAT

t is in the nature of wildlife that species die out and evolve, and the human species' comparatively recent rise to domination, just like whirlwinds, volcanic eruptions and tsunamis, is a natural force. The animal and insect world adapts itself to accommodate us.

We human beings on the other hand have considerable difficulty adapting ourselves to fit in with the natural world. We do not like being threatened by the sea, so we build shore defences which occasionally damage the coast more than the sea would. We do not like having our homes and crops devastated by insects so we devise ways of killing off pests, often provoking another kind of problem.

It is one of the contradictions of our nature as a species that while one human force strides through the world destroying – often accidentally or incidentally – another part of our nature is to conserve. We are the only species which has the slightest conception of responsibility for the results of our actions, along with the capacity to do something about it.

We are appalled by stories of the brutal seamen who, in an orgy of destruction, wreaked havoc among the nests of the dodo in the seventeenth century, and so made the poor flightless bird extinct virtually overnight. We are horrified by the uncaring buffalo-hunters of the nineteenth century who slaughtered so many of the North American bison to feed the leather trade, that herds, which once covered the land as far as the eye could see, were reduced to a few hundred animals.

People living in Aberdeen, Cardiff or Fulham care deeply about the threat of extinction which faces the African elephant, the white rhino or the Siberian tiger, even though they may never have seen one. They form groups such as Elefriends and pass laws to protect birds, mammals and insects.

So if, as a species, we destroy, we also seek to conserve, and the Convention on International Trade In Endangered Species of Wild Fauna and Flora, known all over the world as CITES (pronounced sight-ease), is a testimony to this.

CITES is a worldwide treaty which provides controls on the international trade in species which are considered to be in danger from over-exploitation. It was signed in 1973, came into force in 1975, and was entered into by the United Kingdom in 1976.

It does not prohibit all trade in all species. Of the 1.3 million different species of animals, insects and plants thought to exist, CITES affects only 23,000 (around 2 per cent). Of that 23,000 only 800 of the most threatened are actually banned from trade and, subject to permit, even those can be traded under strict control.

CITES is not by any means perfect. Some signatory countries take it more seriously than others. Indeed, it is said that most of the 124 signatories do little or nothing to enforce CITES in their own territory.

Like the PWLO network in this country, it has to take its place in a scale of priorities, and a country which is wrenched apart by internal turmoil, laid waste

by war or is fighting a desperate battle against, for example, drug barons, is not going to be meticulous about enforcing the international law on the export of exotic parrots, the slaughter of rhinos or the poaching of big cats for their pelt and body parts.

If a shahtoosh shawl can be sold in the Western world's fashion capitals for anything up to £25,000 – and each shahtoosh shawl requires the death of three excruciatingly rare chiru or Tibetan antelope – it is very hard to shut down the trade. This is particularly the case since the remaining 40,000 chiru are being poached at a rate of ten per cent per year by local peasants who eat the meat, sell the skins to make shawls, and the horns for Chinese medicine.

However, the damage being done to native populations in order to feed the international trade in endangered species – sometimes just because it *is* endangered – cannot be ignored, and at least some of the signatories to CITES are doing their best to enforce it.

CHINESE MEDICINE

The European Union regulations aimed at supporting CITES bans the trade in tigers, rhinos, bears and other protected species, including plants. It is illegal to sell, or keep for sale, any product which contains any part of these species or claims to contain them even when it does not. The maximum fine for each offence is up to £5000 or two years in jail.

NB: It is also an offence to buy or offer to buy – that is, to ask for – these products in a shop.

Badger tackled one aspect of CITES in Series I, Episode 5: 'McCabe Gets the Horn'. In this story, Tom McCabe becomes involved in an operation to trace some rhino horn missing from a shipment seized by Customs and Excise in London, and believed to be destined for the Chinese medicine market.

The Chinese medicine market is a real problem for conservationists. It is based on 2000-year-old practices and, because of the Western world's mushrooming interest in alternative therapies, it has suddenly become big business.

The trouble is that Chinese medicine depends on the mystic properties of body parts from a number of species already at a dangerously threatened level.

The tiger is valued for all its body parts, from the hair of its pelt to the ground-up tiger-bone powder, which is used in the treatment of rheumatism. Experts estimate that one tiger is killed each day to feed the demand for such products, and warn that the world population of tigers, partly as a result of this demand, is now reduced to 4000.

The Asian brown bear is 'milked' of its bile for the treatment of infections and inflammations; tortoise shell is thought to have curative properties in reducing fever and even for treating medical problems such as tumours.

One universally prized ingredient in all kinds of potions and ointments is rhino horn. The Chinese use this to treat a list of complaints, ranging from fevers to strokes. Certain Arab states prize it for making dagger hilts and, when made into a tea, consider it to be an aphrodisiac. Since most aphrodisiacs have their strongest effect on the mind, it probably works because they think it will.

In all, there are over 20,000 derivatives in the form of medicinal products, based primarily on tigers, bears and rhinoceroses, although other animals, including snakes and tortoises, are also used. The net result of this demand – now greatly inflated by the alternative-medicine demands of the Western world – is that animals are being hunted to extinction in Asia and Africa. Tigers are dying in Asia in order to be rubbed on poorly knees in Islington. For its horn alone, the black rhino has been hunted to the very edge of existence. The African population of black rhino, for example, has declined by ninety-six per cent since 1970.

Gone forever are seventeen species or sub-species of bears, five of wolves and foxes, four of cats, ten of cattle, sheep, goats and antelopes, five of horses, three of deer. The list simply goes on.

The value of the Chinese medicine market, known to the police more accurately as Traditional East Asian Medicine (TEAM), is estimated at billions. Some animal products sell at anything up to £200 per ounce, and some are as valuable as gold.

What is particularly galling, as McCabe finds out when he goes into the local East Asian community in pursuit of illegal medicines, is that there are perfectly good alternatives to tiger bones, etc., and the vast majority of Chinese suppliers and practitioners manage a thriving trade without ever having handled an illegally procured ingredient. Tiger balm, incidentally, does not contain tigers, or any part of them.

One of the problems in pursuing illegal ingredients in Chinese medicine is that virtually no British policemen can read the labels on the packets, and the sellers may not be disposed to translate for them.

However, Chinese medicine is only a tiny part of the reason for CITES – there are also plenty of other illegal trades in endangered species which are generated by the appetite for exotic animals and plants in the developed West, mainly in Europe, Great Britain and North America.

It is ironic that the very success of CITES has so reduced the supply from the wild of the kind of animals and insects beloved of the West, that the ones already present in those countries have acquired a hugely inflated value.

McCabe discovers that not all Chinese Medicine shops supply illegal products.

The humble common tortoise – once a feature of half the suburban gardens in the country, and imported as ballast in merchant ships – is now worth anything up to £700 per specimen. Criminals, as a result, have not been slow to realize that rich pickings from a children's section of a zoo requires only a bulky sports holdall to net £7000 worth of slow-moving tortoises.

Of course, not all tortoises are worth quite this inflated amount, so the villains do need to know how to recognize the ones that are and where to sell them. So, like art works, animals are increasingly being stolen to order. Collectors, desperate to get a specimen to complete their collection, are occasionally pushed over the edge of the law, and the supply will always follow the demand to its logical conclusion.

In this country, one of the men most concerned with this kind of theft from zoos is John Hayward, former PWLO for Thames Valley, and now the Theft Co-ordinator for the Federation of Zoological Gardens of Great Britain and Ireland.

One of Hayward's last jobs before he retired from the police was to gather information on travelling criminals, and, since his beat extended over Buckinghamshire, Berkshire and Oxfordshire, and was consequently the force with the most central location in the country, he was in a plum position to oversee them.

Over the years, he has watched the nature of his work change almost beyond recognition, and the major factor causing this change has been the onslaught on exotic species of the demand from the West, and the effect of CITES itself.

Twenty years ago, for instance, the hyacinth blue macaw – a huge bird, a metre long in the body with a lovely, deep blue plumage – was so prolific in its native forests of South America that it had no intrinsic value at all. Now, an individual bird can be worth up to £30,000.

Similarly, a breeding pair of Lear's macaws has been estimated at £40,000 upwards; and even the African grey parrot – caught in tens of thousands and exported in crates so cramped that thousands die en route – sells in the West for anything up to £800.

Last year alone, researchers in Brazil discovered that twelve million animals, ranging from ants to jaguars, were snatched from the country's rainforests to feed the illegal international markets. At least 300 gangs run the trade, and officials estimate that it is worth around £25 million a year at Brazilian prices, and that in scope it comes just behind the drug and illegal arms traffic.

Birds are the most trafficked animals, and all of them are transported in conditions so hideously cruel that it is hardly surprising that many do not survive the process. Practices include piercing the eyes of smuggled birds so that they cannot see the light and therefore will not sing. The blinded bird will then give birth to progeny which is not blind, so its value for breeding purposes is not affected. Others are doped to keep them silent.

The dealers never go into the rainforests themselves, and, while raking in huge profits for themselves, pay only tiny amounts to native peoples. They do not, therefore, even have the excuse that they are helping to relieve local poverty.

In 1996, John Hayward, who knows plenty about parrots, handled twenty-seven thefts of exotic birds, involving 351 birds valued at £153,000, which makes it big business. Nine people were arrested.

Bird-nappers have to be highly skilled. They cannot simply kick down the door of an aviary, grab the bird and stick it in a bag. It will die of shock, leaving them with a bundle of feathers instead of a living, breathing and beautiful bird worth tens of thousands of pounds.

Beautiful and extremely valuable: a pair of hyacinth blue macaws.

Stealing a large, noisy, strong bird is no picnic. Most parrots have very sharp beaks with which they can crack a brazil nut, so a human finger is no challenge to them, as two would-be bird-nappers discovered when they tried to grab a parrot from a pet shop in South London.

When they caught him and started to stuff him in a Santa Claus sack, the parrot, called Max, kicked up such a din and attacked them with such ferocity that they had to let go and then prise him out from under a rabbit hutch. When they did eventually get him in the sack, they looked up, and, realizing the whole incident had been filmed on a CCTV camera, dropped the bag and ran off. At least the video tape provided the local police with some amusing Christmas viewing.

These days, one safeguard for birds is to inject them with a micro-chip containing a registration number. Then when a scanner is run over the bird, its number will come up on the screen identifying its origins and legality. On the legitimate market: no chip, no sale.

There is a different problem with identifying tortoises. Regulations, which are aimed at having them 'chipped', run into the problem that tortoises are virtually impossible to chip.

The chip itself is the size of a rice grain, which is negligible when you have the body weight of a human being, but is considerable when you are the size of a baby tortoise. Size for size, it is the equivalent of trying to implant a mobile phone in a human being. As an interim measure, the chips are now being sold along with a certificate to prove that the tortoise has been bred in captivity and not imported from the wild.

The problem is that small animals, like baby tortoises, can easily be transported within the clothing of a traveller. A man was arrested recently trying to smuggle fifty-five rare red-footed tortoises into the United States down his trousers. He had manufactured a hiding cache by putting on one pair of trousers covered with pockets, which he filled with baby tortoises, and then put a second pair of plain trousers over the first.

It was his greed which gave him away because, with fifty-five of the animals about his person, he had developed some very odd bumps in very peculiar places. The US Customs are an unusually sharp-sighted bunch of people; they noticed, and they arrested him.

EPISODE GUIDE

SERIES I

CORE CAST

Tom McCabe – Jerome Flynn

Claire Armitage – Rebecca Lacey

Jim Cassidy – Adrian Bower

Steph Allen – Phillippa Wilson

Catherine 'Wilf' Mannion – Alison Mac

David Armitage – Kevin Doyle

Julia – Jayne Charlton MacKenzie

Liam – Scott Karalius

EPISODE 1

It's a Jungle Out There
by Kieran Prendiville
Producer Murray Ferguson
Director Paul Harrison
The introductory episode in which we meet DC Tom McCabe, former Marine turned Police Wildlife Liaison Officer, and his side-kick, DC Jim Cassidy.
■ McCabe and vet Steph Allen raid the council house in which Ray (Brendan P Healy) lives with his wife and a nine-foot alligator called Patsy. McCabe investigates a case of venison poaching, and RSPB Investigations Officer Claire Armitage, who is also married to McCabe's boss, pursues a birds' egg raider. The cases coincide when the 'egger' (Harrison Philips) is poisoned by the poached venison exposing the poaching ring.

McCabe discovers he has a nineteen-year-old daughter called Catherine 'Wilf' Mannion, of whose existence he was totally unaware until the death of his ex-wife.

EPISODE 2

I've Got Glue Under My Skin
by Nick Hicks-Beach and Shelley Miller
Producer Murray Ferguson
Director Paul Harrison
■ While investigating a series of burglaries, McCabe and Cassidy discover a recently stuffed puma, a protected animal, among the hoard of antique booty in a criminal's cache. Yet it does not appear on the list of missing antiques from owner Damon Soames (Stewart Howson), and when challenged Soames denies all knowledge of it.

Meanwhile, Claire is on the trail of a gunman who wounded a rare red kite. The kite is treated at Steph's wildlife sanctuary and, while visiting Steph, McCabe captures the gunman, who is trying to retrieve his prey.

McCabe forces a confession out of the gunman and tracks down the illegal taxidermist, who is waiting to supply a customer with the red kite.

The taxidermist confesses that he is working for the antique dealer who, on the side, is running a highly illegal trade in stuffed protected wildlife.

Tentatively, McCabe and Steph start to deepen their relationship, and McCabe tries to win over Steph's son, Liam. Claire meanwhile does not seem to approve of their relationship.

Wilf moves in with her father, but the atmosphere between them continues to be prickly.

Certain to complicate McCabe's life: Alison Mac as his daughter, Wilf.

EPISODE 3

The World According to Carp
by Kieran Prendiville from a story by Bryan B. Thompson
Producer Murray Ferguson
Director Paul Harrison

▓ While investigating a shipment of counterfeit money, McCabe and Cassidy keep watch on Frankie Moncur (George Costigan), an arrogant local villain who also runs an apparently respectable restaurant. Moncur is aware of their surveillance, and constantly mocks their efforts.

McCabe is excited when he realizes that otters are moving back into local water, but infuriated when he finds a dead one in a local fishing lake.

The lake belongs to Moncur who is organizing a fishing competition there. Characteristically, he is cheating by seeding the lake with prize fish stolen from more populated water in the south, in an attempt to raise the reputation of his own water and make it more desirable to the professional competition fishing set.

Meanwhile, McCabe catches Moncur's agent shooting cormorants and poisoning otters, apparently because of their raids on Moncur's fish farm.

However, during the competition, Cassidy catches another otter tugging a packet of counterfeit money out of its holt where it has been hidden by Moncur.

True love, or just an illusion? Jim Cassidy (Adrian Bower) and Julia (Jayne Charlton MacKenzie).

Meanwhile, Claire deliberately sabotages McCabe's date with Steph, but McCabe manages to ingratiate himself with Steph's son, Liam.

Wilf and Cassidy start to become close, despite the fact that Cassidy already has a long-term relationship with Julia who runs the Goose and Gargle pub.

EPISODE 4

Setts, Lies and Videotape
by David Ashton
Producer Murray Ferguson
Director Martyn Friend

▓ Chris and Jackie Mason (Mark Scott and Chris Connel), two teenage hoodlums, terrorize a council estate and run a protection racket which preys on the local traders, mocking the police when they try to intervene. But when they decide to step into the big time by running a badger bait in a wharfside warehouse, they incur McCabe's wrath.

The badger is supplied by a disaffected building worker whose boss pays him to 'accidentally' destroy a badger sett which is inconveniently positioned on a site currently undergoing development. However, the use of Smart Water, a chemical fingerprint agent, helps McCabe to track down all the participants and he and Cassidy raid the badger-baiting site.

Wilf and McCabe decide to go for a fun run in support of Claire's organization, the RSPB. Meanwhile, Claire and David's marriage is in trouble over the question of children, but McCabe's affair with Steph is definitely beginning to pick up speed. His relationship with both her son, Liam, and his own daughter, Wilf, is also progressing.

EPISODE 5

McCabe Gets the Horn
by Kieran Prendiville
Producer Murray Ferguson
Director Martyn Friend

▓ Following a seizure of over two million pounds' worth of rhino horn in a London lock-up, McCabe is warned by a friend in the Customs service, who knows that some was missed, to look out for signs of the rhino horn in the Chinese medicine market in the Northumberland area.

The scene is set for McCabe to investigate a shipment of rhino horn in 'McCabe Gets the Horn' (Series I, Episode 5).

At first, McCabe's heavy-handedness alienates Susan Chang (Jaclyn Tse), a Chinese shopkeeper, but she later agrees to help him and leads him to a dealer in the powdered horn.

Meanwhile, McCabe and Cassidy are on the trail of stolen laptop computers. When he discovers that Steph has unwittingly bought one of them, McCabe finds himself blamed for it, causing a rift between them.

McCabe's troubles are not over. Claire's niece has allowed the family pet peke to swallow a valuable rare coin from her father's collection, and Claire seems to expect McCabe to talk Steph into operating on the dog to recover it.

Cassidy's growing relationship with Wilf is getting dangerously inflammable, and even Julia is beginning to suspect all is not well.

EPISODE 6
Low Fidelity
by Kieran Prendiville
Producer Murray Ferguson
Director Martyn Friend

■ Unintentionally, McCabe causes trouble in a gamekeeper's home when he gives a lecture to a school class and says that some gamekeepers are killing rare birds of prey on the moors. When a rare hen harrier is actually killed on a local moor, the locals and the school pupils, including the gamekeeper's own daughter, blame Dominic McGuire (Alan Williams), the local gamekeeper. However, they later discover that it was not the gamekeeper but his ambitious younger deputy who was responsible.

McCabe also faces trouble at home, when Steph discovers drugs in Liam's bed and expects McCabe to handle the ensuing row. But McCabe's attention is distracted by a growing feud on a local housing estate in which a local man, whose garden and car have been vandalized, has taken the law into his own hands and attacked and hospitalized a teenager.

It is not until Liam gives away the source of his illegal drugs that Tom realizes the hospitalized teenager is also the local dealer and was beaten up in a drugs-related incident.

McCabe finally finds out about Wilf's growing relationship with Cassidy, causing him to pick a fight with his partner. The exposed relationship also causes a rift between Cassidy and Julia.

But, when McCabe finally releases the badger he has been nursing back to health into the wild, it brings about a moment of true closeness with his new-found daughter, Wilf.

SERIES II

CORE CAST

As Series I, with the addition of:

Ralph – Conor Mullen

Ray – Brendan P. Healy

EPISODE 1

Inside Story
by Nick Hicks-Beach and Shelley Miller
Producer Annie Tricklebank
Director Keith Washington

■ Zelenka, a local factory, is suspected of polluting the environment and harming the nearby wildlife. But, just as McCabe is beginning to gather proof of their involvement a bomb goes off, destroying all the evidence against them.

Steph and Claire get increasingly worried about the local wildlife and attempt to find the source of the pollution. Meanwhile, McCabe and Cassidy try to track down the culprit of the bombing with the assistance of Annabel Staunton from the CPS (Crown Prosecution Service).

Aidan Fletcher, an employee at the factory, is persuaded to give evidence against his employers and McCabe and Cassidy promise him police protection. But then Aidan and his family come under attack and are taken from their safe house by the very people that McCabe thought he could trust.

Meanwhile, McCabe's relationship with Steph is getting steadily more close and they discuss moving in together.

EPISODE 2

The Price of a Daughter
by Kieran Prendiville
Producer Annie Tricklebank
Director Tom Clegg

■ A dead badger is dumped into McCabe's now unoccupied badger run and, together with other clues, leads McCabe and Cassidy to believe that Wilf may be in danger. This fear is confirmed when Wilf disappears,

kidnapped by Vic Kerrigan who blames McCabe for the death of his own daughter, crippled during a police chase and since dead of pneumonia. McCabe races to Wilf's rescue.

Meanwhile, to McCabe's fury, Steph's husband, Ralph, turns up and tries to woo his way back into the affections of his former wife and their child. Steph also takes on a new helper – Ray, the man McCabe arrested for keeping an alligator in his bedroom in the first episode of Series I – who takes a bird with a broken wing to her and stays to work in the sanctuary.

EPISODE 3

Holding On
by Colin MacDonald
Producer Annie Tricklebank
Director Tom Clegg

■ A violent gang is rustling hill sheep and slaughtering them to sell the meat on the clandestine market. McCabe succeeds in tracking down the rustlers by hiding himself in the van next time there is a raid and guiding the police task force to the illegal slaughterhouse by radio.

A desperate boy brings Steph a wounded racehorse to treat. She discovers that he hopes to nurse the horse back to health and win a trotting race, but his father is dangerously ill and owes money to men who want to take the horse as settlement of the debt. Instead, the boy pays off the debt by racing the recovered horse himself.

Ralph, Steph's lawyer ex-husband, is hired to defend a violent criminal arrested by McCabe, and defeats McCabe in court by a technical trick, which increases the hostility between them. Ralph tries even harder to get Steph back, while the trouble between Claire and her husband is made worse when he finds he's unable to have children.

EPISODE 4

Cock o' the Walk
by Sam Lawrence
Producer Annie Tricklebank
Director Tom Clegg

■ A shepherd's daughter, playing in a ruined pele tower on the moors, is poisoned by a mystery liquid in a lemonade bottle. This has been left behind by a

McCabe gets tough with the cockfighters in 'Cock o' the Walk' (Series II, Episode 4).

cock-fighting ring who use the tower for their illegal meetings. The girl lies close to death in hospital.

Investigating the poisoning, McCabe and Cassidy are also trying to track down some specialist burglars, and are antagonized by the arrogant attitude of some of the victims. However, the two storylines coincide when McCabe realizes that the victims of the serial burglaries are the same people who attend the illegal cock fights – and that the man who organizes them is also tipping off the thieves about whose houses are going to be empty on which nights.

The rift in Claire's marriage continues to get worse, while Ralph appears to be succeeding in his attempt to win back his former wife and son. When McCabe sees Ralph in Steph's bedroom he jumps to the obvious, but in this case wrong, conclusion.

EPISODE 5

Predators
by Nick Hicks-Beach and Shelley Miller
Producer Annie Tricklebank
Director Paul Harrison

■ Harrington, the owner of a private collection of dangerous wild animals, reports that his animals – an iguana, a racoon, two wolves and a leopard – have all been released into the countryside. McCabe brings in a professional big-game hunter and, during their mutual pursuit of the animals, learns to respect the man's expertise. They capture the wolves but are hampered by a local farmer and his sons who appoint themselves

vigilante hunters and are subsequently attacked by the leopard, forcing McCabe to kill it.

Trying to make up with Steph, McCabe takes an expensive gift to Liam's birthday party, but allows Ralph to needle him into a fight. McCabe knocks Ralph down, and wipes out his chances of a reconciliation with Steph. Claire decides to make a clean break with David and tells him she no longer loves him.

EPISODE 6

Flight
by Nick Hicks-Beach and Shelley Miller
Producer Annie Tricklebank
Director Paul Harrison

■ Bronco Sullivan, a violent criminal who has been sent to prison after stabbing Cassidy, breaks out to recover his stashed loot and see his daughter. McCabe and Cassidy keep watch on his house but are distracted by a mysterious teenage boy, who brings them an injured bird, and Sullivan's daughter, who tries to throw them off the scent.

Meanwhile, Liam is bullied at school and Ralph's genuine concern makes Steph warm to him. When he takes on the bully's parents and gets beaten up himself, she is touched and they end up in bed together.

Claire leaves both her husband and Newcastle to find a new life elsewhere.

EPISODE 7

Finders Keepers
by David Ashton
Producer Annie Tricklebank
Director Keith Washington

■ When Boyd, a local fisherman, is found dead after a storm around the Farne Islands, his severe head wounds make the police suspicious. His boat is missing, but his lobster gear is still in his shed and his wife obviously has something to hide. Then his drinking mate, an old beachcomber called Reuben, devoted both to the seals and the islands, goes missing, and McCabe and Cassidy are called in to investigate what looks like a murder. McCabe is certainly glad to be going away, following Steph's confession that she slept with Ralph.

Cassidy tries to get back together with Julia, while McCabe returns from the Farne Islands to talk with Steph and attempt to patch things up.

ACKNOWLEDGEMENTS

So many people contributed by word, deed and advice to this book that a full acknowledgement to each one would require another volume.

Thanks to all the Police Wildlife Liaison Officers, starting with Paul Henery because it was he who first introduced me to the wonders of the world of the Police Wildlife Liaison Officer, Terry Rands and Mick Brewer who corrected at least most of my misconceptions, and all the other PWLOs up and down the country and at two PWLO conferences, who put up with what must have been some pretty damn-fool questions.

To the dedicated people at the RSPB and RSPCA who filled me in on their adventures.

To the hard-working people who devote their lives and incomes to running Wild Life Sanctuaries, and took time off to help.

To the busy, busy people at Feelgood Fiction who made the series for the BBC and kept being interrupted to give me details.

To Laurence Bowen who saw my article in the *Daily Telegraph*, and to the man who threw the party which gave him the hangover and made him reach for the abandoned paper in the train back from Brighton, in which he read about Paul Henery and from which he got the idea to make *Badger*.

PICTURE CREDITS

BBC Books would like to thank the following for providing photographs and for permission to reproduce copyright material. While every effort has been made to trace and acknowledge all copyright holders, we would like to apologize should there have been any errors or omissions.

BBC 2, 11, 14, 15, 18, 19, 22, 23, 24, 27, 33, 34, 36, 37, 55, 56, 57, 58, 59, 69a, 76a, 76b, 77, 81, 83, 104, 105, 108, 109, 112a, 112b, 113, 119, 123, 124, 125, 127; BBC/Moira Conway 6, 10, 29; BBC Natural History Unit 3, 51; courtesy Mick Brewer 42; Bruce Coleman Collection 54, 73, 89, 95a, 101, 106, 117, 121; courtesy Joan Childs 60; courtesy John Cross 32; Andy Fisher 68, 69b, 96, 100; Frank Lane Picture Agency 53, 63, 66, 107; courtesy Garth Coupland 74; Simon Everett 49, 50; Hedgehog Care/Ian Holmes 95b; courtesy Kim McDonald 114; courtesy Steve Kourik 46b; Vanessa Latford 43, 128; National Birds of Prey Centre 92, 93; National Federation of Badger Groups 45; Graeme Peacock 7, 25, 30, 35, 38, 39, 84, 85, 88; courtesy Terry Rands 42; courtesy Quentin Rose 97; Andy Rouse 62; RSPCA 46a, 47, 78l, 78r, 79, 82; Scope Features 12; Vale Wildlife Rescue Centre 87; Sheila Wright/Richard White 52.

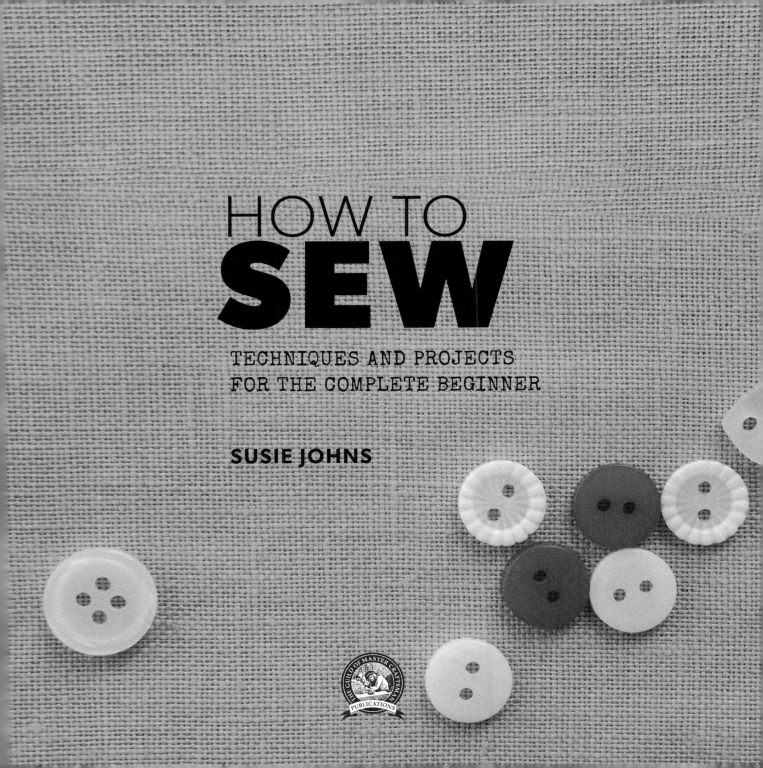

HOW TO
SEW

TECHNIQUES AND PROJECTS
FOR THE COMPLETE BEGINNER

SUSIE JOHNS

THE GUILD OF MASTER CRAFTSMAN
PUBLICATIONS

First published 2013 by
Guild of Master Craftsman Publications Ltd
Castle Place, 166 High Street, Lewes,
East Sussex BN7 1XU

Text and designs © Susie Johns, 2013
Copyright in the Work © GMC Publications Ltd, 2013

ISBN 978-1-86108-911-3

A catalogue record for this book is available from the British Library.

PUBLISHER Jonathan Bailey
PRODUCTION MANAGER Jim Bulley
MANAGING EDITOR Gerrie Purcell
SENIOR PROJECT EDITOR Wendy McAngus
EDITOR Caroline Sanders
MANAGING ART EDITOR Gilda Pacitti
ILLUSTRATIONS Peter & Zabransky
PHOTOGRAPHERS Sarah Cuttle and Rebecca Mothersole
DESIGNER Rebecca Mothersole

Set in Gibson
Colour origination by GMC Reprographics
Printed and bound in China

CONTENTS

INTRODUCTION

One of the best things about creating your own hand-sewn items is that you can customize them with your choice of fabrics and trimmings, and tailor them to suit your home and lifestyle. You can also make them exactly the right size and shape to fit certain items: for example, on pages 94–7, you will find step-by-step instructions for making a cosy cover for your coffee pot, and on pages 60–63 you will find out how to make a liner to fit a basket exactly.

All the projects in this book are easy to sew, requiring only the most basic equipment. If you have a sewing machine, you may find it useful for some of the processes, but you should be able to complete any of the projects by hand.

This book, divided into sections, helps you to build your knowledge and confidence, providing you with a straightforward introduction to a craft that, until now, you might have thought was too difficult to attempt.

Each section comprises a technique, carefully written and laid out in a way designed to help build your skills. To practise each technique, you'll find a project, once again broken down into clear step-by-step stages, helping to simplify the processes involved. So, for example, after introducing the technique of hemming and binding edges, there is an apron to make that has bound edges; and following the section showing you the principles of appliqué, there is a cot cover to make, with an appliqué design.

In order to get the most from this book, especially when trying a new technique for the first time, read through the instructions very carefully, then gather together all the materials and tools you will need to complete the project. You'll find that being organized makes such a difference.

Fabric is a wonderful way to add colour, texture and interest to your home and creating items from fabric and thread requires only the most basic of sewing skills. Follow this simple course from beginning to end or, if you already have some sewing experience, use some of the chapters as a revision guide and others to build on existing skills. Hand sewing is fun, creative and a lot easier than you might think.

Susie

BEFORE
YOU START

BASIC TOOLS AND EQUIPMENT

1 NEEDLES

It is essential to have the right needle for the task. You need to choose one that is suitable for the thickness of the fabric and thread. The smaller the number, the finer the needle. Sizes 7–10 should suit most purposes.

A Sharps are medium needles with a small, round eye, useful for general sewing. Lengths vary; choose a longer length for basting and gathering. For thicker thread or when using two or more strands, choose a needle with a longer eye.

B Betweens are shorter than sharps and good for fine fabrics and tiny stitching.

C Crewel needles are designed for embroidery, having a longer eye to take several thicknesses of thread. You can use them for general sewing too.

D A darning needle is sharp with a large eye, and is used with thick threads. **Tapestry needles** are similar but with blunt tips and are used for threading cord and elastic.

E A bodkin is a large, blunt needle that can be used for turning narrow ties inside out (see page 83), or threading ribbons, tapes or elastic through fabric casings.

2 SCISSORS

For cutting fabric, you will need a pair of good-quality **dressmaking shears F** which should be reserved for cutting fabric only. Cutting paper with them will make them blunt, which will make cutting fabric difficult and inaccurate. Invest in a good pair of dressmaking shears and have them sharpened professionally on an annual basis if you use them often.

You will also need a **small pair of scissors G** with pointed blades, for snipping threads, and a pair of **all-purpose scissors H** for cutting paper and card when making templates. **Pinking shears I**, with zigzag blades, are useful for cutting fabrics that have a tendency to fray.

3 BIAS BINDING MAKER

This clever gadget can be used to fold the edges of a bias-cut strip of fabric, transforming it into a length of bias binding, ready to use to cover fabric edges (see page 45).

4 STITCH RIPPER

A craft knife or a stitch ripper is handy if you need to unpick a seam. A stitch ripper has a hooked end containing a small blade that will cut threads between seam layers.

5 ROTARY CUTTER

Used in conjunction with a steel ruler and a cutting mat, this is a useful tool for cutting multiple layers of fabric. The blade must be sharp, so replace this regularly.

6 THIMBLE

A thimble, whether metal or plastic, can be a useful accessory, protecting your finger's end as it repeatedly pushes the needle through fabric. It is especially useful where the fabric is stiff or you are using a very fine needle.

7 NEEDLE THREADER

Threading a needle can sometimes be frustrating, so it is useful to keep a needle threader in your workbox. You push the wire loop through the eye of the needle, then pass the end of the thread through the loop. Now draw the loop out of the eye, bringing the thread with it.

8 PINS

Buy good-quality steel pins that will not rust or become blunt. Store them in a lidded box. Glass-headed pins are useful as they are easier to see and so less likely to get lost in the weave of a fabric. Safety pins are handy instead of a bodkin for threading elastic or tape through a casing.

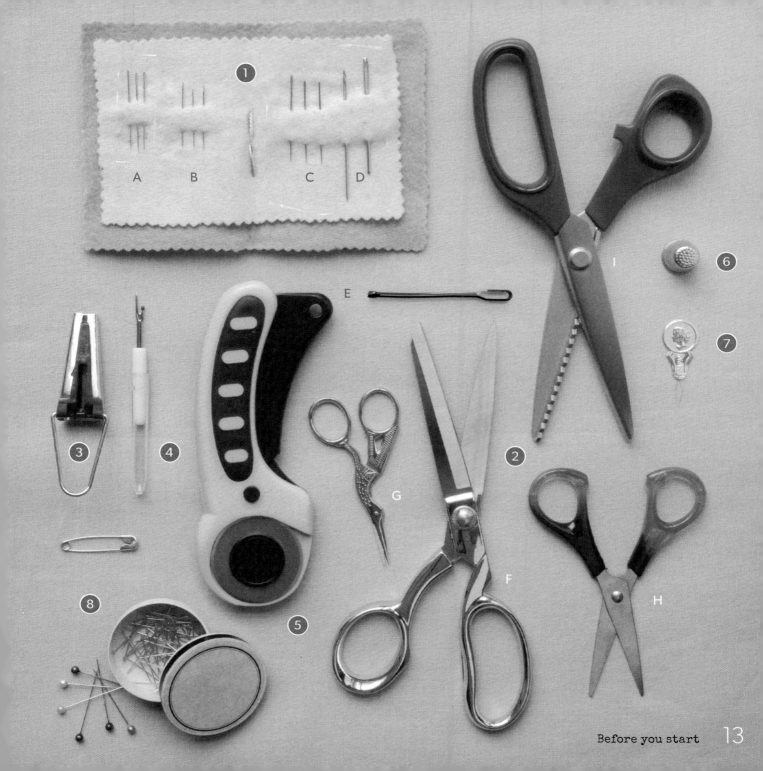

A   B   C   D

E

G

F

H

I

1
3
4
8
5
2
6
7

1 MARKERS

Tailor's chalk A (a flat square or triangular-shaped block) and **chalk pencils** B (with a brush on the end for erasing chalk marks) are the traditional marking tools, available in various colours. Choose a light colour for dark fabrics and vice versa.

For marking the wrong side of most fabrics, where it won't show, an ordinary graphite pencil is adequate, but for making marks on the right side of the fabric, which can later be removed, look out for **erasable pens** C. Some of these simply vanish after a number of hours, while others can be erased with water.

2 MEASURING DEVICES

A **tape measure** D is essential; you will also need a **long ruler** E for drawing lines accurately. A **sewing gauge** F or small ruler is also useful, for measuring small areas such as seam allowances, and a **set square** G will help you achieve neat right-angled corners.

Tip Keep a blunt knitting needle in your workbox, as it can be handy for things such as getting into awkward spaces when turning your work inside out.

IRONING EQUIPMENT

A good steam iron is invaluable for pressing your work at various stages. Use the steam setting when you are pressing folds to ensure that they are nice and crisp. When sewing a project, pressing properly is as important as stitching. It helps to smooth out wrinkles, of course, but it also helps to shape the fabric and set the seams.

Make sure your iron and ironing board cover are clean, as dirt and scorch marks can easily be transferred to your fabric and spoil the appearance of your finished creation. Always set your ironing board at a comfortable height, to avoid causing backache.

When pressing delicate fabrics, always place a clean piece of cloth over the area you are about to iron, as direct contact with the base plate of the iron can cause scorching or unattractive shiny marks.

BASIC MATERIALS

FABRICS

These days, you are not limited by the fabrics available in your local shop: there is a dazzling choice of fabric available to purchase online. Before you go out and spend money, however, search through the workbox or cupboard of any friends or family members who are seasoned stitchers, as they will, no doubt, have some fabric scraps that they might be persuaded to part with.

Fabrics can be made from natural fibres (such as cotton, linen, silk or wool), or manufactured from plant-based cellulose (such as modal), or synthetic fibres (such as polyester). The projects in this book use mostly medium-weight cotton fabrics, of the type a shirt might be made of, or medium-weight furnishing fabrics in cotton or a cotton-linen blend, such as curtains might be made from. The exception is the bunting on page 28, which is made from a lightweight, almost see-through, cotton fabric.

Natural cotton and linen fabrics can feel nicer than synthetics and they are available in a multitude of plain colours, stripes, checks and prints. Before cutting and stitching these fabrics, check whether they are pre-shrunk. If you're not sure, it is advisable to wash the fabric before you work with it, to allow for shrinkage.

1 PLAIN COTTON

This is the most widely used natural fibre. Woven cotton fabric is soft, breathable and comfortable to stitch because the needle passes through the fabric very easily. It is available unbleached (as shown here), bleached white, or dyed in a wide choice of solid colours.

2 PRINTED COTTON

From spots, stripes and checks to florals, geometrics, abstracts and novelty motifs, cotton prints are popular and versatile.

3 MUSLIN

A strong woven fabric that is thin, supple and sheer.

4 GINGHAM

A plain-weave fabric, usually in cotton or a polyester-cotton mix, with a regular checked pattern.

5 LINEN

A strong fabric woven from the fibres of the flax plant, usually with a distinctive, sometimes coarse, weave.

6 WOVEN STRIPES

Stripes woven into a fabric are more even than printed stripes, as they follow the weave. Woven striped fabric is available in various weights; ticking is a heavy, closely woven cotton fabric, usually with a distinctive striped pattern, most commonly used to cover mattresses and cushion pads.

7 INTERLINING

A soft, non-woven material, mostly used when making curtains to create a lightly padded effect, add thermal insulation, and help block out light. It is a good substitute for cotton batting when making quilts, though for a thicker effect, choose a wadding made either from cotton or synthetic fibres such as polyester.

8 VOILE

A light, plain-weave fabric made from cotton or synthetics, often used to make sheer curtains.

Tip It's advisable to use washable fabrics for items that will be in regular use. You will usually find information about this printed on the finished, unfrayed edge of the fabric, known as the selvedge. If you are unsure if the fabric is pre-shrunk, it's best to wash it before you start sewing so it won't shrink later.

SEWING THREADS

As a general rule, whether sewing by hand or machine, choose a sewing thread with a fibre content that matches the fabric. Try to match the colour of the fabric as closely as possible and, if an exact match is not possible, choose a shade slightly darker.

For basting (tacking) – long stitches used to hold fabric together temporarily – choose a contrasting colour thread that shows up well against the fabric, making it easier to remove.

TYPES OF SEWING THREAD

1 **Button thread** is made from cotton-covered polyester thread. It is thick and strong, ideal for sewing on buttons.

2 **Mercerized cotton thread** is strong and firm, and the best choice for natural-fibre fabrics such as cotton and linen.

3 **Polyester thread** is marketed as a 'sew-all' thread, suitable for most types of fabric, and in a choice of thicknesses. Choose extra-fine for stitching lightweight fabrics, all-purpose for general sewing, and buttonhole thread for hand-stitched buttonholes.

4 **Silk thread** is ideal for stitching silk fabrics and is also a good choice for basting on most fabrics as it is very fine and less likely to leave a mark once removed.

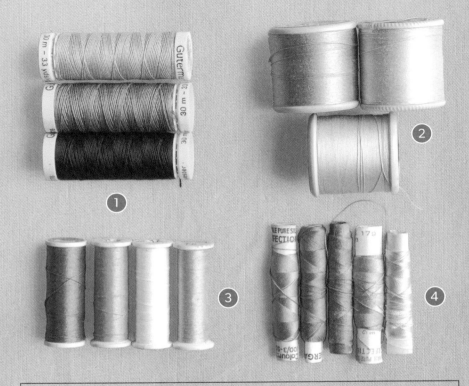

AVOIDING KNOTS

When sewing by hand, the thread has a tendency to twist and become tangled or knotted. To avoid this, try these tips:

- When threading a needle, use the free end of the thread from the spool and make sure that the end you cut is the end that is secured to the fabric.

- Use a length of thread about 18in (45cm). This is a manageable length for most purposes.

- As you sew, pull the needle in the direction in which you are sewing – usually from right to left.

- If the thread does become twisted, let go of the needle and allow it to dangle, so that the thread spins and untwists itself.

OTHER MATERIALS

Haberdashery suppliers offer a tempting selection of trims and embellishments to add practical and decorative details.

❶ BIAS BINDING

Strips of fabric, cut on the bias with the long cut edges folded towards the centre, are used to finish a raw edge by forming a neat border. Bias binding is stretchy and can be eased around curved edges.

❷ FUSIBLE WEB

These non-woven fabrics with a heat-activated adhesive can be applied to fabric cut-outs to create iron-on, non-fraying appliqué motifs.

❸ RIBBON AND BRAID

Available in a great choice of colours, fabrics and finishes, and in widths from ⅝in (1.5cm) to 3in (8cm), these have bound edges and can be used to make ties or embellishments.

❹ COTTON TAPE

This has a straight weave and bound edges and can be used in place of bias binding on a straight edge, or as decorative ties or trims.

❺ BUTTONS

Buttons that have a loop underneath are called shank buttons, while those with holes are called sew-through buttons.

BASIC PRINCIPLES

MEASURING

When embarking on any home sewing project, accurate measuring can be the key to a good result. A tailor's tape measure is vital for measuring objects, as it is flexible and can therefore be wrapped around curves. For measuring seam allowances and hems however, it is usually better to use a rigid ruler as it will lie flat.

Accurate measuring is important at every stage in a sewing project, to make sure that seams line up, that hems are straight, and that the finished object fits. Measuring is also important when buying materials, to avoid too much wastage.

Fabrics are sold in several standard widths, the three most common being 36in (90cm); 45in (115cm); and 60in (150cm). Bear in mind the width of the fabric when deciding how much material to purchase: you may need to buy a longer length if your fabric is a narrow width.

GETTING ORGANIZED

Once you have assembled the tools and materials you need for hand sewing, it is advisable to store them all in one place, so that you are ready to tackle any sewing project without having to rummage around in various drawers and cupboards. By keeping everything together, not only are you ready to start a project from scratch but also to tackle other small jobs such as sewing on a button, taking up a hem, or mending a tear, at a moment's notice. Keeping things in order can save you a lot of time and frustration.

Fabrics can be folded and stored on shelves, in drawers or in storage boxes, depending on how much fabric you have. Another solution is to drape lengths of fabric over the bar of a coat hanger and hang them from a rail in your wardrobe.

Then you need to decide where to keep your basic sewing kit. Because there are so many small items involved, it is important to keep them organized. You could allocate one or two drawers in a chest or cabinet, perhaps putting in dividers to keep items separate. You may prefer to use a sturdy box or basket, or check online or in your local sewing shop for a purpose-made sewing box or work basket that will meet your needs.

UNDERSTANDING THE ILLUSTRATIONS

Use the key below to help you follow the illustrations in this book.

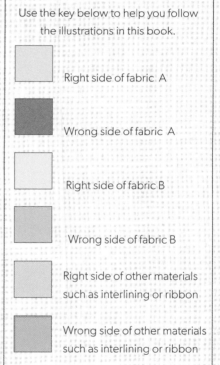

Right side of fabric A

Wrong side of fabric A

Right side of fabric B

Wrong side of fabric B

Right side of other materials such as interlining or ribbon

Wrong side of other materials such as interlining or ribbon

TECHNIQUES
& PROJECTS

BASIC STITCHES

LEARNING A FEW BASIC STITCHES IS THE KEY TO BEING ABLE TO SEW ALMOST ANYTHING.
BEFORE EMBARKING ON A PROJECT, TRY OUT THESE SEWING TECHNIQUES ON SCRAPS OF FABRIC.
ONCE YOU FEEL CONFIDENT, THEN YOU CAN MOVE ON TO SEWING YOUR OWN CREATIONS.

Here are the hand stitches you are most likely to use, and that you will need to complete the projects in this book.

Running stitch is probably the most basic stitch of all. It is most commonly used for gathering and basting (long stitches used to hold two pieces of fabric together temporarily, sometimes referred to as tacking), and also for embroidery.

Backstitch is a secure stitch that is ideal for sewing seams by hand.

Oversewing joins two edges together, so that the stitches will be visible on both sides. Slipstitch can also be used to join two folded edges together, but more discreetly, so it is useful for applying trims and appliqué shapes to fabric. It is also used to stitch hems. (Or you can use hem stitch to sew neat, almost invisible hems; this is described on page 41.)

Blanket stitch can be used in a practical way, to secure a single hem on thick fabric – hence the name. It can also be used decoratively, as an embroidery stitch.

Tip Most hand stitches are worked from right to left. If you are left-handed, you may need to work in the other direction.

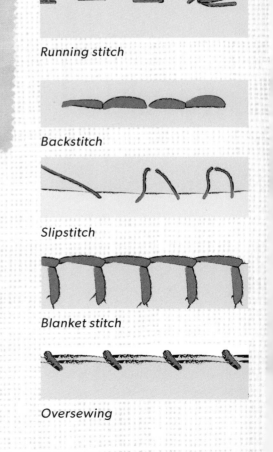

Running stitch

Backstitch

Slipstitch

Blanket stitch

Oversewing

MACHINE STITCHING

For seams, machine stitching is usually more secure than hand sewing. It is also faster, but for small projects, and ones that won't undergo much wear and tear, it can be just as quick to hand sew them.

A sewing machine has two threads: a top thread that goes through the needle, and a bottom thread that is wound around a bobbin. As you sew, the two threads interlock. Use a straight stitch for stitching seams, basting and gathering. Adjust the length of the stitch according to which of these purposes you require and also the weight of your fabric. A zigzag stitch is ideal for neatening edges.

As each machine is slightly different, it is best to refer to your machine's manual for advice on all aspects of machine sewing, from initial set-up to forming stitches.

SECURING THE THREAD

After you have threaded your needle, and before you start stitching, you will need to secure the end of the thread on the wrong side of the fabric. You can do this simply by tying a knot at the end of the thread, or, preferably, by working several small stitches in the same place.

When you have finished sewing, or when you are nearly at the end of your length of thread, pass the needle through to the back of the work and make a few small stitches to secure it. Snip off the thread end close to these stitches for a neat finish.

HOW TO SEW RUNNING STITCH

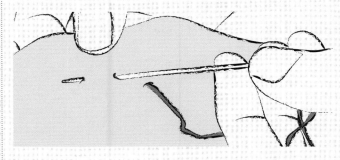

1 Bring the needle out to the right side of the work. Push the needle in and out of the fabric. Repeat at regular intervals, aiming to make each stitch and each gap between stitches the same length. For basting, or 'tacking' (which is used to keep two pieces of fabric together when pins would get in the way), the stitches and gaps should be about ½in (1.2cm) long; for gathering, make them slightly smaller.

HOW TO OVERSEW

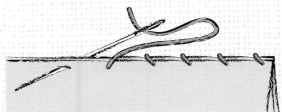

1 This is used to join two folded edges. With wrong sides of the fabrics together, insert the needle from back to front through both pieces, slanting the needle from right to left and picking up only a few threads. Pull through. Insert the needle from the back, just behind the place where the thread is emerging and, slanting the needle as before, bring it through to the front about ⅛in (3mm) along for a neat finish on fine fabrics, or about ¼in (6mm) on coarser fabrics.

HOW TO SEW BACKSTITCH

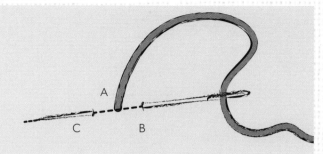

1 Bring the needle up to the front of the work (A) and insert it about ⅛ in (3mm) to the right (B), then bring it back out again about ¼ in (6mm) to the left (C).

2 Pull the thread through and then insert the needle ⅛ in (3mm) to the right, next to where the thread emerged before. Bring the needle up again ¼ in (6mm) to the left. Continue in this way, working half a stitch length backwards and a whole stitch length forwards.

HOW TO SEW SLIPSTITCH

1 When joining two folded edges, bring the needle out through one edge, then make a small stitch into the fold on the opposite edge. Pull the thread through, then make a small stitch into the fold on the opposite edge. Continue in this way, stitching into each edge in turn and pulling the thread to draw the two folds together.

2 When attaching one piece of fabric to the surface of another – for a patch pocket or an appliqué motif, for example – catch a few threads of the background fabric and a few threads on the folded edge of the applied fabric.

HOW TO SEW BLANKET STITCH

1 With the edge of the work facing you, work from right to left or left to right, whichever you find easier. Bring the needle up as near to the edge of the fabric as possible or else at the fold of the hem. Push the needle into the fabric a little way along and the same distance in from the edge. The point of your needle should come out on top of the thread.

2 Pull the needle through the loop of the thread as shown. Pull the thread taut but not too tight as this will pucker the fabric.

3 Repeat the process so that your stitches lie flat with the loop of thread forming a bar across the edge of the fabric. Make sure you space your blanket stitches at regular intervals.

Tip When blanket stitch is worked closely, with no gap between the stitches, it becomes buttonhole stitch (see page 92).

BUNTING

WITH COLOURFUL HOMEMADE BUNTING YOU WILL ALWAYS BE READY FOR A CELEBRATION. CHOOSE LIGHTWEIGHT FABRIC THAT WILL FLUTTER IN THE BREEZE AND USE THIS PROJECT TO PRACTISE BASIC RUNNING STITCH – IT'S REALLY EASY.

YOU WILL NEED

- Pieces of lightweight cotton fabric (such as voile or muslin), each measuring at least 7 x 6in (18 x 15cm)
- A length of cotton tape, ½in (1.3cm) wide (see 'Measuring' for length needed)
- Light card, at least 6 x 5in (15 x 13cm)
- 2 plastic, wooden or metal rings (optional)
- Sewing thread to match tape
- Sewing needle
- Tape measure
- Fabric scissors
- All-purpose scissors
- Ruler
- Pencil

TECHNIQUE USED

Running stitch (see page 25)

MEASURING

You can make your bunting any length you like. Once made, the fabric pennants are 5in (13cm) wide and are spaced 2in (5cm) apart. To calculate how much tape you need for the number of pennants you have, allow 7in (18cm) for each pennant plus at least 1yd (90cm) to give you enough free tape at each end for fastening.

Conversely, if you know what length you want your bunting to be – say, 16ft (5m) to stretch across a room or between two trees – deduct 1yd (90cm) for the ends then divide the remaining length by 7 (18), to calculate how many pennants to cut. As a rough guide, you will need 11 pennants for a 10ft (3m) length; 22 for a 16ft (5m) length; and 61 for a 39ft (12m) length.

If you do not have scraps of material to use up, a piece of fabric measuring 12 x 39in (30 x 100cm) will give you about 26 pennants, with careful cutting.

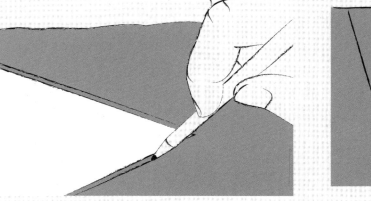

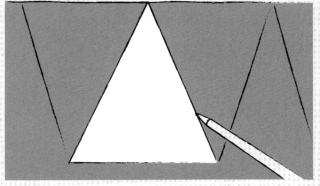

1 Make a card template for the pennants, using the diagram on page 99. Place the card template on each piece of fabric in turn and draw round all three sides.

2 If your fabric scraps are big enough, or if you are using one larger piece of fabric, move the template along and draw round it as before. Flip it as shown in the illustration, to reduce waste. As a guide, you will need 11 pennants for a 10ft (3m) length – see Measuring on page 28.

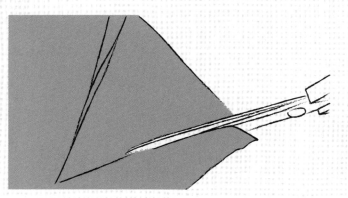

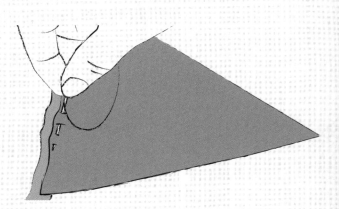

3 Cut along the lines you have drawn. By placing the template on two or more layers of fabric, you can cut out several pennants at a time – pinning the layers of fabric together will make this easier.

4 Position the first pennant at least 18in (45cm) from one end of the tape (or more if you want longer ties at each end). Thread a sewing needle and, with the top (short) edge of the triangle along the centre of the tape, baste the pennant in place, using a long running stitch.

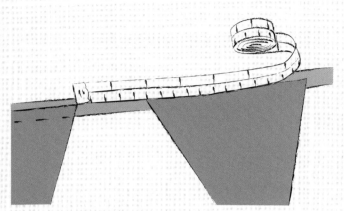

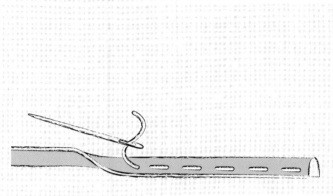

5 Position the second pennant 2in (5cm) from the first and baste as before. Repeat along the length of the tape, leaving the same amount of tape free at both ends.

6 Starting at one end, fold over the tape so that the long edges are aligned, and stitch together with neat running stitch (shorter than in step 4).

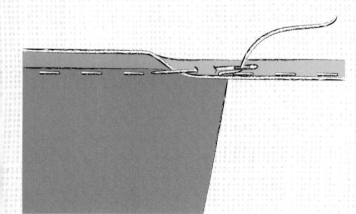

7 Fold over the tape to enclose the top of each pennant in turn, stitching through all three layers. Continue stitching along the free end of the tape. Once all the pennants have been securely stitched in place, remove the basting thread from the top of each one.

8 Fold over each end of the tape to form a loop, and stitch in place. If you wish, you can loop the tape through a plastic, wooden or metal ring before stitching.

SEAMS

A SEAM IS USED FOR JOINING TWO PIECES OF FABRIC TOGETHER. AS SEAMS CAN BE SUBJECTED TO A CERTAIN AMOUNT OF STRAIN, IT IS IMPORTANT TO USE A STRONG STITCH – NAMELY BACKSTITCH – AND TO MAKE SURE YOUR STITCHES ARE SMALL AND EVEN FOR A NEAT FINISH.

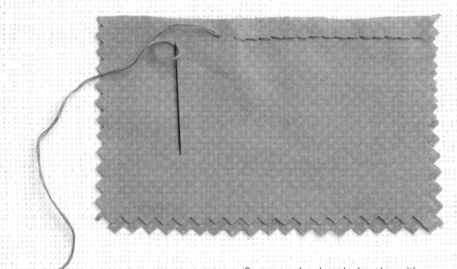

SEAM ALLOWANCES

The distance between the edges of the fabric and the line of stitching is called the seam allowance, and it will be specified in the instructions for your project. For most purposes, the seam allowance is ½in (1.2cm) or ⅝in (1.5cm), depending on the project and the weight of the fabric. If you are new to sewing, it is a good idea to draw a pencil line this distance from the raw edges of the fabric pieces, using a straight edge (such as a long metal ruler), to help you to stitch a straight seam.

You must be consistent when you are measuring seam allowances, or you may find that fabric pieces will not align properly when you join them together.

Seams can be done by hand or with a sewing machine. A hand-sewn seam, in backstitch, is adequate for most projects, especially when making small items, and certainly for those in this book. For larger projects, and when the seam will be subjected to a lot of pulling or wear and tear, it might be advisable to stitch seams using a machine instead.

HAND STITCHING A SIMPLE SEAM

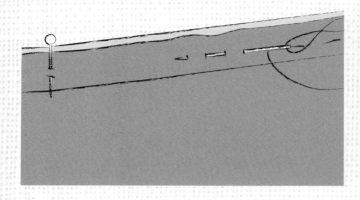

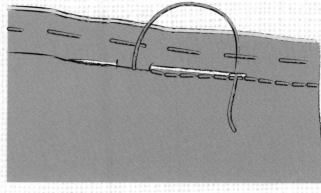

1 Place the two pieces of fabric to be joined right sides together, aligning the edges. Pin the pieces together and draw a pencil line that is the distance of the seam allowance in from the edge. Baste using a long running stitch, with this line of stitching running inside the seam allowance.

2 Secure the end of the thread with a few stitches, then stitch along the pencilled seamline in backstitch (see page 26). When you reach the end of the seam, secure the thread again with a few stitches, then cut the thread close to the fabric.

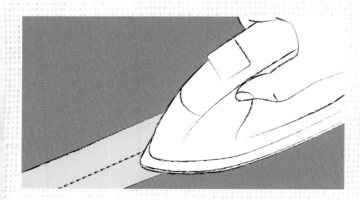

Tip When stitching several thicknesses of fabric together, after sewing the seam it is a good idea to trim away the excess fabric within the seam allowance, to reduce bulk. Where there is a choice, trim away the excess from fabrics that are less likely to fray, such as interfacing or interlining.

3 Remove the basting threads and press. Sometimes the instructions will tell you to press the seam open, with the edges pressed flat either side of the seam. Occasionally they will tell you to press the seam to one side, with both edges pressed flat in the same direction.

COPING WITH CURVES

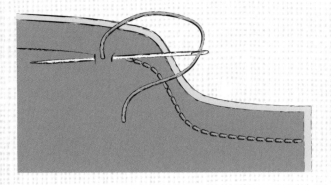

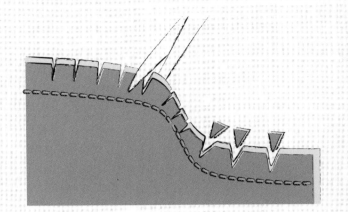

1 When sewing a curved seam, it helps to have a line to follow, to keep the line of the seam at the correct seam allowance you are working to, from the edges of the fabric. Draw on a line using a fabric marker or pencil.

2 After stitching the seam, snip into the seam allowance on outward-facing curves; on inward-facing curves, snip little V-shaped notches from the seam allowance. This will help to form a smooth line on the right side of the work; it will also allow you to press the seam flat, if you need to do so.

STITCHING A NEAT CORNER

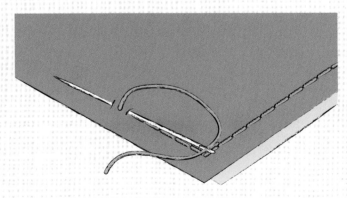

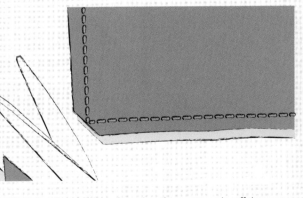

1 Stitch along the seamline until you come to the corner, then sew a few extra stitches on the same spot before turning the corner, to add strength.

2 When you have finished sewing the seam, snip off the corner diagonally; this helps to reduce bulk when turning right sides out.

LEAVING A GAP

Some projects require you to leave a gap in part of the seam, so that you can turn a piece of work right sides out (as in the coffee cosy on page 97).

To do this, start stitching your seam at one end of the gap and continue until you reach the other end of the gap. Fasten off the thread securely, stitching several stitches in the same place before snipping off the thread. Turn the work through the gap you have left.

If there are sharp corners on your item, push a knitting needle or similar blunt-ended object into the corners, to give a neat result. Use an iron to press the seam allowance to the inside on both sides of the gap, then oversew the two edges together, making the stitches as small and discreet as possible.

NEATENING RAW EDGES

In most cases, you can leave the raw edges of seams as they are, especially on items that are lined, such as the basket liner on page 60, or the tote bag on page 36. If, however, the seam is exposed, you may wish to neaten it; and on fabrics that fray easily, it may be necessary to finish the edge in a way that will prevent fraying.

The quickest and easiest method of finishing an edge to stop it fraying is to cut along the edge with pinking shears (see above). Another option is to oversew the edges, creating a line of small diagonal stitches (see page 92, step 4). (If you have a sewing machine, you can work a zigzag stitch along the edge of the fabric.) Binding (see page 40) gives a neat finish to the edges of seams that will be visible (such as unlined curtains).

TOTE BAG

SIMPLE TO MAKE AND MUCH BETTER THAN A PLASTIC CARRIER, THIS SMALL BAG IS DECEPTIVELY ROOMY AND IDEAL FOR CARRYING SHOPPING OR FOR TAKING TO THE BEACH. FIND INTERESTING FABRICS TO MAKE IT FROM AND USE THIS PROJECT TO PRACTISE SEWING SEAMS.

YOU WILL NEED

- 20in (50cm) medium-weight printed cotton fabric, at least 36in (90cm) wide
- 20in (50cm) medium-weight woven checked cotton fabric, at least 36in (90cm) wide, for the lining
- 40in (1m) Petersham ribbon, 1in (2.5cm) wide
- Sewing thread to match fabric
- Sewing needle
- Pins
- Tape measure
- Fabric scissors
- Pencil
- Sewing machine (optional)

Tip You could stitch a button to the base of each handle at the top of the bag, stitching right through all thicknesses of fabric. This will help to hold the handles in place, and looks decorative too.

FINISHED SIZE

19in (48cm) long x 15in (38cm) wide

TECHNIQUES USED

Running stitch (see page 25)
Backstitch (see page 26)
Slipstitch (see page 26)
Hand stitching a simple seam (see page 33)
Stitching a neat corner (see page 34)

MATERIALS TO USE

A medium-weight cotton furnishing fabric is ideal for this bag. The vintage fabric shown here is just the right weight – look out for similar fabrics at flea markets. Do make sure that whatever fabric you buy is washable, so that the finished bag can be laundered.

Grosgrain or Petersham ribbon has a distinctive ribbed texture across the width of the ribbon. It is a good choice for bag handles as it is firm, strong and stable but also easy to stitch as it is not too thick.

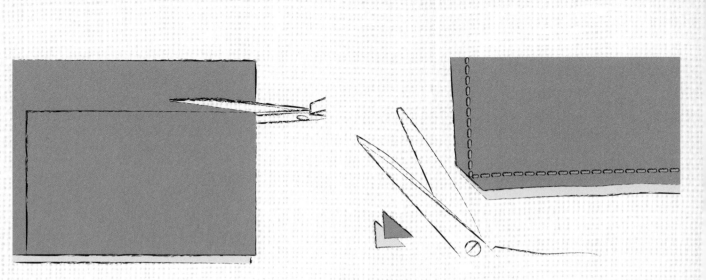

1 Cut two pieces each of main fabric and lining fabric, 19 x 15in (48 x 38cm). If you are using fabric with a one-way pattern make sure the design runs from top to bottom.

2 Place the main fabric pieces right sides together. Pin and baste the sides and base, then stitch them with a ⅜in (1cm) seam allowance, using backstitch (draw a line on the fabric to help you sew straight). Clip the two bottom corners. Do the same with the lining.

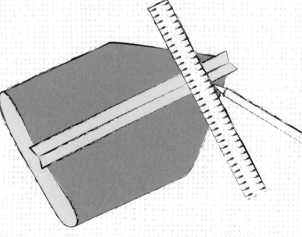

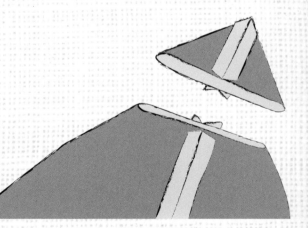

3 To create the gusset, press the base and side seams of the corners together to create points. Measure 2¾in (7cm) in from each point and draw a line across perpendicular to the seam.

4 Stitch along these lines, then cut off each corner ⅜in (1cm) from the stitch line. Do the same with the lining.

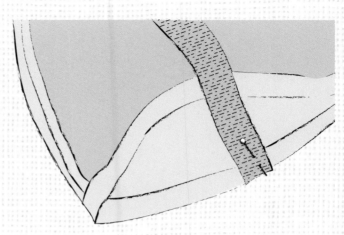

5 Fold the top edge of the lining over to the wrong side, creating a ⅝in (1.5cm) single hem all the way round. Press the hem flat.

6 To make the handles, cut two lengths of ribbon 20in (50cm) long. Stitch both ends firmly in place on the top edges of the lining, one handle on each side. Position them so the ends are ¾in (2cm) down from the top folded edge, and the outside edges are 4½in (12cm) in from the side seams.

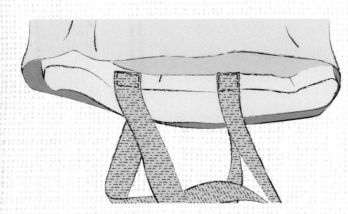

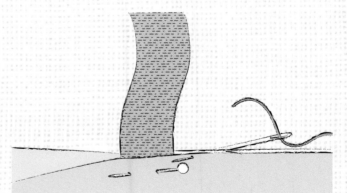

7 Now slip the lining inside the bag, so that the wrong sides of each are against each other and the right sides are showing inside and out.

8 Fold under ⅝in (1.5cm) on the top edge of the main bag. Slipstitch (see page 26) or machine stitch it to the lining, trapping the ends of the handles between the two fabrics.

HEMS AND BINDING

FABRIC WILL FRAY IF YOU DON'T FINISH OFF THE EDGES IN SOME WAY AND THAT'S WHERE HEMS AND BINDING COME IN. WHICH ONE YOU DECIDE TO USE WILL DEPEND ON WHAT SUITS YOUR PROJECT, THE FABRIC YOU ARE USING AND THE LOOK YOU WANT TO ACHIEVE.

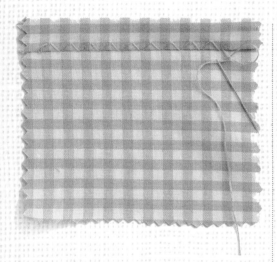

Tip Consider other ways of finishing the edge of an item, depending on the type of fabric used. For thick fabrics, for example, blanket stitch (see page 27) is very effective.

Hems and binding are two ways of finishing the raw edge of a fabric. For a hem, the edge of the fabric is folded over, while binding involves sewing a strip of fabric over to cover the edge.

HEMMING

A hem is used to finish a raw edge on an item. The edge of the fabric is folded over to the wrong side. One fold makes a single hem (used for an item that is to be lined, for example); fold it a second time to form a double hem (used for tablecloths and garments).

A hem can be stitched in place by hand or machine. The simplest hem is made by securing the folded edge with running stitch or a straight machine stitch. For curtains or the lower edge of a garment such as a skirt, however, it is preferable to work with stitching that is so discreet as to be virtually invisible (see opposite).

Hand stitching a hem is easy to learn. The technique shown in this section is for a double hem. For a single hem, it is best if you trim the raw edge with pinking shears, to help prevent fraying. When hemming an item with square corners, the simplest solution is to fold the hem on one edge, then the hem on the other edge. This can be done neatly but will not create the most professional finish. A mitred corner (see page 42) is a neater method.

BINDING

Bound edges are a useful and often decorative alternative to hemming. This technique involves sewing on strips of fabric, with the long edges folded towards the centre, to cover a raw edge. Binding gives a neat finish and can create less bulk than a hem.

Binding fabric that has been cut on the diagonal or 'bias' is known as bias binding. It is stretchy and so can be eased around shaped edges. It can be used to edge an apron, for example, or the top of a pocket, and is a useful way of finishing the perimeter of a quilt.

HAND STITCHING AN 'INVISIBLE' HEM

1 Fold the edge of the fabric to the wrong side to form a single hem ⅜in (1cm) wide. Press.

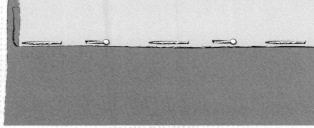

2 Fold a second time to form a double hem, this time folding over ⅝in (1.5cm). Press again and pin in place.

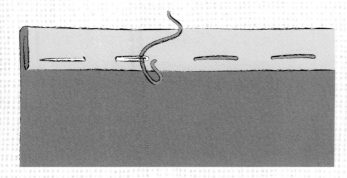

3 Baste the hem in place, using running stitch (see page 25). Remove pins.

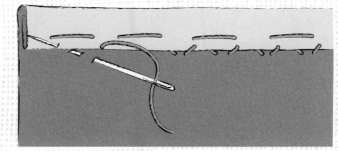

4 Using thread that matches your fabric, bring the needle through the fabric just above the fold, at the right-hand side. With the tip of the needle, pick up one or two threads from the fabric and then one or two threads from the edge of the fold about ⅛in (3–4mm) to the left. Draw the thread through, then repeat all along the edge of the hem.

MITRING A CORNER

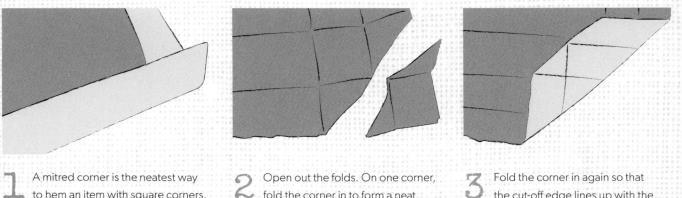

1. A mitred corner is the neatest way to hem an item with square corners. Fold a double hem on all four sides of the fabric. Press.

2. Open out the folds. On one corner, fold the corner in to form a neat right-angled triangle, with the folds lining up. Press and then cut off this triangle.

3. Fold the corner in again so that the cut-off edge lines up with the inner fold.

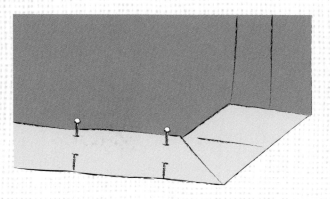

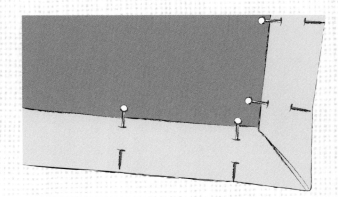

4. Fold the double hem again along the original fold lines. Pin in place.

5. Fold in the adjoining double hem so that the corner edges meet in a neat diagonal. Pin in place then slipstitch these folded edges together. Repeat with the remaining three corners, then stitch the hem all round.

BIAS BINDING

Bias binding can be purchased in several standard widths. It is widely available in cotton, poly-cotton and satin finishes, and in a range of colours. It is also available in some specialist shops in other fabrics, such as velvet, and in cotton prints.

If you want to match a particular colour or print, however, you may prefer to make bias binding from your own fabric (see page 45).

BINDING AN EDGE

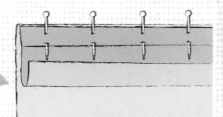

1 Open out one of the folded edges of the bias binding and place it along the edge of the fabric, with right sides together and raw edges matching. Pin in place.

2 Baste the binding in place, just above the fold line. Remove the pins. Stitch along the fold line using thread that matches the binding, in a neat backstitch.

3 Fold the binding over the fabric edge to the wrong side, and line up the folded edge of the binding tape with the line of backstitch. Pin and baste the binding in place.

4 Using slipstitch (see page 26), stitch the folded edge of the binding to the fabric, inserting the tip of the needle under the line of backstitching.

JOINING THE ENDS OF BIAS BINDING

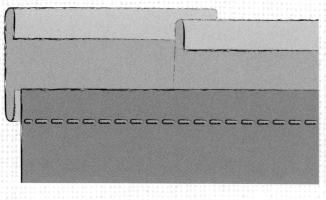

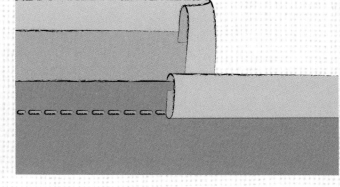

1 When you bind all the way round an item, you will need to use more than one length of binding, so you will need to join the two ends of the binding. To do this, once you have stitched one (long) edge of the binding in place, trim it, leaving about ⅝–¾in (1.5–2cm) for turning.

2 Where the two ends of binding overlap, fold the end that will lie underneath over the fabric edge, and slipstitch it to the fabric.

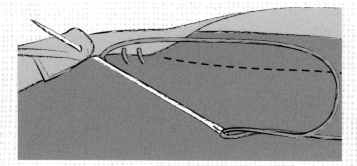

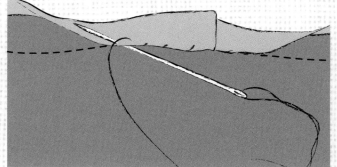

3 Turn under the end of the second length of binding tape and lay it on top, overlapping so that it covers the cut end of the first piece.

4 Slipstitch along the folded edges neatly. Slipstitch the folded end to finish it off tidily.

MAKING BIAS BINDING

To make bias binding from your own fabric you will need a long straight edge, a pencil or fabric marker, fabric scissors and a small gadget called a bias tape maker (see below).

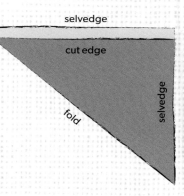

selvedge

cut edge

fold

selvedge

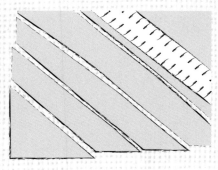

Tip The best fabrics to use for making bias binding are light or medium-weight cottons and cotton blends with a close weave.

1 Cut across the width of your fabric, carefully following the grain (see page 59). Then fold the fabric diagonally, lining up your cut edge with the selvedge (the long straight edge). Press firmly along the diagonal fold with an iron to make the bias grain clear.

2 Open out the fabric and draw lines parallel to the fold line using a ruler or straight edge. The lines should be spaced evenly apart. The spacing is determined by how wide you want your bias binding to be: the strip should be twice as wide as the finished binding: 1¼in (3cm) for ⅝in (1.5cm) binding, and 2in (5cm) for 1in (2.5cm) binding, for example. Use fabric scissors or a rotary cutter to cut along the lines to form strips.

BIAS TAPE MAKER

This small, useful device helps to fold both edges of a bias strip of fabric neatly and evenly. It has a loop on top, which you pull with one hand, gently and slowly, as you iron the strip, holding the iron with the other hand.

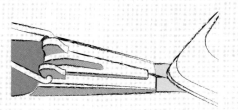

3 Feed the strips through the bias tape maker, one by one. As the folded strips emerge from the tip, press them with a hot iron.

APRON

THIS SMART, NO-NONSENSE APRON IS EASY TO MAKE, WITH NO SEAMS TO SEW. IT'S A GREAT WAY TO PRACTISE WORKING WITH BIAS BINDING, WHICH IS USED TO NEATEN THE EDGES AND MAKE THE TIES. CHOOSE A BRIGHTLY COLOURED BINDING TO CONTRAST WITH YOUR FABRIC.

YOU WILL NEED

- 1yd (90cm) medium-weight woven striped cotton fabric, at least 35–36in (90cm) wide
- 5 ½yd (5m) bias binding, 1in (2.5cm) wide
- A big piece of paper for the template (newspaper is fine)
- Sewing thread to match binding
- Sewing needle
- Pins
- Tape measure
- Fabric scissors
- All-purpose scissors
- Sewing machine (optional)

FINISHED SIZE

33 ½ in (85cm) long x 27in (68cm) wide

TECHNIQUES USED

Running stitch (see page 25)
Backstitch (see page 26)
Slipstitch (see page 26)
Oversewing (see page 25)
Binding an edge (see page 43)

MATERIALS TO USE

A woven striped cotton fabric is ideal for this apron. Do make sure that the fabric you buy is washable, as an apron will need regular laundering.

Tip
Mattress ticking (see page 16) would be a good fabric choice for this project, but may need to be pre-shrunk. To do this, simply wash and iron the fabric before cutting out.

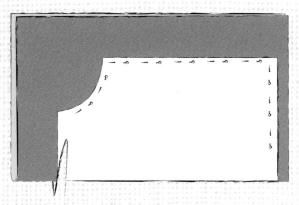

1 Using the diagram and instructions on pages 100–101, make a paper pattern template for the apron. Then fold your fabric in half lengthways and place the template on top with the dotted line running along the fold. Pin the template to the fabric and cut out the apron shape.

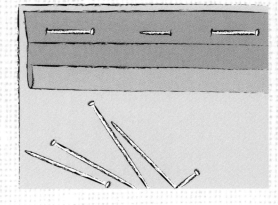

2 Cut a length of bias binding about ¾in (2cm) longer than the short straight edge at the top of the apron. Pin this piece of binding in place on the right side of the fabric, following the method shown on page 43, then baste just above the crease in the binding. Remove the pins.

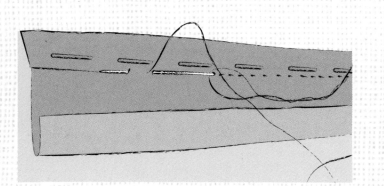

3 Stitch along the crease in the binding, by hand (in backstitch) or using a machine.

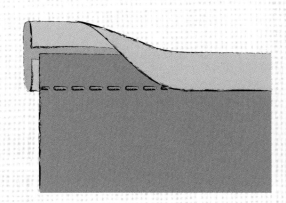

4 Remove the basting thread and fold the binding over to the wrong side, matching the folded edge of the binding to the stitch line.

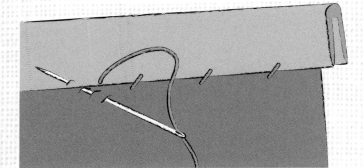

5 Slipstitch the folded edge in place. Trim off the excess binding at each end. Press. Apply binding in the same way along the straight sides and bottom edge of the apron, easing it around the curves on the lower corners.

6 Cut the remaining binding in half. Pin it in place along the curved edges of the apron, positioning the centre point of the binding in the centre of each edge, so that you have equal long free ends either side to form the waist and neck ties. Baste and stitch the binding, as in steps 2 and 3.

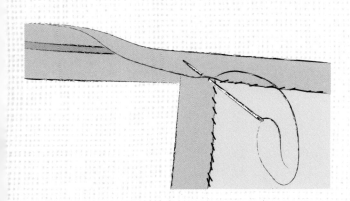

7 Remove the basting thread and fold the binding over to the wrong side, matching the folded edge of the binding to the stitch line. Slipstitch the folded edge in place.

8 Oversew the folded edges of the long free binding ends together, to form the ties. Press.

Technique four

GATHERING

GATHERING IS A WAY OF BUNCHING UP FABRIC TO CREATE A RUFFLED EFFECT. YOU MAKE A LINE OF STITCHES CLOSE TO THE EDGE OF THE FABRIC AND PULL ON THE THREADS TO DRAW UP THE FABRIC INTO FOLDS. THE STITCH LENGTH DETERMINES THE FULLNESS OF THE GATHERS.

Gathering can be done by hand or with a sewing machine. Using a machine can be quicker, but hand stitching will produce a softer, more even effect.

To gather fabric by hand, you will need to sew a line of running stitch (see page 25). To do it with machine stitching, you will need to sew two lines of straight stitch next to each other; the stitches should be longer and looser than if you were sewing a seam.

USES FOR GATHERING

Gathering can be used to create ruffles. A strip of fabric is neatened on one long edge by hemming or binding, then the other long edge is gathered. Ruffles can be used to edge a cushion or pillowcase, or a deep ruffle can be used on the edge of a bed sheet to create a valance. For the coat hanger on page 52, gathering stitches are used when making the fabric cover, to help ensure a snug fit at the ends, and also to create the decorative rosette.

COVERING BUTTONS

You can use gathering to make a covered button. Stitch a line of running stitch around a circle of fabric, place a self-covering button in the centre, then pull the threads to gather the fabric and enclose the button. Place the metal plate over the button shank and snap in place to secure and hide the raw edges of fabric.

GATHERING FABRIC BY HAND

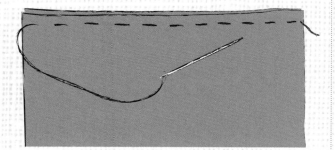

1 Thread a needle with a double thickness of thread and
tie the ends together in a knot. Push the needle in and out
of the fabric at regular intervals: the stitches and gaps
should be about ¼in (6mm) long. When you reach the other
end, do not fasten off the thread but leave a tail of thread
at least 6in (15cm) ong, still attached to the needle.

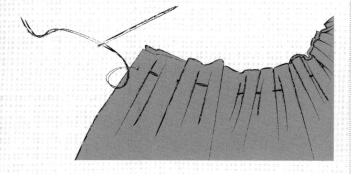

2 Pull up the tail of thread so that the fabric becomes ruched.
Keep pulling until the fabric has been gathered sufficiently,
then fasten off the thread securely.

GATHERING FABRIC BY MACHINE

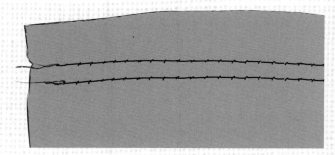

1 Secure the stitches at the beginning by going over the first
few stitches. Stitch a line of machine stitching along the
gathering line. At the end, do not secure the stitches. Stitch
a second line about ¼in (6mm) from the first, in the same
way. Cut the threads, leaving a tail about 6in (15cm) long.

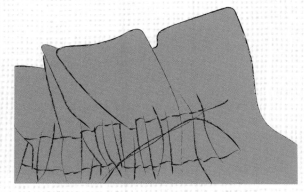

2 Pull up the tails of thread so that the fabric becomes ruched.
Keep pulling until the fabric has been gathered sufficiently,
then fasten off the threads securely by tying knots.

PADDED COAT HANGER

COVERED HANGERS ARE PRACTICAL AS WELL AS DECORATIVE. THEY ARE IDEAL FOR HANGING DELICATE ITEMS SUCH AS KNITWEAR, AS THE PADDING HELPS THE SHOULDERS TO KEEP THEIR SHAPE. THE FABRIC ALSO CREATES A LESS SLIPPERY SURFACE – IDEAL FOR STRAPPY GARMENTS.

YOU WILL NEED

- Woven striped cotton shirting, at least 28 x 8in (70 x 20cm)
- Cotton batting (wadding), at least 20 x 4in (50 x 10cm)
- Wooden coat hanger, 17½in (44cm) long
- Large button, 1in (2.5cm) diameter
- Small button, ½in (1.2cm) diameter
- Sewing thread to match fabric
- Sewing needle
- Pins
- Tape measure
- Fabric scissors
- Sewing machine (optional)

TECHNIQUES USED

Running stitch (see page 25)
Oversewing (see page 26)
Gathering fabric by hand (see page 51)

Tip Search junk shops and markets for vintage buttons, or remove old buttons from worn-out clothes.

MATERIALS TO USE

A woven striped cotton shirting fabric is ideal for this coat hanger. The fabric used here is double-sided with the colours reversed on each side – use one side for covering the hanger and the other side to create a contrasting rosette. Vintage buttons in colours to match the fabric create a stylish finishing touch.

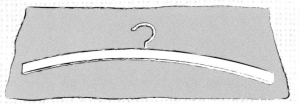

1 Trim the cotton batting (wadding) if necessary, so that it is wide enough to wrap around the hanger with a ⅛ in (2mm) overlap, and is about 1½ in (4cm) longer overall.

2 Wrap the batting around the hanger, with the long edges meeting on the top edge of the hanger. Beginning at the centre and working outwards towards each end, overlap the edges of the batting and oversew them together.

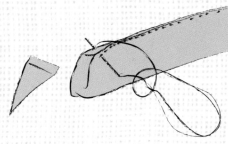

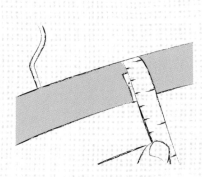

3 At the ends, tuck in the batting, trimming off any excess to avoid too much bulk, then oversew neatly.

4 To calculate the size of fabric to cut, first measure the girth of the hanger. Cut a strip of fabric that is ¾ in (2cm) wider than this amount, and the same length as the lower edge of the hanger plus ¾ in (2cm).

5 Turn under ⅜ in (1cm) on all four edges of the fabric, and press.

6 Place the fabric on the hanger, with the long folded edges meeting on the top edge of the hanger. Pin in place – one pin at either end and one in the centre should suffice. Beginning at the centre and working outwards, oversew the folded edges together.

7 When you get to each end, thread the needle with a double length of thread and sew a running stitch along the fold, then pull up to gather the fabric so that it fits neatly around the end. Oversew the gap with a few stitches and fasten off firmly.

8 To make the rosette, cut a strip of fabric measuring 28 x 3½in (70 x 9.5cm). Fold under ⅜in (1cm) on all four edges and press them flat (baste them if you wish). Fold the strip in half lengthways and press it again. Open out the fabric.

9 With double thread, making sure that your thread is more than 28in (70cm) long, stitch a running (gathering) stitch along the centre fold. Make sure you fasten one end of the thread securely and leave the other end free.

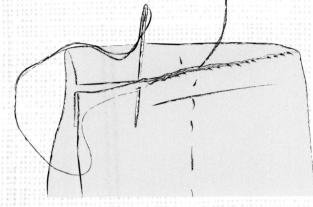

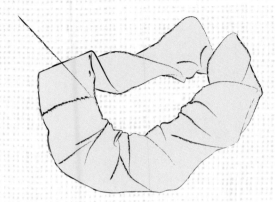

10 Oversew the short folded edges together (creating a circle of fabric), leaving the ends of the running thread free. Then fold the fabric and oversew the long folded edges together.

11 Pull the ends of the gathering threads so that the centre of the rosette is tightly gathered; fasten off securely. There will probably be a small hole in the centre, depending on the thickness of the fabric.

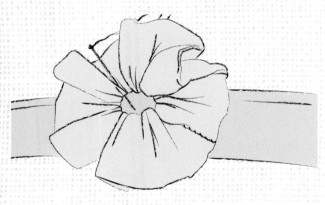

12 Stitch the centre of the rosette to the centre of one side of the hanger. Make sure it is stitched firmly in place; do not cut the thread.

13 Stitch the larger button securely to the centre of the rosette. Then sew the smaller button in place in the centre of the larger button.

CUTTING

CAREFUL CUTTING IS VERY IMPORTANT – YOU NEED TO PAY ATTENTION TO THIS EARLY STAGE OF A PROJECT TO MAKE SURE THAT CUT EDGES ARE NEAT AND SEAMS LINE UP. MAKE SURE YOUR SCISSORS ARE SHARP, AS BLUNT BLADES WILL RESULT IN UNTIDY EDGES AND INACCURATE CUTTING.

Most of the projects in this book do not require paper patterns, but you will need to measure and cut fabric, and sometimes – with the bunting, for example – create a card or paper template as a cutting guide.

When cutting fabric, always lay it out on a large, flat, firm surface. For small- and medium-sized projects, like those in this book, a table top should be adequate, but if you get the sewing bug and progress to larger items, such as curtains and bedcovers, you may need to lay out your fabric on a hard floor.

Tip Whether cutting on a table or on the floor, try laying a blanket out first and placing the fabric on top. The blanket will protect your fabric from marks, help to smooth out any bumps in the work surface, and help to prevent the fabric from slipping around. Be careful not to cut through the blanket at the same time as your fabric, however.

USEFUL EQUIPMENT

A cutting mat can be useful when cutting small and medium-sized pieces of fabric. It has lines and measurements marked on it at regular intervals, to help with measuring and cutting straight lines and accurate right-angled corners. Its rubber surface also helps to grip the fabric and prevent it from slipping around.

A straight edge (such as a metal ruler) is also essential for accurate straight cutting, especially if you are using a rotary cutter (see below).

ROTARY CUTTER

You might want to invest in a rotary cutter (a small gadget with a sharp circular blade) to use with a cutting mat and a steel ruler. It is useful for cutting through several layers of fabric and for cutting long, straight strips when making bias binding (see page 45).

CUTTING ON THE GRAIN

The grain of a fabric runs along its length and width. The lengthwise grain refers to the threads that run the length of the fabric, parallel to the long woven edge (the selvedge). The crosswise grain refers to the threads that run across the width of the fabric. When making something like a cushion cover, it is important to cut the fabric in straight lines along the lengthwise and crosswise grains. If you don't, the edges of the fabric will pull in different directions, making it difficult to stitch, and the finished item may become distorted. (See Tip on page 86 for how to pull out a thread to help you cut along the grain.)

The bias grain runs diagonally across the fabric. If you cut fabric on the bias grain, the edge of the fabric will be liable to stretch, but it will also be less likely to fray.

Tip The stretchy nature of fabric cut on the bias can be used to your advantage when making bias binding (see page 45) as it makes it easier to shape around corners.

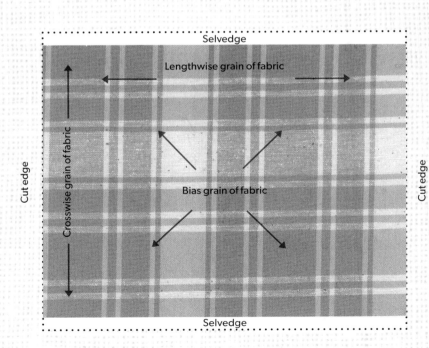

Selvedge

Lengthwise grain of fabric

Cut edge

Crosswise grain of fabric

Bias grain of fabric

Cut edge

Selvedge

BASKET LINER

A CUSTOM-MADE FABRIC LINER IS PRACTICAL AND LOOKS PRETTY WHEN USING A BASKET TO DISPLAY FOOD SUCH AS BREAD ROLLS, CAKES OR FRUIT. THIS LINER IS DETACHABLE FOR WASHING AND REVERSIBLE SO YOU CAN CHANGE WHICH SIDE IS ON SHOW.

TECHNIQUES USED

Running stitch (see page 25)
Backstitch (see page 26)
Oversewing (see page 25)
Hand stitching a simple seam (see page 33)
Cutting (see page 58)

MEASURING

To calculate the size of your basket liner, first measure your basket. Measure the inside length and width, including the sides. Add 1¼in (3cm) to the length and 1¼in (3cm) to the width.

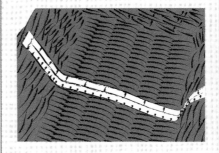

YOU WILL NEED

• Medium-weight printed cotton fabric, approximately 18 x 16in (45 x 40cm)*
• Cotton gingham check fabric, approximately 18 x 16in (45 x 40cm)*
• Sewing thread to match fabric
• Sewing needle
• Pins
• Tape measure
• Fabric scissors
• Ruler
• Pencil
• Large darning needle (optional)

* Fabric amounts are approximate as basket sizes will vary (see Measuring, right). Be sure to allow enough fabric to fit your own basket.

MATERIALS TO USE

A medium-weight cotton furnishing fabric with a small or medium-scale print is ideal for this project. Here it has been paired with a traditional gingham fabric on the reverse side. Make sure the fabric you buy is washable, so the finished liner can be laundered if necessary.

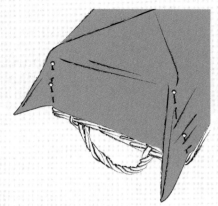

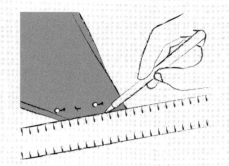

1 Cut out a rectangle of main fabric to your basket's measurements (see page 60). Fold it in half diagonally and press, then fold diagonally the other way and press again. Turn the basket upside down and position the centre of the fabric, wrong side up, on the centre of the basket's base. Pinch each corner of the fabric in turn, making sure the cut edges line up with each other. Pin them close to the corners of the basket, so that the fabric fits the outside of the basket snugly.

Tip Throughout these instructions, the printed fabric is referred to as the 'main' fabric and the gingham as the lining, but the finished liner is reversible and you can use just one fabric if you prefer.

2 Remove the fabric. Using a ruler and pencil, draw a line on each corner, ⅝ in (1.5cm) from the pins. Cut off the corner of the fabric along this line. (The line of pins indicates the stitching line.) Do this on all four corners, then remove the pins.

4 Pin, baste and stitch each corner seam of the main fabric, ⅝ in (1.5cm) from the edge, then press the seams open. Do the same with the lining fabric as well.

3 Open out the fabric and press it flat. Lay the lining fabric on a flat, firm surface. Place the main fabric on top and pin the two together, then cut around the edge, so that the lining fabric is the same size and shape.

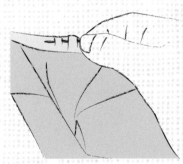

5 Turn ⅝ in (1.5cm) to the wrong side all round the top edge of the lining, and press. Pin and baste this hem. Do the same with the main fabric.

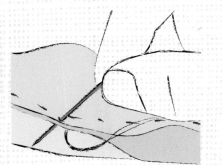

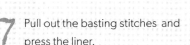

6 Place the main fabric and the lining together, with the right sides facing out. Pin together (and baste if necessary), then oversew the edges to join the two parts together.

7 Pull out the basting stitches and press the liner.

8 Place the finished liner inside the basket, pushing the corners into the corners of the basket. Your basket is now ready to use.

STITCHING THE LINER IN PLACE

If you wish to secure the liner to the basket, thread a large darning needle with a double thickness of thread. Secure the ends of the thread to the top edge of the liner at one corner and push the needle through a gap between the canes of the basket, then take the needle back through another gap in the basket, a little way along, using the tip of the needle to catch a few threads of fabric at the edge of the liner. Continue all round the basket. The stitches, which should be quite

long (and so easy to remove if you wish to take out the liner to wash it), will be hidden in the weave of the basket.

Tip A fabric liner, stitched in place, turns a plain basket into a gift basket. If you intend to use the basket for food, you may prefer not to stitch it in place, so that it can be removed and washed more easily.

APPLIQUÉ

APPLIQUÉ IS A TECHNIQUE OF ATTACHING ONE PIECE OF FABRIC TO ANOTHER TO ADD A PRETTY DECORATIVE MOTIF. CHOOSE ALMOST ANY SHAPE YOU LIKE IN A CONTRASTING OR COMPLEMENTARY FABRIC TO ADD A PERSONAL TOUCH TO YOUR PROJECTS.

A fabric cutout or motif is one of the easiest and quickest ways to apply decorative detail to a background fabric. You can choose a contrasting fabric to add colour and interest, and use any shape you like – although simple shapes work best.

Slipstitch or oversewing are useful methods of attaching fabric shapes (for step-by-step instructions on slipstitch, see page 26). Another method involves bonding fabric shapes to the background fabric using a special bonding material and a hot iron. When you buy this kind of material, it will come with instructions. It is important that you follow these, but here is a simple guide (right).

FUSIBLE BONDING WEB

This is, as the name suggests, a heat-reactive adhesive material that permanently bonds one fabric to another. Applying motifs using this material usually involves tracing an outline shape on to the paper backing, bonding one side to the appliqué fabric, then cutting out the shape and fusing it to the backing fabric. Pay attention to the manufacturer's instructions to ensure a good result and to avoid minor mishaps such as bonding pieces of adhesive to the base plate of your iron.

BONDING SHAPES

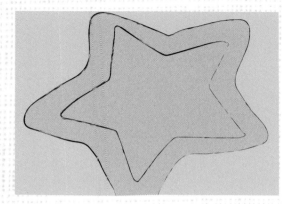

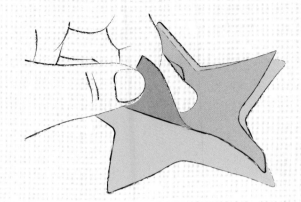

1 Trace your motif onto the paper backing of the bonding material and cut t out roughly, leaving a small margin around the traced outline. Place the bonding material, paper side uppermost, onto the wrong side of the fabric you have chosen fcr your appliqué.

2 Press using a hot iron, following the instructions provided with the bonding material. Cut out the motif, following the lines you have drawn, then peel off the backing paper.

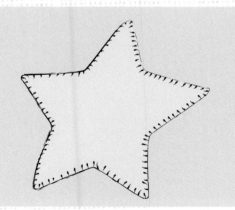

3 Place the motif face up on the background fabric, then press with a hot iron to bond it to the fabric.

4 Embellish the motif with stitching, using embroidery thread. Simply oversew the edges, or use blanket stitch (see page 27).

SLIPSTITCH APPLIQUÉ

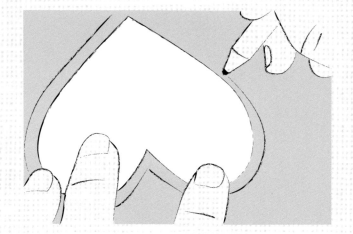

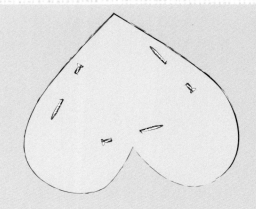

1 This is a method where you finish the edge of the cutout and stitch it to the fabric in one go. First cut out your motif, adding ¼ in (6mm) all round for the turnings.

2 Cut out your shape and pin it to the item to be decorated. Alternatively, you can hold it in place with a few basting stitches, keeping these stitches clear of the edges.

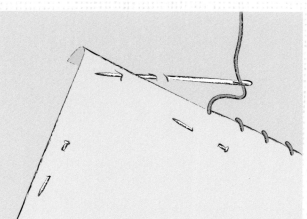

3 Use the tip of your needle to tuck the raw edge under by no more than ⅛ in (3mm). Slipstitch the folded edge of the cutout to the background fabric, using the tip of the needle to pick up a tiny piece of the background fabric and the edge of the appliqué motif at the same time.

HEMMING METHOD

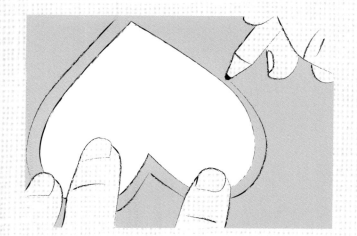

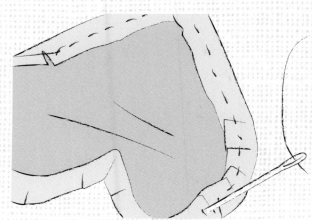

1 If you find it difficult to tuck the edge of a cutout under and stitch it to the background fabric in one step, you may find it easier to turn the edges under first. To do this, first cut out your motif, adding ¼in (6mm) all round for the turnings.

2 Snip into the turning allowance on curves and corners, then turn the edges to the wrong side and baste.

3 Pin the motif to the background fabric, then baste it in place and remove the pins. Slipstitch the folded edge of the motif to the background fabric.

COT COVER

A SCATTERING OF FLOWERS ADDS A DECORATIVE TOUCH TO A COT COVER THAT CAN DOUBLE AS A PLAY MAT – AND IT'S VERY QUICK AND EASY TO MAKE. FOLLOW THE APPLIQUÉ DESIGN SHOWN HERE OR, AS YOU GET MORE CONFIDENT, CREATE YOUR OWN PATTERNS.

YOU WILL NEED

- Cotton fabric in four plain colours, each approximately 36 x 14in (90 x 35cm)*
- Woven check muslin fabric, at least 48 x 36in (120 x 90cm)*
- Cotton batting (wadding)
- Scraps of printed cotton fabrics
- 28in (70cm) narrow bias binding
- Thin card
- Sewing thread to match fabrics
- Sewing needle
- Pins
- Tape measure
- Fabric scissors
- Ruler
- Pencil

* Fabric amounts given here allow for the rectangular strips that make up the top of the cover, with pieces left over for cutting the appliqué shapes. Craft cotton is usually 44in (110cm) wide, so if you are buying fabric from the roll and the retailer sells the fabric in multiples of 10cm, you may have to buy 40cm.

FINISHED SIZE

44½in (113cm) long x 30in (76cm) wide

TECHNIQUES USED

Running stitch (see page 25)
Backstitch (see page 26)
Slipstitch (see page 26)
Hand stitching a simple seam (see page 33)
Mitring a corner (see page 42)
Slipstitching appliqué (see page 66)

MATERIALS TO USE

Checked fabric is a good choice for backing the cover, as the woven lines give an accurate guide to cutting. Choose a lightweight fabric – muslin has been used here – as the edges need to be folded several times to create a softly padded edge to the cover, and a thicker fabric would be too bulky. Make sure that the fabric you buy is washable, so that the finished cover can be laundered. Also check whether or not the fabric is pre-shrunk; if not, or if you're not sure, it is advisable to wash it before cutting.

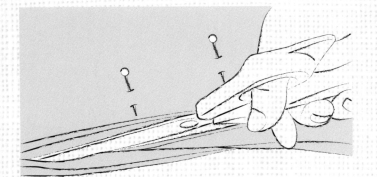

1 Measure and cut a piece of cotton batting (wadding)
44 ½ x 30in (113 x 76cm). Measure and cut the plain cotton
fabric: two pieces measuring 12¼ x 30in (31 x 76cm) and
two measuring 11¾ x 30in (30 x 76cm).

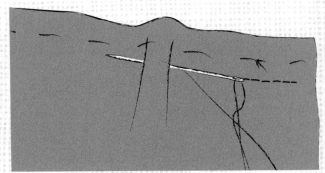

2 The seam allowance for this project is ⅝in (1.5cm). It is a
good idea to draw a pencil line this distance from the raw
edges of the fabric pieces, using a straight edge, to help
you stitch a straight seam.

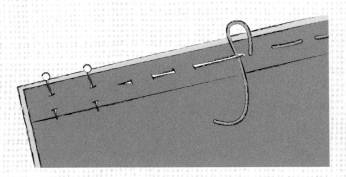

3 Place the first two fabric pieces to be joined, right sides
together, and pin. Baste through both thicknesses, within
the seam allowance.

4 Stitch the two pieces together using thread that matches at
least one of the fabric colours as closely as possible. Sew a
backstitch seam, following the line you have drawn. Repeat
until all four strips are joined together: the wider ones in
the centre and the narrower ones at each end. Press all the
seams to one side. This forms the top of the cover.

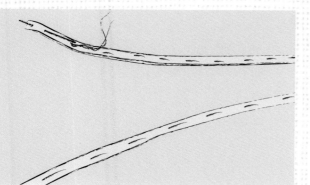

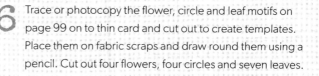

5 Cut three lengths of bias binding for the stems, 7½in, 9½in and 11in (19cm, 24cm and 28cm) long (see page 45). Fold each one in half lengthways. Pin them in place, radiating out from one corner and using the picture of the finished appliqué on page 69 as a guide. Baste and remove the pins.

6 Trace or photocopy the flower, circle and leaf motifs on page 99 on to thin card and cut out to create templates. Place them on fabric scraps and draw round them using a pencil. Cut out four flowers, four circles and seven leaves.

7 Arrange the fabric shapes in the corner of the blanket, with three of the flowers overlapping the ends of the bias binding stems. Play around with the arrangement, using the picture of the finished appliqué on page 69 as a guide. Pin each piece in position, then baste, and remove the pins.

8 Use the point of your needle to tuck under a small amount – about ⅛in (3mm) – of fabric on the edge of each appliqué shape, and slipstitch the fold to the main fabric. Do this all round each shape. Slipstitch the edges of the folded bias binding stems to the main fabric. When all shapes and stems have been stitched in place, remove the basting threads.

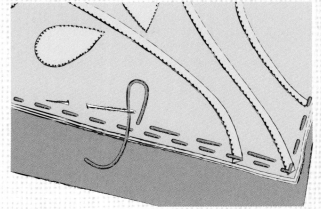

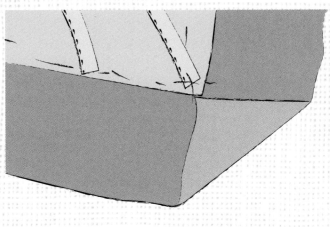

9 Place the finished piece on top of the batting, right side up, lining up all the edges, then pin and baste the two layers together.

10 Place the backing fabric on the work surface, wrong side up, and place the basted batting and top fabric centrally on top, right side up. Baste through all three layers, about ½ in (1.2cm) from the raw edges. Cut the backing, with a margin of 2in (5cm) all round.

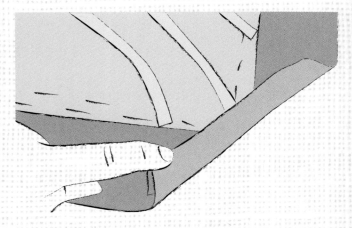

11 To make neat mitred corners, fold the corner of the backing fabric to the corner of the main fabric, then cut along the fold line.

12 Fold the cut edge of the backing fabric twice, letting it overlap the corner of the cover.

13 Fold the edge of the backing to meet the edge of the main fabric and batting, then fold the folded edge in to the same point. Now fold this edge in over the top fabric; it will create a softly padded binding, with four thicknesses of backing fabric. Pin it into position (and baste if you wish), then slipstitch the folded edge to the top fabric all round.

14 At each corner, slipstitch the diagonal folded edges together neatly.

Tip Get into the recycling habit. Save leftover scraps of fabric from any of the projects in this book for future appliqué projects. Scraps of ribbon, lace and bias binding should be saved too as they can also be incorporated into appliqué designs.

Technique seven

POCKETS

EVERYONE KNOWS HOW USEFUL POCKETS CAN BE ON ITEMS OF CLOTHING. THEY CAN ALSO BE AN ATTRACTIVE AND PRACTICAL ADDITION TO ALL KINDS OF HOME SEWING PROJECTS, ADDING INTEREST AND HANDY STORAGE ON ALL KINDS OF ITEMS.

Patch pockets are the easiest to make and a good way to use up fabric scraps. You can make a pocket from a single thickness of fabric, hemming it all round before stitching it to the item. Or you can make a pocket from a double thickness of fabric, creating a lined pocket. Lined pockets can be stitched down securely to the background fabric, or attached at the top only, so that it is more like a small semi-detached bag.

The peg bag on page 78 features a patch pocket on the front, using the same fabric as the main bag – but you could use a contrast fabric. You could also add a pocket to the apron on page 46 or the tote bag on page 36.

Tip Instead of hemming the top of a pocket, bind the edge with bias binding (see page 43). A contrast coloured binding looks decorative. On thicker fabric, binding also has the advantage of being less bulky than a double hem.

Tip Once you know how easy it is to make a pocket you can add pockets to various household items. It's a good way to use up scraps of fabric too. Stitch a simple patch pocket (with or without lining) to an apron or bag, or stitch several pockets to a piece of fabric and hang it up for handy storage.

MAKING A SIMPLE PATCH POCKET

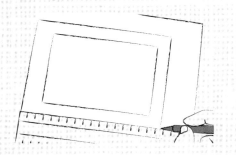

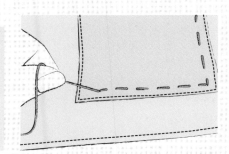

1 Mark out the desired dimensions of the pocket on a piece of paper. Add ⅝in (1.5cm) to the two sides and base and 1in (2.5cm) to the top edge.

2 Cut out the paper to make a template, pin it to the fabric, and cut out around the template.

3 Turn under ⅝in (1.5cm) on the two sides and the base. Press the hems flat. Baste the single hems you have just created. For a neat finish, mitre the two lower corners (see Hems, page 42).

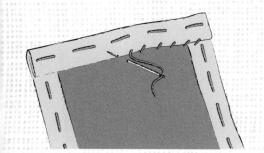

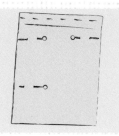

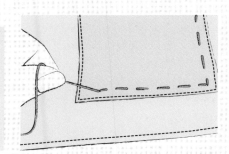

4 On the top edge, turn under ⅜in (1cm) and press, then fold a further ⅝in (1.5cm) to the wrong side and press again. Baste, then stitch hem as shown on page 41.

5 Place the prepared pocket on the background fabric and pin in place, then baste.

6 Using backstitch or a close running stitch, stitch down the right side, across the base and up the left side of the pocket. Remove the basting stitches and press.

MAKING A LINED POCKET

1 Make a template and use it to cut out two pieces of fabric (see steps 1 and 2, page 75). Place the two pieces right sides together and baste inside the seam allowance. Mark the seamline in pencil.

2 Stitch along the seamline using backstitch. Leave a gap at the centre of one of the short edges, so that you can turn the pocket inside out. Snip off each corner.

3 Remove basting. Turn the right sides out through the gap you left in the seam.

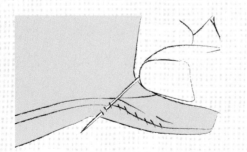

4 Press the pocket. At the gap, press the seam allowance to the inside. Oversew the folded edges neatly to close the gap.

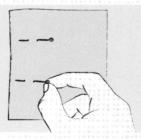

5 Place the prepared pocket on the background fabric and pin it in place.

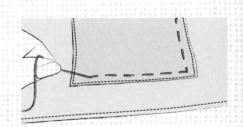

6 Baste, then stitch, using a neat backstitch or close running stitch, down the right side, across the base and up the left side. Remove the basting stitches and press.

PEG BAG

THIS BAG CAN BE CARRIED OUT TO THE GARDEN AND HOOKED OVER THE WASHING LINE, SO THAT PEGS ARE TO HAND. THE LITTLE POCKET IS USEFUL FOR STORING A CLOTH FOR WIPING THE LINE. THE BAG IS EASY TO MAKE, USING FABRIC REMNANTS AND A CHILD'S COAT HANGER.

YOU WILL NEED

- Woven checked medium-weight cotton fabric, at least 28 x 16in (70 x 40cm)
- Woven checked dress-weight cotton fabric, approximately 36 x 16in (90 x 40cm), for the lining and pocket
- 60in (1.5m) of ⅝in (1.5cm) cotton bias binding
- Wooden coat hanger, 12in (30cm) long
- Sewing thread to match fabric
- Sewing needle
- Pins
- Tape measure
- Fabric scissors
- Ruler
- Pencil
- Sewing machine (optional)

FINISHED SIZE

12in (30cm) long x 13 ¼in (33.5cm) wide

TECHNIQUES USED

Running stitch (see page 25)
Oversewing (see page 25)
Backstitch (see page 26)
Slipstitch (se page 26)
Hand stitching a simple seam (see page 33)
Binding an edge (see page 43)
Making a simple patch pocket (see page 75)

MATERIALS TO USE

A woven check fabric is ideal for this project, as the lines of weaving help with measuring and cutting out. Bias binding in a contrasting pattern adds an extra stylish twist. Choose a medium-weight furnishing cotton that is washable, so that the bag can be laundered, but remember to remove the hanger from the peg bag before washing.

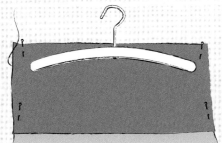

1 Cut two rectangles from each fabric: one of each measuring 20½ x 13¼in (52 x 33.5cm) and one of each 13¼ x 6¼in (33.5 x 16cm). Place all four pieces together, with four of the narrower edges lined up. Centre the coat hanger at the top.

2 Draw along the top curve of the hanger, then cut along the line you have drawn, through all four thicknesses.

3 Now place the hanger close to the lower edges of the two larger pieces of fabric (both main and lining). Draw along the lower curve of the hanger, then cut along this line through both thicknesses.

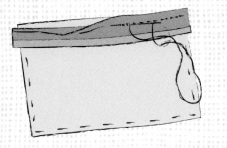

4 Cut a pocket 7 x 4¾in (18 x 12cm) from the lining fabric. Turn under ⅜in (1cm) on both of the short edges and one long edge, and baste. Bind the top (raw) edge (see page 43).

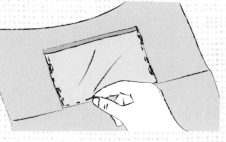

5 Fold up 6⅝in (17cm) on the larger piece of main fabric from the lower hanger curve (so that the wrong sides meet). Press. Align the bottom of the pocket with the fold, centre and pin, then baste. Attach the three sides of the pocket to the bag by oversewing (see page 25).

6 Place the two main fabric pieces right sides together, with the top curved edges aligned. Baste them together close to the top curved edge, then find the centre and place two pins, one on either side of the centre point, 1in (2.5cm) apart. Do the same with the two lining pieces.

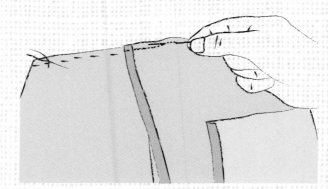

7 Stitch the two main fabric pieces together, ⅜ in (1cm) from the top edge; do not stitch between the pins but leave a gap. Clip the seam allowance at intervals on the curved edge. Do the same with the lining fabric.

8 Place the lining inside the main section, wrong sides together. Pin and baste the curved raw edges of the main fabric and the lining together, and bind with a length of bias binding. Do the same with the straight raw edges on the small section. Fold the lower section of the peg bag along the fold created in step 5, so that the bound curved edge overlaps the bound straight edge slightly, then baste the sides of the bag together, through all thicknesses.

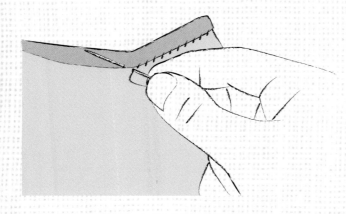

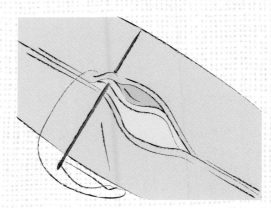

9 Stitch the sides, then bind the two side edges of the bag with bias binding.

10 To neaten the opening at the top of the bag, slipstitch the folded edges of the lining and the main fabric together. Insert the coat hanger, with the hook poking through this opening.

TIES

TIES ARE A WAY OF CLOSING A GAP OR SECURING TWO EDGES TOGETHER, BUT THEY CAN ALSO FORM A DECORATIVE DETAIL. WHEN MAKING TIES, USE THE SAME FABRIC AS THE MAIN PART OF THE ITEM, OR A CONTRASTING FABRIC, DEPENDING ON THE LOOK YOU WISH TO ACHIEVE.

If a fabric tie is to be stitched into a seam, leave this end of the tie unfinished but finish the other end neatly. This can be done when making the tie (as described here), or after the tie has been turned right side out by tucking in the raw edges and oversewing the end neatly.

Instead of making ties, you may want to use something ready-made, to save time and effort. There is a great selection of ribbons and braids available. Make sure the one you choose is suitable for the purpose, such as grosgrain ribbon, cotton or linen braid, or a ribbon with firm woven edges that can stand up to some wear and tear.

MAKING A FABRIC TIE – METHOD 1

For this simple technique, the fabric tie is folded and stitched from the outside.

1 Cut a strip of fabric the required length of the finished tie plus ¾ in (2cm). Fold in ⅜ in (1cm) on each side and press.

2 Now fold the strip in half lengthwise, right sides out, with the edges folded to the inside. Oversew the folded edges together along the whole length of the tie. Alternatively, you can stitch through all layers, close to the double fold, with a running stitch or straight machine stitch, then add a line of stitching down the other side to make it look more balanced.

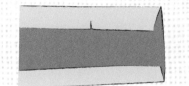

MAKING A FABRIC TIE - METHOD 2

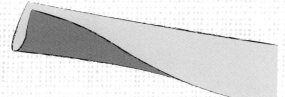

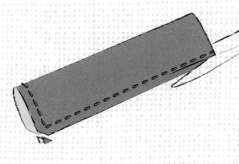

1 Cut a strip of fabric the required length of the finished tie plus ⅜in or ⅝in (1cm or 1.5cm), depending on the seam allowance you are working with. Fold the strip of fabric in half lengthwise, with the right side on the inside and the raw edges aligned. Stitch a seam across one of the short ends and down the length of the tie.

2 Clip the corner and trim away the excess fabric from the seam allowance, to reduce the bulk and make it easier to turn the tie right sides out.

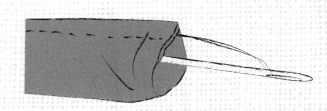

3 Push the stitched end of the tie inwards, then, using a knitting needle push it all the way down until the fabric can be turned inside out, with the right side showing. Press the tie flat.

4 Alternatively, you could use a bodkin or a safety pin to turn the tie inside out. In this case, do not stitch across one end of the tie but leave both ends open. Attach a double thickness of strong thread to one of the open ends and attach the thread to the bodkin or pin. Push the bodkin or pin all the way down the tube of fabric and out of the other end and pull, so that the end attached to the thread is pulled down inside the tube, thereby turning it inside out.

Project eight

CUSHIONS

CUSHIONS WITH REMOVABLE COVERS MAKE LAUNDERING EASY, AND TIE FASTENINGS ARE PRACTICAL AS WELL AS STYLISH. THE RECTANGULAR CUSHION USES TIES MADE FROM THE SAME FABRIC, WHILE THE SQUARE CUSHION HAS TIES MADE FROM RIBBON.

YOU WILL NEED
RECTANGULAR CUSHION WITH FABRIC TIES

• ½yd (50cm) printed linen furnishing fabric
• Cushion pad, 20 x 14in (50 x 35cm)
• Sewing thread to match fabric
• Sewing needle
• Pins
• Tape measure
• Fabric scissors
• Ruler and pencil

SQUARE CUSHION WITH RIBBON TIES

• ½yd (50cm) printed linen furnishing fabric
• 2¼yd (2m) ribbon, 1½ –2in (4–5cm) wide
• Cushion pad, 17 x 17in (43 x 43cm)
• Sewing thread to match fabric
• Sewing needle
• Pins
• Tape measure
• Fabric scissors
• Ruler and pencil

FINISHED SIZES
Rectangular cushion 20 x 14in (50 x 35cm)
Square cushion 17 x 17in (43 x 43cm)

TECHNIQUES USED
Running stitch (see page 25)
Backstitch (see page 26)
Hand stitching a simple seam
(see page 33)
Hand stitching an 'invisible' hem
(see page 41)
Cutting on the grain (see page 59)
Making a fabric tie (rectangular cushion)
(see page 83)

Tip Cushion covers look best when they fit quite snugly. When cutting out fabric for covers, allow no more than ⅜in (1cm) extra all round than the dimensions of the cushion pad. The seam allowance is ⅜in (1cm).

RECTANGULAR CUSHION WITH FABRIC TIES

Tip To ensure a straight cut along the grain of the fabric, first pull out a thread. Where the thread has been removed you will see a line; cut along this line and you will have a nice straight edge.

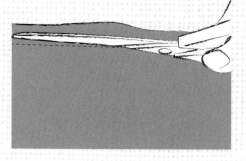

1 Cut three rectangles of fabric, one measuring 21 x 14½in (53 x 37cm), one measuring 20½ x 14½in (52 x 37cm), and the other 14½ x 6¼in (37 x 16cm). For the ties, cut four strips of fabric, each 20½ x 1 ¾in (52 x 4.5cm).

2 Fold each tie strip of fabric in half lengthways. Stitch across one short end, then down the long side, ¼in (6mm) from the edge; leave the other short end open. Clip the stitched corner, turn the tie right sides out and press.

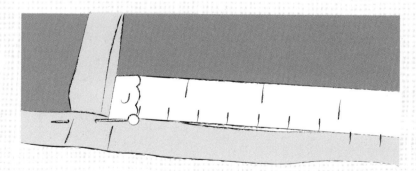

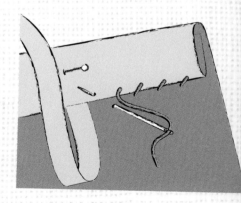

3 On the largest of the three rectangles, turn under one of the short ends by ⅜in (1cm), then ⅝in (1.5cm), to make a double hem and press. Tuck the raw ends of two of the ties under the hem, 4⅓in (11cm) in from each side and pin in place.

4 Stitch the hem (by hand or machine), trapping the ties in place as you go.

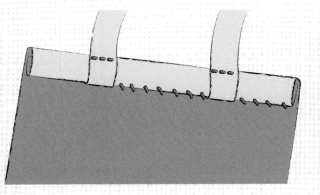

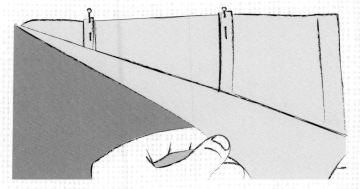

5 Fold the ties back on themselves, over the hem, and stitch over them again. this time close to the cushion edge. This helps to hold the ties in place and makes them more secure when they are being tied and untied.

6 Hem one long edge of the smallest piece of fabric. Pin the raw ends of the remaining two ties to the shorter edge of the remaining piece, then line up the long unhemmed edge of the smallest piece with this edge, right sides together, trapping the ends of the ties between the two layers. Pin, baste and stitch, either by hand or machine.

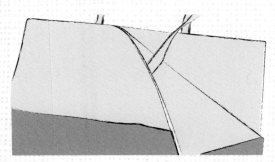

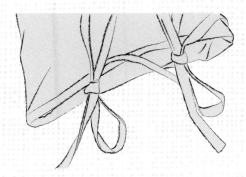

7 Place the largest piece (from step 3) right side up and place the second piece, right side down, on top, lining up the edges with the ties. Pin, baste and stitch around three sides, leaving the edges with the ties open.

8 Clip the corners and turn the cushion cover right sides out. Insert the cushion pad through the opening, then tuck the end of the pad under the flap inside. Tie the pairs of ties together in neat bows.

SQUARE CUSHION WITH RIBBON TIES

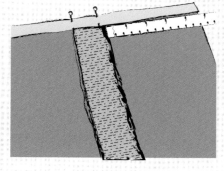

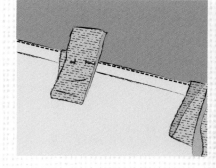

1 Cut three pieces of fabric, one measuring 17¾ x 17¾in (45 x 45cm), one measuring 17¾ x 12¾in (45 x 32.5cm) and the other 17¾ x 10in (45 x 25cm). On the middle-sized piece, on one of the long sides, turn under ⅜in (1cm), then ⅝in (1.5cm), to make a double hem. Press and pin, then stitch.

2 On the smallest of the three pieces, on one of the long sides, turn under ⅜in (1cm), then ⅝in (1.5cm) and press. This piece will form the cushion flap. Cut the ribbon into four equal lengths. Trap the ends of two of the pieces of ribbon under the hem, 4¾in (12cm) in from each side, then pin, baste and stitch the hem.

3 Lay the largest piece of fabric (which forms the cushion front) right side up on a flat surface. Place the piece with the ribbon ties on top of it, right side down, lining up the raw edges. Roll up the ribbons and pin them, so that their ends do not get in the way when you stitch the seams.

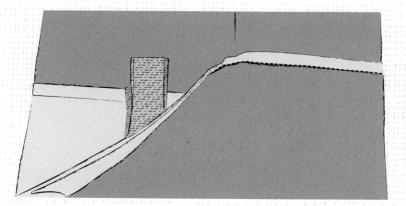

4 Place the remaining piece (the middle-sized piece) on top, wrong side up, overlapping the second piece, and lining up the raw edges with the cushion front. Pin, baste and stitch all three fabric pieces together around all four sides. Clip the corners and turn right sides out.

6 Insert the cushion pad through the opening, and tie the pairs of ribbon ties together in neat bows.

5 Remove the pins from the rolled-up ribbon ties. Fold over one end of each of the two remaining pieces of ribbon twice to make a narrow double hem. Line up these ends with the ties on the edge of the flap, pin and stitch securely in position.

CUSHION PADS

Ready-made cushion pads are available to buy in various shapes and sizes, and with different fillings. Feather and down is the most luxurious and expensive filling, but may not be suitable for anyone suffering from an allergy. Cushion pads with polyester fillings are cheaper, and pads stuffed with foam chips are cheapest of all, but can be a bit lumpy.

Alternatively, you could make your own cushion pad. One advantage to this is that you can make it to any size you choose and fill it with your choice of filling. Choose a fabric with a close weave, especially if you are filling it with feathers, so that the filling doesn't poke through: calico and mattress ticking are good choices for this.

FASTENINGS

YOU CAN MAKE ALL SORTS OF CREATIVE CHOICES WHEN IT COMES TO FASTENINGS. BUTTONS AND BUTTONHOLES CAN BE A DECORATIVE DETAIL, AS WELL AS BEING PRACTICAL, WHILE OTHER OPTIONS, SUCH AS PRESS STUDS, CAN BE DISCREET OR MADE INTO AN ATTRACTIVE FEATURE.

BUTTONS

Buttons and buttonholes are not only one of the simplest and most practical ways of fastening two pieces of fabric together, they can also be made into a decorative feature.

Tip If you don't want to sew buttonholes, an alternative method is to make button loops, as in the coffee cosy project on page 94.

TYPES OF BUTTON

When using medium-weight or thicker fabrics, you will need to use a button with a shank (a raised area on the back). If you use a button with holes you can create a shank with thread as you stitch the button in place (see opposite page).

ATTACHING A SHANK BUTTON

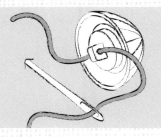

1 Bring the needle through to the front of the fabric at the position for the button to sit. Pass the needle through the shank, then back through the fabric close to where it came out.

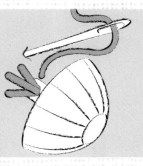

2 Bring the needle out again at or near the same place as before, and back through the shank. Repeat this about five or six times, then take the needle back through to the wrong side and fasten off with a few secure stitches before snipping the thread.

CREATING A STITCHED SHANK

1 Mark the position where you want the button to be on the fabric. Bring the needle through to the front of the fabric at this point. Pass the needle through one of the holes in the button, then lay a matchstick or toothpick across the centre of the button. Take the needle over the stick, down through another hole and back through the fabric, trapping the matchstick in place. Pass the needle through the fabric and the holes in the button in this way about five or six times, then slide the stick out.

2 Now bring the needle up through the fabric beneath the button. Pull the button upwards, then wind the thread around the stitches underneath the button several times to form the stitched shank. Take the needle back through to the wrong side of the fabric and fasten off.

Tip When stitching buttons in place, they need to be stitched firmly and securely. It is a good idea to use a double thickness of sewing thread or, even better, a strong specialist button thread.

STITCHING A BUTTONHOLE

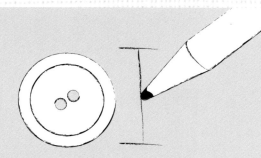

1   In the position you want your buttonhole to be, mark a line on the fabric the length of the finished buttonhole, which should be the same length as the diameter of the button.

2   Stitch a line of running stitches either side, ⅛ in (3mm) from the line. Make a few stitches either end of the line, at right angles to it.

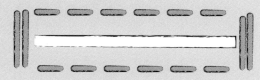

3   Cut along the marked line using small sharp scissors or a craft knife, taking care not to cut through the stitches at either end of the buttonhole.

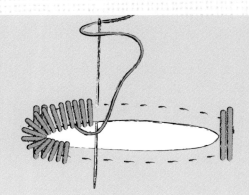

4   Oversew the raw edges of this slit. Now work all round the buttonhole, in buttonhole stitch, which is a variation of blanket stitch (see page 27).

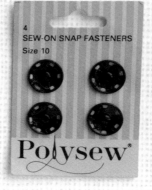

Press stud tape   Press fasteners (poppers)   Hooks and eyes

OTHER TYPES OF FASTENING

PRESS FASTENERS (POPPERS)

These come in a variety of sizes. The smallest are suitable for thin fabrics and the largest for thicker, heavier fabrics. They can be a good substitute for buttons. Each press fastener has two parts: a ball and a socket. Stitch the part with the ball to the overlapping fabric and the part with the socket to the fabric that will be on the underside. Each part should be positioned at least ¼in (6mm) from the edge of the fabric. You will find a hole in the centre of both the ball and socket, which is useful for lining up the two parts. Stitch each part to the fabric by oversewing, inserting your needle into each of the four corner holes in turn.

PRESS STUD TAPE

You can buy tape with metal or plastic press studs fixed to it at regular intervals, and it is available in a choice of widths. This tape saves time stitching individual press fasteners in place and is particularly useful for cushion covers.

PRESS-AND-CLOSE FASTENING

This tape (brand name 'Velcro') consists of two sides, one with hooks and one with loops which, when pressed together, form a strong bond. It is available in various widths, in a range of colours, and also as small spots that are a good substitute for buttons or press fasteners. To apply, oversew the edges to the fabric, or use a straight or zigzag machine stitch.

HOOKS AND EYES

A hook-and-eye closure is a simple and secure method of fastening two fabric edges together. The hook and the eye are each made of flattened wire, one bent in a hook shape and the other in a loop into which the hook fits. A single hook and eye is often sewn above the top of a zip, to help ease the pressure on the zip; a row of several hooks and eyes can be used on a garment such as a shirt or dress, instead of buttons, where a more discreet or unobtrusive fastening is required.

COFFEE COSY

WITH ITS THERMAL INTERLINING, THIS STYLISH WRAP HELPS TO KEEP YOUR COFFEE HOTTER FOR LONGER. THE PATTERN CAN BE ADAPTED TO FIT ANY SIZE OF CAFETIÈRE AND THE BUTTON FASTENING ENSURES A SNUG FIT. CHOOSE A FABRIC TO MATCH YOUR KITCHEN COLOUR SCHEME.

YOU WILL NEED

- Medium-weight woven striped cotton fabric, approximately 14 x 8in (35 x 20cm)
- Medium-weight plain cotton or linen fabric, approximately 14 x 8in (35 x 20cm)
- Thermal interlining or lightweight cotton batting, approximately 14 x 8in (35 x 20cm)
- 12in (30cm) medium-weight ribbon
- Three 1in (2.5cm) buttons with shanks
- Sewing thread to match fabric
- Sewing needle
- Pins
- Tape measure
- Fabric scissors
- Pencil

TECHNIQUES USED

Running stitch (see page 25)
Backstitch (see page 26)
Hand stitching a simple seam (see page 33)
Coping with curves (see page 34)
Leaving a gap (see page 35)
Attaching a shank button (see page 91)

MATERIALS TO USE

A medium-weight cotton furnishing fabric is ideal for this cosy. Here it has been paired with a plain linen fabric. Make sure that the fabric you buy is washable, so that the finished cosy can be laundered.

MEASURING

To calculate the size of your cosy, measure the glass portion of your cafetière. Add 1¼in (3cm) to both the height and the girth, and cut out rectangles of the main fabric, backing fabric and interlining in these measurements. This cafetière measures 12¼in (31cm) around, and 6¾in (17cm) tall, giving a fabric size of 13½ x 8in (34 x 20cm).

Tip Fabric that has woven stripes, evenly spaced, will help with measuring and cutting, and with sewing straight seams.

1 Place all three rectangles of fabric on top of each other, lining up all the edges. Place a circular object, such as a cup or a glass, on one corner and draw around the edge in the corner to create a curve. Cut out along the line you have drawn, to create a neat curve. Repeat on the other three corners.

2 For the button loops, cut three 3½in (9cm) lengths of ribbon. Lining up both ends of one piece of ribbon with the raw edge on one short side of the main fabric, pin the ribbon in position so that it will sit just under the top part of the handle. Repeat with a second length of ribbon so that it sits just above the bottom part of the handle. Check the positions against the cafetière.

3 Baste the two button loops in place. The basting stitches should run within the seam allowance. Position the third ribbon loop halfway between the first two and baste.

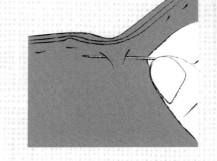

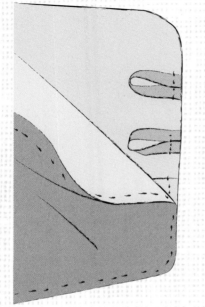

5 Stitch all round, ⅝in (1.5cm) from the edge, through all layers. Leave a gap along the short edge without the button loops, so that the cosy can be turned right sides out.

6 When you have finished stitching, cut away the excess interlining from the seam allowance and snip notches at each corner, taking care not to cut the stitches.

4 Matching raw edges, baste the backing fabric and interlining together. Place the main fabric right side up, then place the basted fabrics on top, with the interlining uppermost and the button loops sandwiched between the main fabric and the backing fabric.

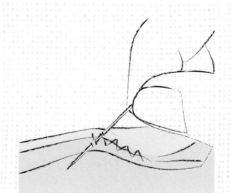

7 Turn the cosy right sides out. Fold the raw edges of the gap to the inside by ⅝in (1.5cm) and press, then oversew the edges neatly to close the gap.

8 Mark the position of the buttons on the opposite edge to the ribbon loops, then stitch each one in place.

TEMPLATES AND PATTERNS

THE SHAPES ON THESE PAGES ARE FOR YOU TO COPY TO USE AS TEMPLATES WHEN CUTTING OUT YOUR FABRIC. THE APPLIQUÉ SHAPES FOR THE COT COVER (PAGE 68) ARE ACTUAL SIZE, WHILE THE TRIANGLE FOR THE BUNTING (PAGE 28) WILL NEED TO BE COPIED OR DRAWN AT TWICE THE SIZE.

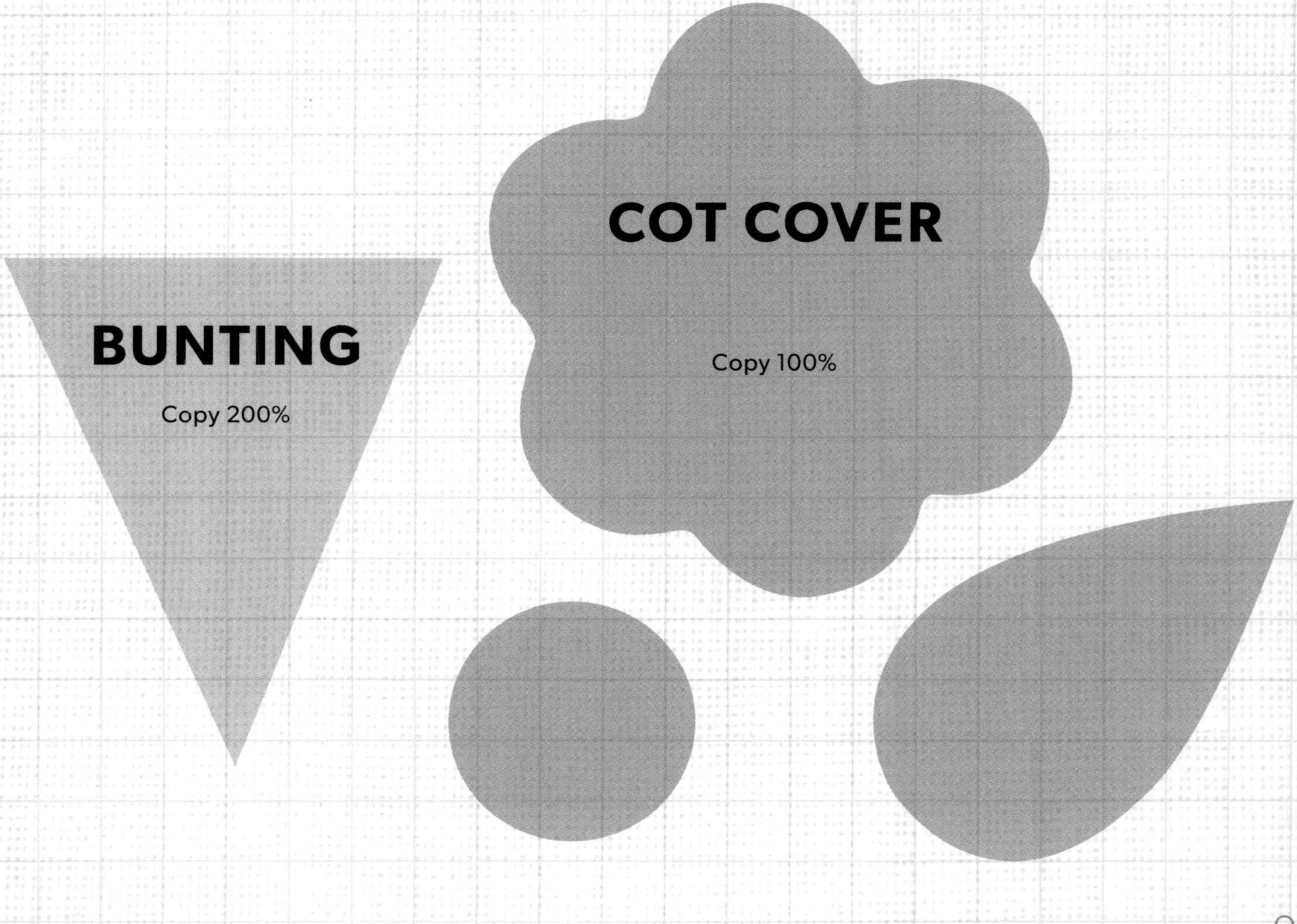

COT COVER

Copy 100%

BUNTING

Copy 200%

APRON
EACH SQUARE = 1in (2.5cm)

This template shows the pattern shape for the apron on page 46. You need to make a paper pattern that you can pin to your fabric (which you should fold in half lengthwise) and use as a cutting guide. You can either photocopy the template at 250% (you will need to print it out on several sheets of paper and join them together with sticky tape) or you can copy the shape on to a large sheet of pattern paper.

Pattern paper with a printed grid is available to buy from most haberdashery suppliers. The squares on this grid are designed to help you transfer the shape onto the pattern paper. Each square here represents 1in (2.5cm). You can scale up the shape on the pattern paper by drawing whatever is in the corresponding square on this grid at actual size. Where this apron is concerned, though, you could cut a rectangle of fabric to the overall dimensions of the apron – 33½in (85cm) by 27in (68cm) – then fold this in half lengthwise. You can then mark the cutting lines of the curve, using tailor's chalk or an erasable pencil, directly on to the fabric, using the measurements on this template as a guide.

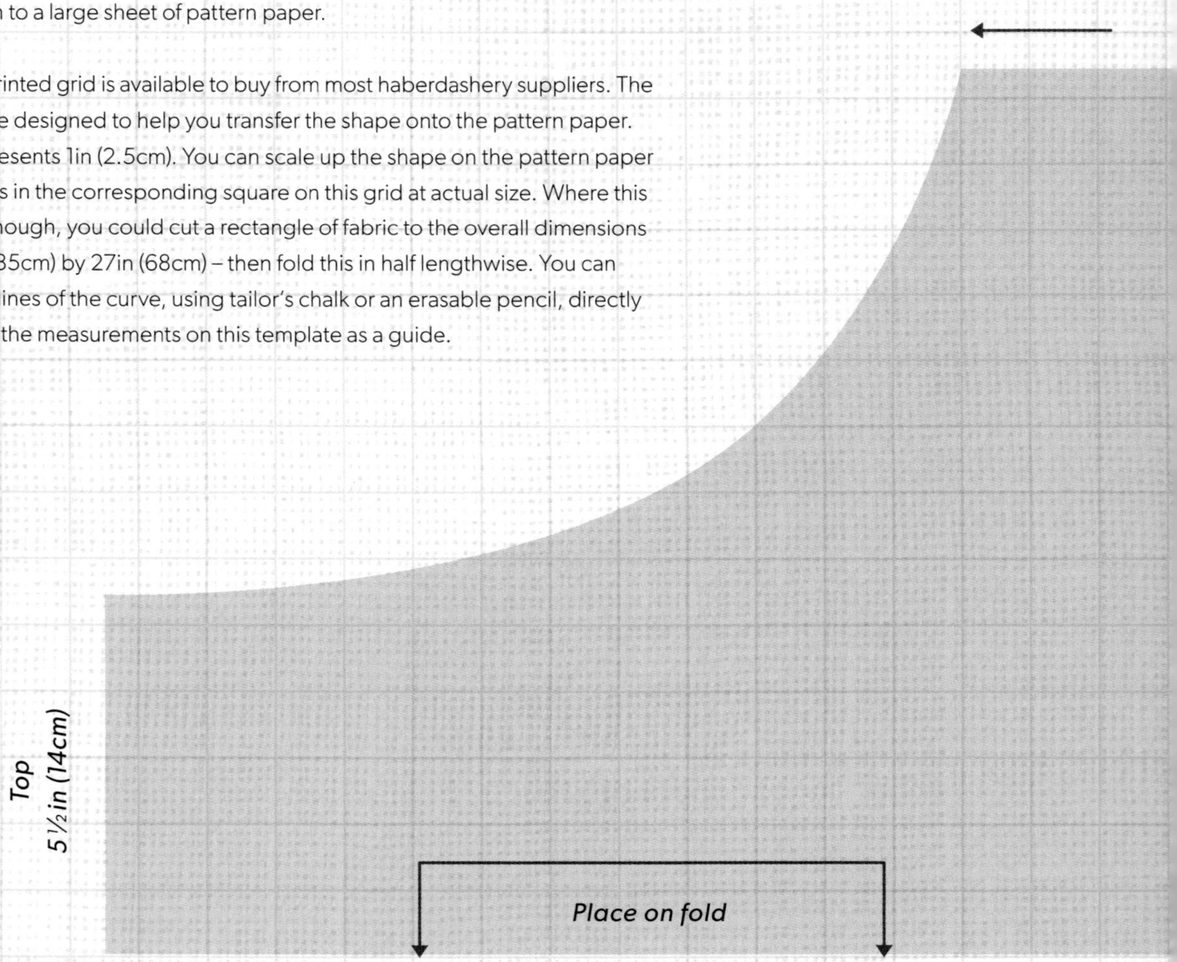

Top
5½in (14cm)

Place on fold

21in (53.5cm)

Place on straight grain of fabric

APRON

Copy 250%

Bottom edge
13½in (34cm)

Place on fold

Glossary

appliqué
The decorative technique of sewing fabric shapes on to a background fabric.

background
A fabric onto which other fabrics, trims or embellishments are sewn.

backing
A second layer of fabric placed behind a main fabric, with or without a layer of wadding or interlining in between.

backstitch
Stronger than basic running stitch and used to sew seams by hand. Stitches are formed by working backwards in relation to the normal direction of hand stitching.

baste
To sew pieces of fabric together temporarily, using a long, loose line of stitches. Also known as tacking.

bias cut
A cut made on the diagonal, across the fabric's lengthwise and crosswise grain.

bodkin
A blunt needle with a large eye, used for threading ribbon, tape or elastic through a casing or a tube of fabric.

bond
To attach one fabric to another, either by gluing or by using a heat-activated (iron-on) bonding fabric.

casing
A hollow channel into which a cord, elastic or drawstring is inserted.

crosswise
Threads running across the width of a fabric (see 'grain').

fray
A cut made across the lengthwise or crosswise grain of a fabric exposes thread ends that are then prone to unravel – or fray. A cut made across the bias (diagonal) of a woven fabric is less likely to fray.

gathering
The technique of sewing a line of stitches then pulling up the thread so that the fabric is formed into folds or pleats.

grain
The arrangement of threads in a woven fabric, where weft (crosswise) threads are woven back and forth between warp (lengthwise) threads.

hem
A method of turning under and stitching the cut edge of a piece of fabric to neaten it and prevent fraying.

interlining
Dense, soft fabric, similar to wadding, used between two layers of fabric when making curtains and other items, to increase bulk, block light or insulate.

lengthwise
Threads running along the length of a fabric (see 'grain').

mitre
Creating a neat effect with a diagonal line when hemming or binding a corner.

motif
A decorative shape that can be cut from fabric or embroidered, for example.

neaten
This applies to a method used to turn under or otherwise finish off a raw edge.

non-woven fabric
A material with fibres bonded together by chemical, mechanical or heat treatment – such as interfacings, wadding and felt.

oversewing
Using small stitches to join two edges. For the neatest result, the needle picks up only a few threads of fabric.

pattern
Refers both to the design printed or woven into a fabric, and a paper template used as a guide to cutting fabric pieces.

press
Refers to ironing fabric, which is done at various stages in a project.

print
A design applied to a fabric using dyes (as opposed to a pattern woven into the fabric).

raw edge
The cut edge of fabric, without a selvedge or hem.

ribbon
A thin strip of fabric with woven edges.

right side
The surface of the fabric that will show on the outside of the finished project, usually the printed side. On most plain fabrics or those with woven stripes or checks, either side can be the right side.

ruched
Fabric gathered into tight folds or pleats.

ruffle
A strip of gathered fabric for decoration.

seam
A line of stitching that joins two pieces of fabric together.

seam allowance
The area between the raw (cut) edge of the fabric and the seamline. The most common seam allowances are ¼in, ½in and ⅝in (6mm, 1.2cm and 1.5cm).

seamline
The line along which you stitch a seam.

selvedge
The finished edge on either side of a piece of fabric, which will not fray or unravel.

shank
The protrusion on the back of a button with a hole through which thread is passed to attach the button to the fabric.

slipstitch
A small stitch used to join two fabrics together, such as when attaching an appliqué shape or creating a hem.

snip
To make a small cut in fabric, usually with the tips of a pair of scissors.

straight edge
A tool such as a ruler that has, as the name implies, a straight edge, used for drawing or cutting straight lines.

tail
The end of a length of thread.

template
A shape that can be cut from a material such as paper, card or plastic and used as a guide for cutting fabric.

topstitch
A line of stitching, such as running stitch, used on top of a seam, close to the seamline, or close to the folded edge on a hem, to create a neat appearance.

wadding
Non-woven sheets of padding, in various thicknesses or weights, usually made from polyester or cotton fibres.

wrong side
The surface of the fabric that will be on the inside of a finished project (see also 'right side').

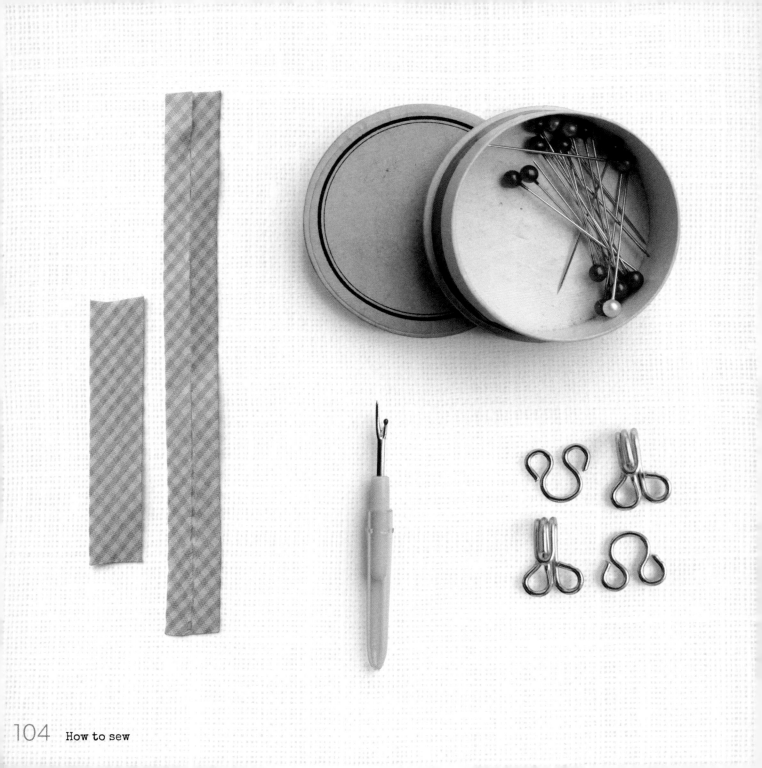

Resources

Fabrics
The Cotton Patch
1283–1285 Stratford Road
Hall Green
Birmingham
B28 9AJ
+44 (0)121 702 2840
www.cottonpatch.co.uk

Fabrics and books on sewing
Laughing Hens
www.laughinghens.com

Haberdashery and craft supplies
Sewing Online
9 Mallard Road
Victoria Business Park
Netherfield
Nottingham
NG4 2PE
+44 (0)115 9874422
www.sewing-online.com

*Haberdashery, fabrics and sewing
classes for all skill levels*
Ray-Stitch
99 Essex Road
London
N1 2SJ
+44 (0)207 704 1060
www.raystitch.co.uk

Online sewing tutorials
Craftsy
www.craftsy.com

Crafty Gemini
www.craftygemini.blogspot.co.uk

Professor Pincushion
www.professorpincushion.com

*Sewing, quilting and embroidery
threads*
Mettler
Amann Handel GmbH
89165 Dietenheim
Germany
www.amann-mettler.com

*Sewing accessories, haberdashery
and paper patterns*
Sew Direct
+44 (0) 884 880 1263
www.sewdirect.com

Sewing supplies
Morplan
Unit 1
Temple Bank
Harlow
Essex
CM20 2DY
0800 451122 (UK only)
www.morplan.com

ABOUT THE AUTHOR

Artist, writer and designer Susie Johns grew up in a household where drawing and making things were very much encouraged – both her parents and all four grandparents were creative people.

Having studied Fine Art at the Slade School, London, Susie began her publishing career as a magazine and partworks editor before becoming a freelance writer and designer. She is the author of more than 30 craft books – including *Knitted Finger Puppets* and *Knitted Pets* – on a range of subjects including knitting, crochet, papier mâché and embroidery. Susie has also contributed to a number of magazines, such as *Let's Knit*, *Crafts Beautiful*, *Embroidery* and *Needlecraft*. She particularly enjoys art and craft activities that involve recycling and reinventing.

Susie is a qualified teacher and runs workshops in drawing and painting, knitting and crochet, embroidery and 3D design near her home in Greenwich, London.

ACKNOWLEDGEMENTS

Many thanks to the following for their help in creating this book: Gerrie Purcell and Jonathan Bailey, for asking me to do it in the first place; Sarah Cuttle and Rebecca Mothersole for the attractive photography and styling, and for making sure the finished book looks so inviting; Caroline Sanders for her impeccable editing skills; and last, but by no means least, Wendy McAngus for her support and her patience under pressure.

Index

To order a book, or to request
a catalogue, contact:

GMC Publications Ltd
Castle Place, 166 High Street,
Lewes, East Sussex,
BN7 1XU
United Kingdom
Tel: +44 (0)1273 488005
www.gmcbooks.com